Mission

We understand "community literacy" as the domain for literacy work that exists outside of mainstream educational and work institutions. It can be found in programs devoted to adult education, early childhood education, reading initiatives, lifelong learning, workplace literacy, or work with marginalized populations, but it can also be found in more informal, *ad hoc* projects.

For us, literacy is defined as the realm where attention is paid not just to content or to knowledge but to the symbolic means by which it is represented and used. Thus, literacy makes reference not just to letters and to text but to other multimodal and technological representations as well. We publish work that contributes to the field's emerging methodologies and research agendas.

Subscriptions

We are pleased to offer subscriptions to *CLJ*—two issues per year:

Institutions & libraries	$200.00
Faculty	$30.00
Graduate students	$20.00
Community workers	$20.00

Please send a check or money order made out to the University of Arizona Foundation to:

John Warnock, *Community Literacy Journal*
445 Modern Languages Bldg., University of Arizona, P.O. Box 210067
Tucson, AZ 85721
Info: johnw@u.arizona.edu

Cover Image

Norris Community Club (circa 1975), Commerce, Texas
Source: Commerce Public Library, Local History Collection

In 1973, the Norris Community Club (NCC) was established by university students in partnership with local citizens to provide what they called "a clear channel of communication" between residents of Norris, the historically segregated neighborhood in town, and the City of Commerce. In a few short years, NCC ushered in unprecedented change. The cover image selected for this collection on Writing Democracy serves as a powerful reminder of the very real, very concrete impact university-community partnerships can have. Soon after this photograph was taken, founding members like MacArthur Evans, Larry Mathis, and Allen Hallmark graduated and moved on to their new lives in far East Texas, Colorado, and Oregon. They never forgot the experience, and community leaders in Norris never forgot them. The conference provided the opportunity to bring them together for the first time in nearly 35 years. For an extended discussion of NCC, please see Carter's "A Clear Channel" in this volume.

Editorial Advisory Board

Jonathan Alexander	*University of California, Irvine*
Nancy Guerra Barron	*Northern Arizona University*
David Barton	*Lancaster University, UK*
David Blakesley	*Clemson University*
Melody Bowdon	*University of Central Florida*
Tara Brabazon	*University of Brighton, UK*
Danika Brown	*University of Texas–Pan American*
Ernesto Cardenal	*Casa de los Tres Mundos, Managua*
Marilyn Cooper	*Michigan Technological University*
Linda Flower	*Carnegie Mellon University*
Diana George	*Virginia Tech University*
Jeff Grabill	*Michigan State University*
Greg Hart	*Tucson Area Literacy Coalition*
Shirley Brice Heath	*Stanford University*
Tobi Jacobi	*Colorado State University*
Lou Johnson	*River Parishes YMCA, New Orleans*
Paula Mathieu	*Boston College*
Regina Mokgokong	*Project Literacy, Pretoria, South Africa*
Ruth E. Ray	*Wayne State University*
Georgia Rhoades	*Appalachian State University*
Mike Rose	*University of California, Los Angeles*
Tiffany Rousculp	*Salt Lake Community College*
Cynthia Selfe	*The Ohio State University*
Tanya Shuy	*National Institute for Literacy*
Vanderlei de Souza	*Faculdade de Tecnologia de Indaiatuba, São Paulo*
John Trimbur	*Worcester Polytechnic Institute*
Christopher Wilkey	*Northern Kentucky University*

fall 2012

COMMUNITY LITERACY Journal

Editors	Michael Moore DePaul University
	John Warnock University of Arizona
Senior Assistant Editor	Sarah Hughes DePaul University
Assistant Editor	Nikki Marie Bartoloni DePaul University
Journal Manager	Daniel James Carroll DePaul University
Copyeditor	Tricia Hermes DePaul University
Design & Production Editor	Kimberly Coon DePaul University
Book & New Media Review Editor	Jim Bowman St. John Fisher College
Social Media Editor	Melissa Pompos University of Central Florida
Consulting Editors	Eric Plattner DePaul University
	Stephanie Vie Fort Lewis College
	Rachael Wendler Univerity of Arizona

Submissions

The peer-reviewed *Community Literacy Journal* seeks contributions for upcoming issues. We welcome submissions that address social, cultural, rhetorical, or institutional aspects of community literacy; we particularly welcome pieces authored in collaboration with community partners.

Manuscripts should be submitted according to the standards of the *MLA Handbook for Writers of Research Papers*, 7th ed. (New York: MLA).

Shorter and longer pieces are acceptable (8–25 manuscript pages) depending on authors' approaches. Case studies, reflective pieces, scholarly articles, etc., are all welcome.

To submit manuscripts, visit our site—communityliteracy.org—and register as an author. Send queries to Michael Moore: mmoore46@depaul.edu.

Advertising

The Community Literacy Journal welcomes advertising. The journal is published twice annually, in the Fall and Spring (Nov. and Mar.). Deadlines for advertising are two months prior to publication (Sept. and Jan).

Ad Sizes and Pricing

Half page (trim size 6X4.5)	$200
Full page (trim size 6X9)	$350
Inside back cover (trim size 6X9)	$500
Inside front cover (trim size 6X9)	$600

Format

We accept .PDF, .JPG, .TIF or .EPS. All advertising images should be camera-ready and have a resolution of 300 dpi. For more information, please contact the Design & Production Editor at kimberly.coon@gmail.com.

Copyright © 2012 *Community Literacy Journal*
ISSN 1555-9734

Community Literacy Journal is a member of the Council of Editors of Learned Journals

COMMUNITY LITERACY Journal

Volume 7 Issue 1 Fall 2012

Table of Contents

Articles

Writing Democracy: Notes on a Federal Writers' Project for the 21st Century... 1
Shannon Carter and Deborah Mutnick

Rediscovering America: The FWP Legacy and Challenge...................... 15
Jerrold Hirsch

Informed, Passionate, and Disorderly: Uncivil Rhetoric in a New Gilded Age..33
Nancy Welch

Gambian-American College Writers Flip the Script on Aid-to-Africa Discourse.. 53
Elenore Long, Nyillan Fye, and John Jarvis

Shakespeare and the Cultural Capital Tension: Advancing Literacy in Rural Arkansas..77
David A. Jolliffe

What's Writing Got to Do with It?: Citizen Wisdom, Civil Rights Activism, and 21st Century Community Literacy......................................89
Michelle Hall Kells

A Clear Channel: Circulating Resistance in a Rural University Town.. 111
Shannon Carter

Book and New Media Reviews

From the Review Desk.. 139
Jim Bowman

Keywords: Community Publishing.. 141
Ben Kuebrich

Literacy in Times of Crisis 149
Reviewed by Patricia Burnes

Community Literacy and the Rhetoric of Public Engagement 155
Reviewed by Christine Martorana

Writing Home 161
Reviewed by Rebecca Lorimer

Writing Democracy: Notes on a Federal Writers' Project for the 21st Century

Shannon Carter and Deborah Mutnick

A general overview of the Writing Democracy project, including its origin story and key objectives. Draws parallels between the historical context that gave rise to the New Deal's Federal Writers' Project and today, examining the potential for a reprise of the FWP in community literacy and public rhetoric and introducing articles collected in this special issue as responses to the key challenges such a reprisal might raise.

One thread of a story that explains the genesis of this special issue of Community Literacy Journal dates back to October 17, 2008, the start of the worst economic crash in seventy-five years. An eerie pall settled over the country as the subprime mortgage debacle unfolded and hardworking people lost their jobs and watched their retirement funds dissipate. Karl Marx's *Das Kapital* gained sudden favor among Wall Street analysts looking for answers to what many observers predicted—at least for a while—might be a total collapse of capitalism. Another thread of the story dates back to October 28, 1929, the mythical, big crash that triggered the Great Depression and the New Deal. Franklin Delano Roosevelt's Works Progress Administration (WPA) put millions of people without jobs—including artists, musicians, actors, and writers—back to work under Federal One. The Federal Writers' Project (FWP) employed more than 6,500 workers nationwide, some like Richard Wright, Zora Neal Hurston, and Studs Terkl who went on to become literary luminaries but also many—the vast majority—who were secretaries, students, lawyers, teachers, and clerks.

The third thread is an idea that began to circulate in late 2008 and early 2009 about trying to revive the WPA. Mark Pinsky, a former writer for the *Orlando Sentinel*, published a piece in *The New Republic*, titled "Write Now: Why Barack Obama Should Resurrect the Federal Writers' Project and Bail Out Laid-off Journalists." In addition to getting picked up by National Public Radio, Pinsky's call circulated on the Internet as Congress was debating the American Recovery and Reinvestment Act of 2009, Obama's stimulus package. Artists, progressive critics, and Washington policymakers discussed the idea of reviving the back-to-work programs of the 1930s that had not only provided a lifeline to the unemployed but had also resulted in major infrastructural improvements like bridges and roads and invigorated the arts with federal funding. After one of us had some initial conversations with representatives from the National Council of Teachers of English, who expressed interest but could not commit to a large-scale project, we organized a small, ad-hoc meeting at a Starbucks in Louisville at the 2010 Conference on College Composition and Communication. About fifteen conference-goers discussed ways we could push the agenda of a new FWP through existing or new channels. Eventually, with the stimulus package clearly earmarked for other uses, it dawned on us that an already existing infrastructure of university-community partnerships, many led by writing faculty, could serve as the basis for a national project. We agreed to organize our own conference a year hence.

In March 2011, over 150 scholars, students, and community members convened at "Writing Democracy: A Rhetoric of (T)here," a three-day conference in Commerce, Texas, sponsored by Texas A&M University-Commerce and the Federation Rhetoric Symposium. Seven keynote speakers—five of whose papers we are proud to include in this issue—addressed the theme of existing and possible ways of "writing democracy" in the United States. Shannon hosted a panel discussion with members of the Norris Community Club, a local group organized in 1973 to foster communication between Commerce's African American residents and university and city officials. (See her article in this issue.) Among the many papers presented were Daylaynne Markwardt's "Composing Democracy: Teaching Genres of Community Action to Collaborate on Understanding Social Problems" and Jeanne Bohannon's "In Their Own Voices: Literacy, Politics, and the Experiences of the Underrepresented." Participants included many from rhetoric and writing studies, but also a number of public and university librarians, local and academic historians, and community activists. Throughout the three days, we heard repeatedly how grateful attendees were to participate in a forum on ways composition studies could take up the pressing issues of income inequality, poverty, racism, and xenophobia—all issues that the FWP had wrestled with in 1935 as they sought to "introduce America to Americans" and "rediscover" our national identity at a time when Jim Crow was on the rise, nearly a third of the country was unemployed, and strict immigration quotas had been recently legislated. Sound familiar?

A Primer on the FWP

The Federal Writers' Project is not widely remembered today, despite having gained critical acclaim in the 1930s and presciently re-envisioned America as a more pluralistic, inclusive society. In addition to serving as a training ground for numerous, important American writers, including several of color, the FWP broke new ground in documenting American life and left a rich legacy of state guides or Baedekers called the *American Guide Series*, oral histories including 2,000 narratives of the last generation of ex-slaves, and searching, ethnographic evocations of everyday life. Yet its reputation faded soon after its final demise in 1943 as a combined result of the national focus on the war effort and persistent accusations of communist infiltration by Texas Congressman Martin Dies, head of the House Un-American Activities Committee, known then as the Dies Committee. Additionally, writers associated with the FWP who went on to gain widespread recognition either eschewed their FWP connection or simply failed to include it in their resumes, perhaps because of the anonymity of the publications or the shame associated with having been on the dole.

Familiarity with the FWP may be on the rise due to the ongoing digitization of thousands of FWP documents made available by the Library of Congress and other repositories as well as the publication of recent books such as historian and conference keynote speaker Jerrold Hirsch's Portrait of America: A Cultural History of the Federal Writers' Project—see his essay in this special issue—and release of films like Andrea Kalin and David Taylor's Soul of a People: Writing America's Story and Ed Bell and Thomas Lennon's Unchained Memories: Readings from the Slave Narratives. Nevertheless, anecdotally, as we continue to explore the potential for a 21st century FWP, we find ourselves repeatedly explaining the precedent for it. Perhaps it is this repeated narration of the Federal Writers' Project's scope and significance that leads us increasingly to see it as a truly remarkable, still largely unmined trove of cultural and social history providing a unique, democratic model for the kind of deliberative public engagement, inquiry, and communication many of us see as a central to our mission as educators.

A Confluence of Forces and Events: One World, One Pain

When we arrived in Commerce in March 2011, the conference was buzzing with conversations about several dramatic events that had transpired since that January: Congresswoman Gabriella Giffords' tragic shooting followed by earnest national calls for civic dialogue and bipartisanship; the groundswell of resistance to political tyranny in the Middle East in what quickly became known as the Arab Spring; and a tumultuous series of events in Wisconsin as working people across the state, along with Democratic elected officials, stood up to protest Governor Scott Walker's attack on collective bargaining rights. With social media playing an ever more critical role in organizing grassroots movements globally, it was not surprising when we clicked open a viral photograph of an Egyptian protester with a sign reading, "Egyptians Support Wisconsin: One World, One Pain."

Then, as if to remind us of the seriousness of the questions we were raising, as the March 2011 conference in Commerce was ending, the Fukushima Daiichi Nuclear Plant, destabilized by a massive earthquake and tsunami, experienced the worst meltdown since the Chernobyl disaster in 1986. Bearing witness to yet another nuclear disaster, devastating to the Japanese people and a grim threat to an increasingly fragile planet, gave us a case in point of the premise of our project, "writing democracy," supporting the idea that history itself is authored, determined at least to some extent by human agency—decisions, policies, plans, actions. As Nancy Welch—another conference keynote speaker—observes in her essay "Informed, Passionate, and Disorderly: Uncivil Rhetoric in a New Gilded Age" in this special issue, militant protests that summer at the Indian Point nuclear power plant in Buchanan, New York, drew criticism from a highly regarded anti-nuclear activist for being "completely disorderly" (34). Welch's point is not only that this denunciation of the protesters was a deliberate attempt to influence the outcome of another scheduled National Regulatory Commission presentation in Vermont by quelling dissent but also that the speaker, who had not been present at the Indian Point meeting, had been contacted directly and manipulated by the NRC unbeknownst to the public.

Thus we note both our capacity to "write" history and "revise" our present course, and also the powerful forces historically arrayed against those who aim to do so under the banner, broadly speaking, of placing human need before profit. That this is a large, diverse amalgam of groups and individuals, with multiple, contested points of view makes deep structural social change a complicated, messy process. That process is further derailed by the dominant culture's strategic exercise of power, overtly through military might and covertly through what Antonio Gramsci called cultural hegemony—a form of domination in which a ruling class convinces the rest of us that we benefit by social arrangements presented as universal, normal, and natural. The Fukushima disaster was clearly not outside the control of human beings but rather the consequence of policy decisions that are neither inevitable nor immutable. For us at our small conference of community members, graduate students, and professors, the momentous events that winter and the Fukushima meltdown on our last day together served almost uncannily to reinforce our sense of the urgency, however quixotic, of our growing band of scholars, teachers, students, and community members "writing democracy."

Add one more surprising phenomenon to the events of 2011 that retroactively inform the conference theme: Occupy Wall Street. Who could have anticipated half a year earlier in March the self-described "people-powered movement" inspired by the protests in Tunisia and Egypt that first occupied Zuccotti Park, also known as Liberty Square, on September 17? Although the momentum of OWS slowed considerably over the winter, this national uprising of the 99% "daring to imagine a new socio-political and economic alternative that offers greater possibility of equality" spread to over one hundred cities across the country and got front page media coverage for months. Whatever the future of OWS may be, its very emergence, its brilliant identification as the 99%, its remarkably fast spreading influence, and its ability to reach across many sectors, including organized labor, demonstrates the latent power of mass collective struggle.

Add, too, one caveat: we have no illusions about the role that "Writing Democracy/FWP 2.0" would or could play in any movement for social change. What we are proposing is a cultural project, which we hope is inclusive, broad, and appealing to students, teachers, scholars, community members, and the general public. Its character is yet to be determined and can only be shaped by those who respond to calls for its creation and the historical context that gave rise to those calls. Like the 1930s' FWP, the one we envision would document cultural and social history through writing about places, communities, and people, and, like its precursor, it would train a corps of writers drawn from the ranks of college students, community members, and ordinary people to tell their own and each other's stories, and once again, some 75 years later, redefine who we are as a country through local guides, oral histories, and now, web-based, multimedia compositions.

Public Writing in the Era of Neoliberalism

The "public turn" in composition studies has taken myriad forms, from service learning and community literacy projects to more traditional letters to the editor and op-editorials (see, e.g., Wells; Herzberg; Weisser; Faigley; Trimbur). Reflective of the field's search for its own identity, the turn to public writing emanates from a widely shared conviction that higher education should prepare students to participate fully in public life, and that literacy skills and knowledge are a prerequisite for such engagement. Yet the obstacles to public writing can be formidable: students' lack of preparedness; the complications of developing and sustaining relationships with community partners; the "do-good" ethos of many service learning programs; the asymmetrical power dynamics that typically define university-community relations; and the illusiveness of the public sphere in a highly stratified, commodified, fragmented society, just to name a few.

Nonetheless, the public turn can be seen in a growing number of university-community partnerships and exercises in civic engagement across the disciplines, including the field of composition. This trend is evinced in four of the essays by our contributors—Michelle Hall Kells, Elenore Long (coauthored by Nyillian Fye and John Jarvis), David Jolliffe, and Shannon Carter—as well as the work of national organizations like Campus Compact, Imagining America: Artists and Scholars in Public Life, and the Kettering Foundation. We see Writing Democracy/FWP 2.0 in this context as well as in response to—or anticipation of—broader, national calls for higher education to return to its larger, public, democratic mission.

These high-level appeals came in January 2012 from the Department of Education and the National Task Force on Civic Learning and Democratic Engagement, which simultaneously released reports calling for higher education "to reclaim and reinvest in [its] fundamental civic and democratic mission." Such calls echo the visions of American democracy that have guided and troubled the U.S. since its inception—guided its promises to enact the values of equality, freedom, and human rights inherited from the European Enlightenment, and troubled its genocidal, racist, xenophobic, anti-labor, profit-driven policies and practices starting with the decimation of the native people whose cultures were destroyed and whose lands were robbed. The calls also come at a moment of extreme income inequality not seen since the Gilded Age, a long global recession that continues to impoverish and deracinate masses of people, and the still ongoing U.S. war in Afghanistan, by far the longest in our history.

Clearly, this crisis regarding the role of higher education in a democracy informed the authors of the National Task Force report entitled "A Crucible Moment" who self-consciously cite the Truman Commission on Higher Education as a source of inspiration for having spurred the development of free, community colleges and "foregrounded democracy as the force for driving higher education's transformation and leadership, and with it, the nation's course toward justice for all" (National 18). We applaud their emphasis on civil rights and other social movements for justice and socioeconomic equality, and we hope to join their efforts to revitalize civic education and rebuild a participatory democracy. However, we also note the report's internal contradictions: this appeal to refocus the nation's attention on democracy and "justice for all" is invited and sanctioned by a government which has led or been complicit in subverting and in some cases destroying precisely those social justice movements at home and abroad cited as exemplary models of democratic engagement.

Nor is this history behind us; current neoliberal policies of austerity, deregulation, privatization, and militarization evident at home and abroad have served to demobilize and demoralize precisely the kind of civic engagement the report endorses, leading to what David Mathews, cited by the National Task Force report, describes as a "citizenless democracy." Notwithstanding the Task Force's rhetorical commitment to civic engagement and democratic processes, and its praise for popular movements for democracy like the Arab Spring elsewhere in the world, it ignores the largest, fastest-growing mass movement in this country, Occupy Wall Street, despite the fact that not two months prior to the report's release, OWS protesters at the University of California at Davis were severely pepper sprayed by campus police.

As UC Davis music professor Bob Ostertag wrote in the Huffington Post, "To begin with, the chancellor could have thanked them for their sense of civic duty. The occupation could have been turned into a teach-in on the role of public education in this country. There could have been a call for professors to hold classes on the quad. The list of 'other options' is endless." The police response to the OWS protests raging across the country from mid-September through December epitomizes the contradiction between grassroots, democratic engagement that leads to social change because it forces those in power to push through divisive laws on the one hand, and academic forums for civic engagement that set out to teach people how to participate in democracy on the other. The one rises up from popular resistance; the other is all too often pedantic and unresponsive if not hostile to community needs, identities, and aspirations.

While the two forms of engagement are clearly not mutually exclusive—and we sincerely agree that the sphere of education can be a critical space for learning about history, politics, government, and the deliberative skills and strategies that enable participation in the public sphere—it seems to us that frequently we in the academy have more to learn from than to teach community members and social justice organizers. Local officials and police attacked the students who sat in at racially segregated lunch counters in the 1960s, and federal support only came late and provisionally. The impact of service learning—restricted in its political reach by academic proprieties and often set up strictly for the convenience of the student, shoehorned into two seventy-five-minute class periods for fourteen or so weeks—pales by comparison.

Thus we envision Writing Democracy/FWP 2.0 as a project that will not only encourage writing in communities responsive to local needs—and communities that recognize and relate to the colleges and universities within them—but also analysis of our era's central contradiction between popular aspirations for socioeconomic justice and the relentless drive for power and profits. This contradiction has been deepened by decades of a particularly inhumane form of neoliberal capitalism. We see its critical interrogation as central to the goals of "writing democracy," and in so doing we anticipate disagreement and debate as we drill deeper into what we mean by the very term "democracy." We assume that the authors of "A Crucible Moment" understand this contradiction, too, just as we recognize the value of forging alliances across all sectors of society. We also hope they will listen to the conversations their report provokes and invite the participation of diverse academic, community, and grassroots organizations in the implementation of their mission. In the meantime, we wonder how civic engagement might be organized in response to what Dwight D. Eisenhower famously dubbed the "military industrial complex" more than 50 years ago, warning against its unfettered growth, and might now be renamed in this era of hedge funds, venture capital, and derivatives the "military industrial financial complex."

Writing Democracy/FWP 2.0

Following the March 2011 conference in Commerce, we co-facilitated a CCCC workshop on "Writing Democracy 2012: Envisioning a Federal Writers' Project for the 21st Century" in St. Louis. At the workshop, Jerrold Hirsch's brief history of the FWP's achievements and impediments, in conversation with more contemporary initiatives like the National Coalition of Writing Across Communities (Brian Hendrickson, University of New Mexico) and the Center for Everyday Writing at Florida State University (Kathleen Blake Yancey), helped ground our exploration of the potential forms our project might take. Steve Parks of Syracuse University reminded us of the popular appeal of such projects, drawing our attention to the Federation of Worker Writers & Community Publishers in Great Britain and current community publishing ventures in neighborhoods surrounding Syracuse, New York. Laurie Grobman of Penn State Berks and Catherine Hobbs of the University of Oklahoma emphasized the role of local history in their pedagogical and scholarly projects, as well as the complexities of capturing and publishing that history: Grobman focused on her ongoing community publishing with students in partnership with a local chapter of NAACP, the Jewish Heritage Center, and the Hispanic Heritage Center, while Hobbs described her ongoing study of a writer for the FWP and her attempts to capture Native American history for the Oklahoma State Guide in the 1930s.

All of these perspectives came together for us when Jeff Grabill from Michigan State University reflected on creating a public in response to specific events or calls to action, which helped situate the project in concrete, historical terms. Drawing on John Dewey's defense of participatory democracy in The Public and Its Problems, Grabill eloquently argued that the "public" we might engage in FWP 2.0 will only emerge, if at all, in the process of an evolving conversation calling it into being. We were struck in particular by the difficulty of defining the very idea of "writing democracy." What, after all, might that mean in practical and political terms? In all of the "turns" academe has taken in the last fifty years, we notice the absence of a "political turn," which we now see as imperative in response to the dire socioeconomic, environmental, and humanitarian exigencies of our times. Like the National Task Force, we see higher education as playing a critical role not only in teaching historical, civic, rhetorical, information, and critical literacy—summed up pithily by what Mary Louise Pratt called "the arts of the contact zone"—but also in joining forces with local communities and emerging social movements, and supporting their efforts to rebuild and retool for a more equitable, just, democratic, environmentally sustainable society. To that end, we proposed a full-day workshop at CCCC 2013 in Las Vegas called "The Political Turn: Writing 'Democracy' in the 21st Century."

Along with a series of panels theorizing what we mean by "democracy," featuring Kurt Spellmeyer, Carmen Kynard, and Nancy Welch, we will be joined by John Carlos, the Olympic athlete renowned for having raised his fist in a black power salute at the 1968 Olympics in Mexico City. A former student of what was then East Texas State University—the institution where Shannon teaches and where, significantly, the first Writing Democracy conference was held—Carlos will be a featured CCCC speaker in Las Vegas (for more on Carlos at ETSU in 1966-67, see Shannon's article). Also planned is a web- and video-based project titled "This We Believe," launching Writing Democracy/FWP 2.0 and giving a more collective spin to Edward R. Murrow's "This I Believe" (revived in 2004 by NPR) as a means of eliciting broader participation—an emerging public—at the conference and beyond.

...

This special issue of the CLJ serves as an opening gambit in developing a theoretical, historical, and practical framework for "writing democracy." We take the unexpectedly large number of submissions and the many interesting community projects we got a chance to read about as a sign of FWP 2.0's potential, and we thank the many authors whose excellent work we could not include due to the limits of space. Divided into three sections—Historical and Theoretical Frameworks, Global/Local Communities, and Civic Engagement—the five articles that follow dovetail in various ways with our sense of the FWP as a prototype for a new national or even international writing project. Our intent is to put the authors in dialogue with each other about the history of the 1930s project in relation to a "public turn" evident across the disciplines and all the issues it has raised so as to probe more deeply into the goals, methods, and forms a 21st century FWP might take.

In Part I: Historical and Theoretical Frameworks, we start with historian Jerrold Hirsch's "Rediscovering America: The FWP Legacy and Challenge," which returns us to our original inspiration for Writing Democracy/FWP 2.0, connecting the historical and cultural dots between 1935 and 2012 as only someone whose own life's work has been profoundly affected by study of the Federal Writers' Project could do. By incorporating his reflections on both the 2011 Writing Democracy conference and the 2012 CCCC workshop, Hirsch helps us think through what a contemporary FWP might achieve as well as some of the pitfalls to bear in mind. He returns again and again to the trope of "the perpetual rediscovery of America" (16, 18, 29), with all of its problematic associations including early stages of exploration and conquest, because, alas, the question of who is an American remains as—if not more—troubling now as it was in the 1930s. Hirsch asks: "Who today are our submerged classes?" (19). Lacing his overview of the history of the FWP with his own "le petite histoire," as he puts it, Hirsch hits on critical reference points for our vision of what the project might look like today: the 1930s' FWP's cross-disciplinary integration of literature and history; the rejection of strict divisions between high and low culture; and the bottom-up approach to history that had begun profoundly to influence the discipline of history by the 1970s, embracing previously excluded groups, and gave rise to new sub-disciplines of oral history and public history.

Also essential to applying the lessons of the FWP to a contemporary landscape is a theoretical analysis of class dynamics. In her essay, "Informed, Passionate, and Disorderly: Uncivil Rhetoric for a New Gilded Age," Nancy Welch analyzes how a ruling class maintains power and perpetuates social inequalities by veiling its own crass, self-serving political and economic interests with the language of reason, order, justice, and democracy. Welch unpacks the rhetoric of civility as serving all too frequently to silence debate and "curtail rhetorical spaciousness" (36), especially noticeable in an era of privatization leading to increasingly fewer public spaces and more limited access to political decision making. Along with telling current examples of how this "wooly rhetoric" is being used to suppress dissent and advance a neoliberal agenda, Welch recounts denunciations of "incivility" by some of the era's progressive reformers of the Bread and Roses strike in Lawrence, Massachusetts, in 1912 to illustrate "how a civil order may be defended not for the good of democracy but against it" (38).

In Part II: Global/Local Communities, Elenore Long, Nyllian Fye, and John Jarvis provide a version of the kind of project FWP 2.0 might support in their exploration of the intersection of the global and the local in "Gambian-American College Writers Flip the Script on Aid-to-Africa Discourse." The authors examine the discourse of aid to Africa in light of the fourth annual Miss Gambia-USA Pageant in 2009, an event hosted by Fye and other Gambian-American students to raise funds for girls' education in the Gambia. Invoking Michael Warner's term, "stranger-relationality"—the social structures that govern relations between self and other—they examine how "rhetors call together a public to address issues of shared concern" when the dominant culture negates the agency of those most affected, in this case, by aid to Africa. By staging the pageant, the Gambian students "disrupted self-other norms toward international aid and activism," exemplifying the rhetorical agency and activity of those outside dominant cultural institutions.

For Fye and her colleagues, the question was not so much whether the fashion show objectified the female body—undercut in any case by the pageant's down-to-earth, critically conscious presentations by female students and supportive, entertaining participation by male Gambian students—as it was "what's an available cultural form" to use for the purposes of raising funds for girls' education in the Gambia. In "flipping the script" on noblesse oblige, celebrity refeudalism, and neoliberal economics—the three types of dehumanizing, "doer-done" stranger-relationality they argue commonly structure aid to Africa—the pageant "invented discursive space" to "co-construct" or "name" "the terms of a yet uncharted future" (55, 63). Such self-sponsored literacy, according to the authors, is the point: "[C]ollege writers like Fye have a lot to teach those of us who teach rhetoric about this highly inventive public discourse that is taking place with or without us" (54).

David A. Jolliffe turns to more local concerns in rural Arkansas in his essay, "Shakespeare and the Cultural Capital Tension: Advancing Literacy in Rural Arkansas." While Jolliffe admits that his own fervent desire to "embed" literacy in community life and thereby "equalize people's chances to live freely and pursue happiness" (77) might subject him to a Bourdieuian critique for having imposed his cultural values on rural, east central Arkansas, his exuberant story of literacy's role in rebuilding an economically depressed community suggests otherwise. The reasons for the economic decline, though slightly different in rural Arkansas, are familiar: an interstate highway that sapped economic vitality from local businesses and the transformation of family farms to big, highly mechanized, globalized agribusinesses.

The demographic data portray widespread job loss and poverty combined with low levels of education, producing "a cycle of decline" exacerbated by the discourse of deficit typically used to describe it. In part because the Augusta Recovery

Initiative had already decided that education rather than jobs per se was the key to economic development, Jolliffe's proposal for a community literacy initiative was enthusiastically embraced, giving birth to the Augusta Community Literacy Advocacy Project. Among other measures of its success, this project has given rise to the Arkansas Delta Oral History Project, the ARCare Shakespeare Festival reviving a century's old tradition of performing the bard's work in rural places—this past year, The Tempest—and the Augusta Veterans' Stories Project. For Jolliffe, the takeaway is twofold: widespread community involvement and recognition and celebration of each and everyone's achievements.

Finally, in Part III: Civic Engagement, we conclude with additional channels for FWP 2.0 suggested by university-community projects closely tied to scholarly research. In "What's Writing Got to Do with It? Citizen Wisdom, Civil Rights Activism, and 21st Century Community Literacy," Michelle Hall Kells theorizes principles for community literacy through the lens of the twentieth century Mexican American civil rights movement. Following up on her book-length study of everyday rhetoric in the life of Mexican American civil rights leader Hector P. Garcia, she examines two rhetorical events—a letter-to-the-editor of the Albuquerque Journal and a telegram protesting the actions of a local chapter of the Daughters of the American Revolution—in the life of Garcia's friend, Vicente Ximenes, who held several strategic positions, including Chairman of the American GI Forum in New Mexico and Commissioner of the Equal Employment Opportunity Commission under President Lyndon B. Johnson.

Kells argues that the letter and telegram represent Ximenes' pragmatic approach to community organizing and his enactment of precisely the kind of community literacy practices she and her colleagues in the Writing Across Communities initiative at the University of New Mexico and the ABQ Community Literacy Center hope to accomplish: "a platform for invigorating the public sphere and cultivating civic literacy among our most vulnerable communities—creating spaces for historically excluded peoples" (99). Her exposition of dissent, deliberation, dissonance, and disputation—what she calls the "four dimensions of democratic discourse"—in relation to Ximenes' work reveals the complex rhetorical exigencies involved in struggling for civil rights within the constraints of post-World War II social realities in New Mexico.

Similarly, in "A Clear Channel: Circulating Resistance in a Rural University Town," Shannon Carter demonstrates what we can learn from public writing generated for and by communities organizing on their own behalf. Like Kells and Welch in the current issue, Carter turns to historical examples of civic engagement, in this case two local efforts to challenge racial injustice in a rural university town—both initiated by African American students, one in 1967, the other in 1973—and both with important implications for contemporary projects like Writing Democracy. In 1967, a year before his heroic, silent protest against racism with Tommie Smith at the 1968 Olympics in Mexico City, then East Texas State University student John Carlos loudly protested the racism he felt as a young black man transplanted from Harlem to an East Texas he found unbearably racist and inhospitable. But while many locals—black and white—agreed with his characterizations of segregation's ongoing challenges, Carlos could not mobilize even minimal local support. Frustrated, he left ET in 1967, going on to stage his dramatic protest at the Olympics the following year.

Five years later in 1973, the Norris Community Club (NCC)—a university-community partnership with deep local roots—was established to provide what NCC organizers called a "clear channel of communication" between residents of Norris, the town's historically segregated neighborhood, and the rest of the city. Because student populations are transient by nature and racism is not a "curable aberration" but rather institutionalized, systemic, and seemingly intractable, civil rights secured by NCC—and the organization as such—began to lose ground as the involved student leadership graduated and city leadership shifted priorities. In addition to instantiating "writing democracy" in a chapter of local history, Carter demonstrates how this university-community partnership ultimately reemerged through the very act of rhetorical recovery and strategic use of public programming, providing again the "clear channel" needed for democratic deliberation and suggesting, by example, the role Writing Democracy/FWP 2.0 might play in providing "a clear channel" for local publics linked together across the nation still struggling to understand America(ns) today.

...

What would a new FWP look like? In his article, Hirsch suggests an agenda that would, among other things: 1) address the tensions between writers and the communities they document; 2) draw on the travel/tourism motif suggested by the state guides but avoid their inherent commercialism; and 3) develop and implement a theory of shared authority among all the stakeholders. Toward that end we hope to continue to expand the conversation we started in 2010, engaging with like-minded local, national, and even international initiatives. Although a full conceptualization of a 21st century FWP will need to be collectively determined, we invite feedback to this issue's delineation of historical and contemporary efforts that we think map out the road ahead. Along with oral history, cultural guides, and folklore projects, FWP 2.0 might also digitize archives, making them available to the public, and use geo-mapping, digital movies, and social media tools to develop interactive sites and disseminate stories. Obviously, technology will transform FWP 2.0 with a Web-based platform accessible to communities across the country if not the world. As we swap local stories in a more global context, we hope, too, to deepen discussions about democracy. Like the original FWP, we will surely encounter conflicting points of view and, most likely, some hostile responses along the way. But a new FWP could also give rise to a new cadre of writers and unify already existing projects that could help "write democracy" as we document everyday life at a critical turning point of world history.

For more information on the current project, see www.writingdemocracy.org

Works Cited

Bell, Ed, and Thomas Lennon. *Unchained Memories: Readings from the Slave Narratives.* HBO Home Video. 2003. DVD.

Bohannon, Jeanne. "In Their Own Voices: Literacy, Politics, and the Experiences of the Underrepresented." Writing Democracy: A Rhetoric of (T)here, 2011. Conference Paper.

Faigley, Lester. *Fragments of Rationality: Postmodernity and the Subject of Composition*. Pittsburgh, PA: U of Pittsburgh Press, 1992. Print.

Gold, David. "Beyond Recovery: Contemporary Challenges in Rhetoric and Composition Historiography." Writing Democracy: A Rhetoric of (T)here, 2011. Keynote. Paper.

Herzberg, Bruce. "Community Service and Critical Teaching." *College Composition and Communication* 45.3 (Oct. 1994): 307-19. Print.

Hirsch, Jerrold. *Portrait of America: A Cultural History of the Federal Writers' Project*. Chapel Hill, NC: The University of North Carolina Press, 2006. Print.

Kahn, Andrea, and David Taylor. *Soul of a People: Writing America's Story*. Infinity Entertainment/Hepcat. 2010. DVD

Markward, Daylaynne. "Composing Democracy: Teaching Genres of Community Action to Collaborate on Understanding Social Problems." Writing Democracy: A Rhetoric of (T)here. 2011. Conference Paper.

Mouffe, Chantal. *The Democratic Paradox*. New York: Verso, 2000. Print.

The National Task Force on Civic Learning and Democratic Engagement. *A Crucible Moment: College Learning and Democracy's Future*. Washington, DC: Association of American Colleges and Universities. 2012. Web.

Ostertag, Bob. "Militarization of Campus Police." *Huffington Post*. 11 Nov. 2011. Web.

Pinsky, Mark I. "Write Now: Why Barack Obama Should Resurrect the Federal Writers' Project and Bail Out Unemployed Journalists. *The New Republic*. 8 Dec. 2008. Web

Pratt, Mary Louise. "The Arts of the Contact Zone." *Profession* (1991): 33-40. Print.

Trimbur, John. "Composition and the Circulation of Writing." *College Composition and Communication* 52.2 (2000): 188-219. Print.

Warner, Michael. *Publics and Counterpublics*. New York: Zone Books, 2005. Print.

Weisser, Christian. *Moving Beyond Academic Discourse: Composition Studies and the Public Sphere*. Carbondale, IL: Southern Illinois UP, 2002. Print.

Wells, Susan. "Rogue Cops and Health Care: What Do We Want from Public Writing?" *College Composition and Communication* 47.3 (1996): 325-41. Print.

Shannon Carter, an Associate Professor of English, is the author of *The Way Literacy Lives* (SUNY Albany, 1998), as well as essays in *College English, College Composition and Communication, Community Literacy Journal*, and *Kairos*. She is currently working on her second book, a rhetorical historiography of race and civic engagement in this rural university community during the last half of the twentieth century. Her interests include digital media, especially video, and her recent work takes up these themes in a series of short video documentaries remixed almost entirely from existing local history collections. She currently serves as PI on Remixing Rural Texas, which received an NEH Office of Digital Humanities Start Up Grant.

Deborah Mutnick, Professor of English and Director of the Writing Program at Long Island University-Brooklyn, has facilitated university-community projects in neighborhoods and public schools to foster intercultural understanding, recover popular histories, and give voice to individuals and groups whose stories have previously been excluded from the public record. Her book *Writing in an Alien World: Basic Writing and the Struggle for Equality in Higher Education* (1996) focuses on underprepared college students whose stories are typically told by others rather than by themselves. She has published articles on basic writing and place-based composition studies in the *Journal of Basic Writing*, *Rhetoric Review*, and *College Composition and Communication*.

The Writing Democracy Project: Next Steps

We are committed to providing regular opportunities to continue the conversations represented in this special issue. To that end, we share two opportunities to join the Writing Democracy Project. "This We Believe/FWP 2.0 Project" is online, ongoing, and will launch with the publication of this special issue. "The Political Turn" is a face-to-face workshop to take place at the Conference on College Composition and Communication in Las Vegas, Nevada, in March 2013. Additional details on these and related activities can be found at our project website: writingdemocracy.org.

Rediscovering America: The FWP Legacy and Challenge

Jerrold Hirsch

Truman State University

This article examines the New Deal's Federal Writers' Project's challenge and legacy to scholars seeking to create an FWP-inspired project today. It explores how scholars in various disciplines engaged in the "public turn," which has contributed to university-community research and teaching projects, can gain perspective and insight from learning about the FWP's goals and accomplishments. The article focuses on the FWP's pluralistic vision of national identity, which led national FWP officials to examine American diversity in encyclopedic guidebooks and through oral history, ethnic, and folklore studies. By exploring why the work of the FWP was ignored for a long time and how its vision and work gradually reemerged, I seek not only to provide a history of the FWPs reputation but also to shed light on the opportunities and responsibilities the FWP offers to current efforts to create new FWP-like projects for a new time.

I always thought my research on the Federal Writers' Project (FWP) was relevant in the broadest sense of that term. Then in the beginning of 2009, in the midst of the high expectations many Americans had for the Obama presidency, and during the severe economic recession of the time that faced the nation, I learned that the FWP was not only relevant but also topical to a degree I had never anticipated. Robin Pogrebin reported in the *New York Times* in early 2009 that "The challenge for culture boosters in Congress was to convince a House-Senate conference committee that the arts provide jobs as other industries do, while also encouraging tourism and spending in general." This echoed the very ideas and language that supporters of the FWP and the New Deal Arts Project used to gain public and congressional support for a New Deal program in the 1930s that employed at its height 6,500 workers.

Ideas and debates about government, the arts, and work relief for artists that had not taken place in over seventy years were recurring after Obama's election. The question remains how deep this discussion can become, although it is now clear that the initiatives in this area are very unlikely to come from the Obama administration. Can those involved in university-community research projects draw on the legacy of the New Deal's Federal Writers' Project to an FWP-like project that meets the cultural needs of a new time that is both similar to and different from that of the 1930s?

...

When I received an invitation to be a keynote speaker at the "Writing Democracy: A Rhetoric of (T)Here" conference in 2011, I was not only honored, flattered, and delighted, but also I was thinking maybe here was an opportunity to move beyond the topical flurry of discussion about new government art projects that had not really gone anywhere, and actually accomplish something. Reviewing the FWP as an effort in writing democracy, as part of the seemingly perpetual rediscovery of America, can help us think about a key question the "Writing Democracy" conference organizers posed: [H]ow might something like the Federal Writers' Project, part of FDR's New Deal in the 1930s, serve to link all our projects nationwide to tell America's story today in its local and global contexts as we enter the second decade of the 21st century? ("Writing Democracy"). Useful comparisons can be made between the way national FWP officials as the leaders of a New Deal agency were able to ignore existing academic boundaries that some of the projects they undertook transgressed and the interdisciplinary work being undertaken by some scholars today. And scholars today in various disciplines engaged in university-community research and teaching projects can gain perspective and insight from learning about the FWP's goals and accomplishments, which by definition were aimed at a public audience and were thus most relevant for the discipline's current "public turn."

We can learn from thinking about the FWP experience as we pursue current projects and plan future ones that seek to broaden the discourse in the public sphere about American nationality, culture, and identity. If the work of the FWP was about anything, it was about, "Introducing America to Americans"—the value of trying to understand the subjective experience of other Americans—in order to create communal solidarity not only by accepting but also by embracing and celebrating American diversity in democratic and egalitarian ways.

The guiding vision of the FWP deserves our consideration. Differences and similarities between then and now merit discussion, as do pitfalls and opportunities to build on the philosophy and work of the FWP. The very term "writing" in "writing democracy" deserves special attention in terms of the work the FWP did in oral history and folklore and the work that would need to be done in those areas in any project that sought to build on the work of Federal Writers.[1] Whether we are fully conscious of it or not, the very idea of reviving an FWP-like project brings that new undertaking into the history of the perpetual rediscovery of America.

The idea of rediscovering America was already old when the country was young. National FWP officials talked about the need to rediscover the United States but they were hardly the first Americans to do so. Nor, in all likelihood, will they be the last. Why is that? Historian Robert Wiebe argued some years ago that one of the permanent issues in American culture is that each generation passes on to the next an unfinished and incomplete answer to who really is an American, who really belongs, who can be included. The struggle over who is an American and over what is American in culture and behavior relates to the constantly changing make-up of our society. Wiebe observes, "[T]ry as they might most Americans in [every generation have] stopped short of encompassing the nation... Each generation passed to the next an open question of who really belonged to American society" (90-91).

The nature of what should be explored is never a product of a broad consensus, but is instead always a highly contested matter. Rediscovery is a social construction metaphorically linked to the exploration of the New World and the geographical expansion of U.S. power and territory and the constant arrival of ever-newer groups of immigrants. In my book *Portrait of America: A Cultural History of the Federal Writers' Project*,[2] I explore these issues in depth; suffice it to say here that efforts—such as those of the FWP—to rediscover an America that includes previously excluded groups always generate conflict. The national editors of the FWP wanted a more democratic, egalitarian, and inclusive society. While such a cultural program during the New Deal was an important component of the Roosevelt administration's efforts for economic and social reform, as conservative critics at the time recognized, after World War II it often served a new uncritical conservative consensus.

Rediscovery has not only been about who should be included in American society, but also about what should be studied, understood, and *appreciated*, when the cultural creations of U. S. residents are examined. The FWP refused to draw firm lines between high and folk expressive culture. They wanted to celebrate both. National FWP folklore editor B. A. Botkin valued interviews with workers and former slaves as lore, literature, and history (Hirsch, *Portrait*). He saw such interviews as a contribution to cultural and artistic renewal. In some of the interviews, he saw art that combined lore and history in a new form of literature. Unlike many folklorists, he did not focus exclusively on the folklore of the past or see folklore as dying out, but lamented that most Americans did not "recognize or appreciate the folklore of the present" (Botkin, *Treasury* xxi-xxii).

Botkin was part of a long tradition of American intellectuals who argued for a broad view of the materials of an American culture, a tradition whose roots can be found in the work of such American Renaissance writers as Ralph Waldo Emerson and Walt Whitman and in the early twentieth century in W. E. B. Du Bois's writings on *The Souls of Black Folks*, Randolph Bourne's celebration of a "Trans-National America" whose diverse people come from around the globe, and Horace Kallen's arguments for celebrating cultural pluralism (Hirsch, "Folklore"; Bourne 86-97; Kallen). It is a tradition that seems never to triumph and never to disappear. Writers, artists, scholars, and others can work to keep that tradition from disappearing, even if we cannot promise it will ever triumph. Like national FWP officials, we too need to contemplate the relationship between government and culture, and ultimately between culture and democracy. Then maybe we can create university-community projects that will contribute to understanding, experiencing, and living those relationships in new ways.

...

My subjective experience studying the FWP is, dare I say it, part of a larger history of the Federal Writers in their times and ours, for as my life crossed paths with the products and records of this New Deal program so did larger historical trends. I did not go to graduate school in history at the University of North Carolina at Chapel Hill in 1971 with the idea that I would study the FWP, but that quickly changed once I arrived in what locals called "the southern part of heaven." Eager to get ahead, I went to the UNC library before the semester started and asked to see what George Tindall had on his reserve list for his seminar on the history of the New South. Perhaps the first step on the path that led to my still ongoing research on the FWP began on an August day, when I discovered on Tindall's list, *These Are Our Lives, As Told By The People and Written By Members of the Federal Writers' Project of the Works Progress Administration in North Carolina, Tennessee, and Georgia* (Federal

Writers' Project). I include the full title here because not only did I reread it several times that day, but also because everything in the title intrigued and puzzled me. I had no idea what a Federal Writer was, nor what the Federal Writers' Project was, nor that stories "as told by the people" could be history, especially if most of "the people" were southern tenant farmers, mill workers, and former slaves. Here I found a group of writers doing interviews that seemed to me to be both literature and history.

I began my graduate studies in a world in which the FWP was not famous and cherished for its many contributions to American culture. The fact that I, a callow twenty-three year old, had not yet heard of it by itself proves little. However, none of my graduate professors, nor my fellow graduate students, would have been shocked to learn that I had never heard of the Writers' Project, for neither had they for the most part. In 1971 one would have been hard pressed to find Americans at any educational level who had heard of the Writers' Project. Aside from a few specialists in various areas of American history who had come across works of the FWP in their studies, and the collectors of FWP state guidebooks, the project was neither praised nor criticized; it was simply forgotten or ignored. My first encounter with an FWP publication changed my life, influenced the research I have done in the years since, and started me thinking in new ways about why and how we study American culture and history. It also led me to think in new ways about who beyond academics could be the audience for such explorations.

My growing interest in the FWP was also affected by the fact that, both during the New Deal and in the America I had grown up in, efforts had been made to create a more inclusive national community. In 1971 I was part of an America in which questions of who was an American, and what could be called American, were issues that had been at the center of electoral politics and the politics of culture for more than a decade and a half. I saw myself as committed to the black freedom movement, the women's movement, the gay movement, and still later the disability rights movement. And these movements were certainly in large ways about whom we include when we use the term "American" and on what terms. In their later stages these movements were also about welcoming and appreciating *difference* as part of the meaning of democracy and equality. At the time, the work of the FWP seemed relevant to the world in which I lived and as it has turned out, continues to be relevant in a United States that still faces the need for a perpetual rediscovery of America in terms of both inclusion and difference. That is part of why I think an FWP-like project today and into the future still has so much to offer.

...

My own research on the Federal Writers' Project grew out of my initial interest in *why* and *how* a book like *These Are Our Lives* had come to be. I wanted to understand why Federal Writers had conducted interviews with groups of Americans often left out of historical writing, and looked at their work as a contribution both to a new literature and history and to a cultural renewal. Given the movement among historians beginning in the early 1970s to look systematically at history from the bottom up and to develop oral and *public* history projects that sought audiences beyond academic walls, one might think the new social historians would be concerned with trying to understand what the FWP was about as well as what it had produced, but that was not the case. For the most part these historians were so preoccupied with "mining" the material for data for a new social history that they largely ignored questions about how and why the documents they were using had come to be. The Project's intellectual and cultural history remained unwritten. It became clear that to address what had been previously ignored required understanding the FWP not only as part of the New Deal and the Great Depression, but also as part of the larger history of romantic nationalism and cultural pluralism. This larger canvas was necessary because the editors in the national office were addressing inherited questions as well as contemporaneous ones. As it turns out, we still find ourselves addressing these inherited questions—questions that seem to be a permanent part of American life.

So now here I am trying to encourage scholars today to undertake new FWP-like projects and to urge them to think about the relevance of FWP publications, such as the state guidebook series, with their broad view of who is an American, their inclusive definition of culture—their focus on the extraordinary in the ordinary and the ordinary in the extraordinary. We need to remember that they thought that to do this, they also needed to collect the life histories of former slaves, textile workers, tenant farmers, ethnic minorities, and industrial workers. We need to be asking who today, as Botkin put it in 1936, are our "submerged classes" (Botkin, *Regionalism* 185). He claimed, "[O]ur many folk cultures are not behind us at all but right under us. Below the surface of the dominant pattern are the popular life and fantasy of our cultural minorities and other nondominant groups--non-dominant but not recessive, not static but dynamic and transitional, on their way up" (Botkin, "The Folk" 126). We are thinking again in new ways about how to "introduce America to Americans" as the FWP tried to do, thinking about asking our fellow citizens as the FWP did, "Have you discovered America?" (Federal Writers' Project). Our thinking about what it would mean to ask such a question today, and about how to ask such a question, would benefit from revisiting the history of the Writers' Project.

...

In 1935 Congressional majorities supported creating the FWP because they favored work relief, not because they supported federally sponsored arts projects. The directors of the FWP, however, seized the opportunity they were given to try to make a contribution to American culture. They worked to come up with projects that could speak to seemingly permanent questions in American life and culture. In effect, they wanted to reopen historical issues that seemed closed but that continued to affect American life. For example, the existing racial order in the South and the North in the New Deal era was linked to the fact that at the end of Reconstruction, blacks were denied the equal citizenship rights that were supposed to follow the end of slavery. By including the newer Americans, the new immigrants and their children, in all their work, the FWP also implicitly challenged the view of who was an American embedded in the immigration restriction laws enacted by Congress in the 1920s. Those laws had not simply lowered the number of immigrants who would be allowed into the country in the future, but specifically restricted immigration of people from southern and eastern Europe who were often thought of as racially inferior to U.S.-born descendants of Protestant northern Europeans.

The goal of these laws was to return the nation to what it was allegedly like before the "new immigration" that began in the 1880s had so dramatically altered the ethnic and religious makeup of the United States. National FWP editors in sharp contrast wanted to acknowledge the tremendous growth and importance of a new post-Civil War industrial working class. The new immigrants and their children born in the United States and the African Americans who left the rural south for northern urban industrial centers were the major components of this new workforce. National FWP administrators rejected the narrow views of the 1920s about who was a real American. It was, however, clear that not everyone supported the FWP approach. Those who with anger and bitterness asked why the nation had changed from their nostalgic image of an older WASP America with blacks in their place—their threatened "real" America--greatly resented any attempt to try to reopen issues regarding race, ethnicity, and labor. Not surprisingly, these same forces criticized all New Deal programs.

Playing with the words "travel" and "tourism," FWP editors tried to defend their agency by locating it in relationship to the goal of economic recovery. They also suggested to mainstream institutions, such as Chambers of Commerce, state universities, public libraries, local and state governments, and the daily newspapers, that FWP guides were an act of patriotism, affirming American culture (Hirsch, *Portrait* 46-47, 51). At the same time, they stressed travel as a form of discovery, a means for enlarging understanding. Travel was not seen as a privilege for the wealthy alone. The FWP invited Americans to use the road to explore American culture. The authors of the guidebooks created new forms of public space for sharing knowledge of American culture. Linked to tourism, it was primarily a space for middle-class travelers and readers, but it also asked them to look at groups who they had rarely been asked to view as fellow citizens. By 1938 many of the guidebooks had been completed. At that stage, national FWP editor Henry Alsberg wanted to examine more deeply American culture and that was one of the reasons he hired Botkin.

National FWP officials sought to reconcile romantic nationalism with cultural pluralism. Romantic nationalism in Europe, and at times in the United States, has often been exclusive, reactionary, illiberal, racist, and focused on homogeneity in its search for a core national tradition. Many European romantic nationalists stressed the traditions of a predominantly rural ethnic group over other groups within a nation's borders in defining the essence of a national identity and culture. This approach created problems for the leadership of the FWP, who were both romantic nationalists and cultural pluralists. They sought to prove to skeptics that although the United States did not have a rural peasantry whose history stretched back to time immemorial, it still had rich cultural traditions. By the time they joined the Writers' Project, most national FWP editors had absorbed anthropologist Franz Boas's concept of cultural pluralism and relativism—cultures are diverse and different but one is not superior to another— and used it to answer their theoretical dilemmas. FWP officials argued American diversity meant that the United States had an abundance of diverse folk traditions and cultures on which to build an American national identity. In their view these traditions and cultures could not be ranked in the hierarchical and racist way earlier evolutionary anthropologists had done.

The national FWP office intertwined the practical goals of providing work relief with dreams of making enduring contributions to American culture. The work it undertook was also designed to employ the ninety percent of project employees who came from the relief rolls and were not creative writers, but unemployed teachers, lawyers, librarians, and other educated middle class individuals. Therefore it is misleading to think of the FWP as a government patronage program for unemployed writers and to search obsessively for the names of writers who would later became famous, although you could find on its rolls such writers as Richard Wright, John Cheever, Ralph Ellison, and Zora Neale Hurston, who had been a student of Franz Boas. At its height, there were as many as 6,500 workers on the FWP. There was an FWP project in every state of the union. Governmental bodies from the national office down to the state and local level were involved in the project.

Local and state officials sometimes disagreed about what they wanted from the FWP and they both often opposed the national FWP office. Officials at the lower levels often opposed the kind of liberal pluralism that the national office embraced. And outside some major northern metropolitan areas, the Federal Writer working for a state project was very often much more conservative than the editors in the national office. For example, officials in almost every southern state opposed giving attention in their state guides to black residents that the national office demanded. Still, there is an overarching vision to the guides that reflects the outlook of the national office despite discordant notes regarding matters of race, ethnicity, and labor. The guides also often oscillate between treating diversity condescendingly as local color to amuse the middle class reader and treating the same material as a reflection of cultural vitality, of a democratic pluralism that needed to be embraced. If the FWP guidebooks did not entirely leave behind the search for the picturesque, they did not simply replicate it as they created work that had elements of both old and new traditions, what we might call a picturesque pluralism (Hirsch, *Portrait* 81-103).

Botkin's concept of folklore was at the center of what might be called the second phase of the FWP. He wanted to examine and share American folklore in all its regional, ethnic, and work related dimensions with a wide audience. In contrast to conservative regionalists who imagined isolated, homogenous, and harmonious groups, which did not actually exist any longer—if they ever had—as the folk, Botkin called attention to the role of conflict in creating lore. For Botkin, conflict and acculturation produced hybrid lore, as not only various groups, but also levels of culture—high, popular, and folk—interacted. He wished to study hybrid lore and how it developed, rather than regard it as worthless evidence of a pure folklore that had been contaminated. As a Popular Front intellectual, Botkin made it clear that he found repulsive the connection between the search for folk purity, the hatred of the allegedly impure, and the growth of fascism. He did not see folklore as vanishing, something to be salvaged before it disappeared, but rather as something still being created, and not only in the rural areas, but also in the cities, not just in the fields, but also in the factories. Botkin maintained that, "for every form of folk fantasy that dies, a new one is being created, as culture in decay is balanced by folklore in the making" (Botkin, "The Folkness" 469). He formulated a left-liberal theoretical position reconciling romantic nationalism and cultural pluralism. "There is," he maintained, "not one folk in [America] but many folk groups—as many as there are regional cultures or racial or occupational groups within a region." He insisted it was time "to recognize that we have in America a variety of folk cultures, representing racial, regional, and even industrial cultures; [and] that this very variety . . . constitutes the strength and richness in American lore" (Botkin, *The Folk* 3).

Morton Royse, national FWP social-ethnic studies editor, addressed the question of who and what is American in memorable terms. He maintained that the Polish, Irish, or Greek population of a town in, for example, traditionally white Anglo-Saxon Protestant New England "is American culture, not merely a contributor to American culture." Put another way, he insisted, "their culture is contemporary American culture as truly as is the culture of Iowa-American farmers or Appalachian American hill-billies" (Royse 86-89).). Royse and Botkin tried to coordinate folklore and oral history interviews in exploring the lives of ethnic minorities. They were convinced that "ways of living and ways of making a living" were deeply intertwined (Botkin, 5). Most of the material gathered under their direction has never been published, although much of it is now available online through the Library of Congress' American Folklife Center.

Henry Alsberg captured the grand liberal, and pluralistic vision of the story that he and his colleagues in the Washington office wanted to tell: "The building up of our country knows no parallel in historical time . . . How a social and cultural unity was achieved ... without stamping cultural differences into one mold, producing the unique American civilization and how the fabric was enlarged is the crux of our story" (Hirsch, *Portrait* 136*)*. In trying to tell this story, Botkin also worked closely with FWP Negro affairs editor Sterling Brown. Both thought interviews with former slaves should focus not only on life in slavery but also on the denial of full citizenship rights since Reconstruction, which stood in the way of the former slaves and blacks born in "freedom" becoming equal citizens. Brown shared Botkin's and Royse's rejection of the "contributions" approach to studying minorities. In the uncompleted "Portrait of the Negro as American," Brown, like Botkin and Royse, stressed what they all referred to as a *participation* over a *contributions* approach They argued that a contributions approach only focused on a few minority group members who had succeeded according to the standards of the dominant group, while ignoring the many who created a culture worthy of respect despite being excluded. Equally important, the minority, though kept separate from the majority, still participated in shaping American history, life, and culture as a whole (Hirsch, *Portrait* 112-131; 138-39).

At the same time, the FWP began these projects, the distinguished Columbia University historian Alan Nevins pleaded in 1938 in *The Gateway to History* "for an organization which [would make] a systematic attempt to obtain from the lips and papers of Americans who had lived significant lives a fuller record of their accomplishments" (iv). What Nevins had in mind differed significantly from what FWP officials wanted to do. Nevins saw history as a form of literature that actively helped constitute a nation and gave it an identity, but his focus was on the role of prominent men. What he feared was that the records that would make it possible to narrate a history focused on the movers and shakers were disappearing as the telephone and modern travel led to the disappearance of written documents. For him oral history was important because it could create the kind of documents that were missing in the modern age, thereby making it possible for historians to still write about leaders. Like Nevins, national FWP officials argued for the key role of history and literature in constituting national identity, but they were more interested in the new social classes modernity created than in how the traditional records usually left by elites were disappearing because of new technology (Hirsch, "Before Columbia" 1-3, 6-10).

Botkin theorized the FWP's blurring the lines among history, literature, and lore. He maintained writers could become ethnographers among the urban working classes American anthropologists and folklorists ignored. He thought they could document "the popular life and fantasy of our cultural minorities and other nondominant groups" to gain the knowledge and insight often missing from much of the thirties' proletarian literature and write about groups that high modernists ignored. Botkin was encouraging writers to create new literary forms (Botkin, "The Folk and the Individual" 128-129.) He also raised important questions—about the narrative nature of history, about who gets to speak, and about the relationship between historical writing and contested memories—that scholars have only recently begun to focus on. This becomes clear in *Lay My Burden Down: A Folk History of Slavery*, a volume one might almost say choreographed excerpts that Botkin edited from the FWP slave narratives (see Hirsch, *Lay*). Botkin insisted "that this book has many authors, who are also its heroes. Together they make one author and one hero—the ex-slave" (Botkin, *Papers*, Box 114). In his drafts for the preface to *Lay My Burden Down*, Botkin provided insights into thinking about the FWP's vision of cultural studies and about how a reader might approach the text:

> Just as it is impossible to read these stories as mere stories, so it was thought that by putting emphasis on story-telling the book would reach a larger audience. Certainly the impact of a document is no less for its being literature and narrative as well as history and statement. It is at once an old and a new kind of literature and history that we have here—something like what we had in the days before writing and something that we may have more of in the future, as it becomes more generally understood that people can talk a kind of literature and that memory is a form of history. (Botkin, *Papers* Box 14)

...

In recent years I have been trying to understand why the work of the FWP was ignored for so long. That the FWP operated outside the circle of university-based, traditional disciplines, that it worked in genres not associated with traditional scholarly formats, and that it deliberately blurred genre distinctions among history, literature, and folklore worked against its legacy making a difference in an expanding disciplinary-driven university system that thrived between 1945 and 1965. Organizers today looking to the FWP for inspiration should also probably expect to have to struggle to gain respect for such work, but that may be less true today than it was in the two and half decades following the demise of the FWP. Perhaps today the situation is different because trends in post-structural theory and cultural studies have called into question the boundaries university departments in post-WWII America worked so hard to create. But beware if you think that engaging in and gaining respect for FWP-like endeavors today is going to be an easy task. The story of the FWP's reputation and legacy is something of a cautionary tale. Even most postmodernist academics write for other scholars whose judgments affect their careers, not for a public audience.

The political landscape of our time is as fraught as it was for the leaders of the FWP. It is possible to understand how the morale of national FWP officials could be bolstered by the feeling that a New Deal-Popular Front bloc would inevitably triumph in public policy and in the politics of culture, but in retrospect that seems a naïve hope. It was, however, a hope that kept them going as they saw the project suffer increasing congressional cuts and the attacks of the Martin Dies-led House Un-American Activities Committee. In addition, some of the national FWP leaders saw themselves as part of an effort at professionalizing a scholarship that would address itself to a public audience—hence their eagerness to explore the possibilities of the FWP working closely with the Library of Congress and the American Council of Learned Societies—and presenting aspects of their research at scholarly conferences and in scholarly journals. As the FWP gradually wound down with the rise of a conservative, anti-New Deal coalition in Congress and with the looming threat of war, Botkin tried to create a permanent FWP-like organization operating through the Music Division of the Library of Congress (Hirsch, *Portrait* 231-236).

Given the path-breaking work the FWP had done, one might assume its work was honored and admired in the post World War II period for its vision and accomplishments; one might assume the project was remembered and honored, but one would be seriously mistaken. We may perhaps too easily forget how uncomfortable and chilling a place post-WWII America quickly became for anything associated with the New Deal and Popular Front cultural politics. The publication of Botkin's *Lay My Burden Down: A Folk History of Slavery* in 1945 provided an occasion for what turned out to be the last flurry of public discussion of the Writers' Project for more than two decades. Despite the positive reviews, there was an undertow of criticism that indicated that in roughly seven short years, the world Botkin had worked in when he joined the FWP in 1938 had changed dramatically. Many reviewers appreciated *Lay My Burden Down* (*LMBD*) as both history and literature. One critic insisted, "[T]he Federal Writers' Project produced a major contribution to the social history and literary heritage of America" (Christman 21). Former Federal Writer Jack Conroy claimed that "the achievements of the FWP were ... being forgotten (Conroy, news clipping in Botkin, *Papers*, Box 14). Despite what he saw as noteworthy accomplishments, he thought that the contributions he and his fellow writers on the project had made to American culture were "too often unsung" (Conroy). Those critics who lauded "the fine legacies of the short-lived Federal Writers' Project" (Christman 21) were by the end of World War II writing with the knowledge that they were defending a "much-maligned" (Brown 574) and, as they correctly feared, a soon to be ignored episode in American history (Christman 21). Thus, one reviewer referred to *LMBD* as "Another excellent fruit of the too-little-appreciated W. P. A. cultural projects" (Reynolds 736).

In 1945, praise for the FWP's work, usually addressed to the intellectual readers of liberal-left journals, often encapsulated a defense of a New Deal legacy that its supporters knew was under attack. Lloyd Lewis captured the mood when he wrote about *LMBD* that "the book is only another one of the things that keep popping up to remind us what all those people accomplished while leaning on shovels during the days of WPA." Thus, the publication of previously unpublished FWP work had provided an occasion for a limited but vigorous attempt at trying to appreciate the project. It is revealing that those who valued the work of the FWP assumed that the public needed to be reminded that a project that had ended only several years earlier had significant accomplishments. The defenders of the FWP and the other arts projects indirectly provided evidence of the diminished status of these programs and the varied nature of the developing hostility toward them and much of the New Deal legacy.

The ambivalence toward the New Deal, the ordeal of living through the Great Depression, and the anti-communist rhetoric of the Cold War tarred New Deal and left domestic politics indiscriminately with the broad-brushed accusation of anti-American disloyalty. Consider what might happen if a new FWP type project published interviews with American citizens of Arab or Pakistani ancestry as an effort to "introduce America to Americans" or collected life histories of resident aliens and residents who are here illegally. And who knows when, if ever, there will be an end to the current war on terror, and whether we will ever enter a post-war-on-terror world. In many ways, it is not an auspicious time for raising the question of who and what we refer to when we talk about being an American. In reality it never is, which is all the more reason why it needs to be done.

...

The inability to appreciate the legacy of the FWP was just as widespread in the academic world as it was among the general public. Neither history departments nor those interested in oral history in particular manifested any significant interest in the FWP before the late 1960s. In this period, historians were more interested in consensus than conflict in American history. While they showed an increasing interest in exploring the concepts of other social sciences, it was within the framework of maintaining a strong disciplinary identity. Oral history projects tended to be located in libraries and archives, which meant the interviews were treated as historical sources, but not as versions of history presented by an interviewee. University history departments showed little or no interest in these endeavors. The vast majority of oral history interviews in this period were with prominent individuals. Most of these oral historians were interested in discussing memory only with the goal of learning how to judge the accuracy of the memory of an individual being interviewed. At the same time, there was practically no interest in how individuals and groups narrated their stories, in how they constructed their memory of the past, nor in the way memory and what was worth remembering were contested. The very things that had led national FWP officials to do interviews were of little concern to oral historians in the post-war 1950s. By the late sixties, more and more oral historians came to share the FWP's concerns. Today, virtually all oral historians are interested in these questions.

At Indiana University in the late 1950s, Richard Dorson created the first doctoral program in folklore. The standard narrative regarding Dorson's role in the history of American folklore studies treats him as a scholar determined to replace amateurism with rigorous scholarship and to carve a solid niche in the academy for folklore as a distinct field with its own disciplinary identity. An emphasis on method trumped theory. This approach led Dorson to dismiss the work of the FWP as amateurish. In addition Dorson, a Cold War liberal, rejected the FWP's Popular Front cultural politics. Furthermore, Dorson saw an emphasis on a public audience as not only a potential lowering of standards, but as a threat to gaining the respect for folklore studies he wanted scholars in other disciplines to show. Thus he both ignored the work of the FWP and opposed the work of folklorists in the 1960s who wanted to create public folklore programs. Although Dorson worked with scholars in other disciplines and considered himself both a historian and a folklorist, it was of the utmost importance to him to create and police boundaries between folklore and academe. Some scholars have argued this led to a lack of innovative theory among folklorists in the 1950s and isolated folklore from other disciplines (Briggs 91-105). A renewed interest among folklorists in the relationship of folklore studies to other disciplines and to a public audience eventually led to a renewed interest in the FWP.

American Studies emerged as a discipline during the height of the Cold War. It owed much of its success not only to some of its early brilliant scholars but also to its search for an American exceptionalism that manifested itself in a national character and culture worthy of international respect. In a sense, American Studies was, as were the humanities and social sciences in general in this period, a form of anti-Marxism (Denning 356-380). National attributes figured largely in these studies, but class hardly at all, and social history, race, and ethnicity not much more. There was no place in this world of American cultural studies for the FWP, which had been interested in aspects of the American experience that the new American Studies usually ignored.

In some ways, this quick tour of these disciplines during the height of the Cold War is unfair to their actual achievements, and ignores pockets of resistance, such as the famous neo-progressive historians at the University of Wisconsin. My point is not to write these disciplines' histories but to explain an academic world that had little interest in the FWP. And we should not kid ourselves about how happy everybody will be if and when a new FWP-like project seems to challenge traditional scholarly habits, administrators see the first signs of controversy involving their institutions, or parts of a community react negatively to how they are portrayed.

...

The FWP story can, I think, be relevant, and even, dare I say, inspirational. As a model, however, it has limitations that we have to acknowledge. Thinking about the limitations of the FWP is also a way in which the New Deal agency can be helpful to us. Like the FWP, we are looking for a practical way to undertake new ways of telling the American story, of identifying, creating, and connecting American places and the variety of Americans who inhabit them. Their vehicle was the Depression's unemployment crisis. Ours is the desire of institutions of higher education to serve the public and the fact that the vast majority of college students take composition classes, along with the initial impetus of the Great Recession and its parallels to the 1930s. We have a sense of some of the opportunities the Depression created for New Deal cultural projects that might help us respond creatively to the economic realities of our time at the local, national, and global levels. Recognizing some of the limitations of the Depression as a vehicle for cultural studies may help us anticipate problems in the student-community model for a new FWP-like venture. Some of these issues concern tourism and travel, place making, organizational authority, and ways of reaching and creating audiences. The FWP had to employ many people in the local projects who made little positive contribution to the work of the organization. Beyond that there was also the problem of the various ways in which the composition of the local FWP workforce was not representative of the community in terms of class, ethnicity, race, and gender. The situation in the South was notorious from the national FWP officials' point of view because few blacks were on the project and where they were, segregation laws dictated how they were organized and employed (Hirsch, *Portrait* 7, 28-29). In general, FWP employees were not a cross-section of the community. Nor did the FWP self-consciously consider the history of gender roles. Regarding class, ethnicity, and gender, the variety of students in composition and rhetoric classes will provide their own special problems *and* opportunities in creating FWP-like projects.

In a time of economic depression, the FWP had little choice but to play on the economic benefits of tourism for local communities and states and at the same time try to transform tourism into a form of travel, exploration, and growth. Perhaps we can avoid the literal tourist appeal the FWP sought to tap into, but can we avoid the modality of tourism? After all, one of the central concerns of cultural anthropologists for the last twenty-five years has been the close relationship between tourist/travel modalities and ethnography, and the way that mode exoticizes subjects who are not given an opportunity to speak for themselves (Clifford). There is no simple answer, but awareness as well as experience can help us develop a self-reflexive critique.

The FWP did not have a community-based discussion about how to engage in place making. Or, put another way, the elements of the community that affected this discussion the most were social and cultural elites. What is to be the relationship between students and community in our time in constructing a sense of place? How do we try to make discussions about such issues representative of varying opinions? How do we avoid a narrative that reflects only the view of one individual or one group? The national FWP office often tried to exert authority to make state and local units conform to their vision of place making, sometimes with more success and sometimes with less.

Is that, however, the way we want to handle the issues of authority today? Should editorial power rest with the students, the community, the professors, or the university administrators? And, with which members of these groups should authority rest? It no longer seems possible, defensible, or desirable to make, for example, the professors the final authority, as the national FWP office *tried* to make itself the final authority. But while it is necessary to give some say to all groups involved, it is not necessary for experts, in this case the professors, to abdicate all authority, for denying experts any role is to deny the value of expertise. As historian Michael Frisch has written, the question is how to have a shared authority, which is no easy matter (xxi-xxii). Nevertheless, unless the idea of sharing authority is entertained from the beginning, it has no chance. In addition, without shared authority, only one group argues about and develops answers to questions about what needs to be said about the places to be included in the work of this new FWP. Students, professors, and community members will all have things to teach and learn from each other. While that is a fine sentiment, it is easier said than done. To be achieved, it has to be worked at consciously.

The communications revolution of our time would need to be fully exploited by a new FWP-like project. Books were at the center of the FWP's effort to disseminate its work, in particular, encyclopedic state guides, local guides, and some collections of interviews. That is not to say that they did not experiment with other forms of communication. There were FWP scripts presented on the radio. There were collaborations between the Federal Theatre Project and the FWP. The Federal Art Project provided materials for FWP book exhibits. Photographs taken by Farm Security Administration photographers appear in FWP publications. The Internet, computers, smart phones, and tablets open up a wealth of possibilities. Indeed, government agencies such as the American Folk Life Center at the Library of Congress have led the way in digitizing unpublished FWP materials, making them available via the Internet. Spark Media, a private documentary film company, has released a film history of the Writers' Project, "Soul of a People," has broadcast radio programs on the subject, and is developing an interactive learning game about it. The possibilities for sharing material seem limited only by our imaginations.

...

Perhaps given that these academic disciplines are to a degree welcoming class and social history back into the discussion, paying attention to the "linguistic turn," and so seeking a public as well as a teaching and scholarly face, all will be clear sailing for a new FWP-like program. I doubt it will be so easy. Nevertheless, the game is worth the candle. It is also necessary to invite public historians, oral historians, and public folklorists into the discussion with rhetoric, communication, and composition professors, as we think about a new FWP-like project. These groups all have extensive experience with both the problems and the opportunities in the presentation of history and lore to a general audience. We need to be aware of the differences between orality and writing, between the performance of lore and the presentation of it in other mediums—and the disciplines mentioned have much to teach us.

We also should not ignore the possibilities for creative writing in a new, FWP-like project. The FWP didn't. Botkin was especially interested in these connections, as the unpublished work of the Living Lore units he created in Chicago and New York City show (Botkin, "*Living Lore*" 252-263; Botkin, *We Called It* 189-201). In effect, he sought to create new types of work that blurred the lines between history, folklore, and creative writing while challenging traditional assumptions of existing discipline-driven work in these areas. A new FWP-like project could end up challenging the fundamental assumptions of disciplines today and contribute to new theoretical understandings while at the same time reaching a diverse public audience. When Botkin spoke to members of the MLA at their 1938 meeting, he declared that the challenge facing a democratic scholarship and art was to study and use folklore to understand and strengthen democracy: "Upon us devolves the tremendous responsibility of studying folklore as a living culture and of understanding its meaning and function not only in its immediate setting but in progressive and democratic society as a whole." If we take up the challenge of creating a new, FWP-like effort of rediscovering America, the responsibility Botkin talked about in 1938 devolves upon us (Botkin, "WPA" 14). Hopefully, it will not take as long for

Americans to appreciate a new project in the FWP tradition as it is taking them to appreciate the old FWP.

...

The need for a perpetual rediscovery of America is seemingly permanent, a challenge for every generation. But now is an especially important time for taking up the challenge. The similarities and differences between now and the 1930s are striking. Take, for example, the issue of "newer Americans." Reading the newspapers and watching television, one would think today that the only immigrants in the nation are illegal Mexicans. And yet anyone who visits a major U. S. city knows that this is not the case. Perhaps the majority today knows less about the culture and experiences of Nigerian, Afghani, Korean, Lebanese, and Jordanian immigrants than the majority in the 1930s knew about Italian, Polish, and Jewish immigrants.

So much need, so much opportunity. We should look forward to accepting the challenge and seeing what we can do. Let us make the FWP a living legacy.

Endnotes

1. "Folklore is a body of traditional belief, custom and expression handed down largely by word of mouth and circulating chiefly outside of commercial and academic means of communication and instruction. Every group bound together by common interests and purposes, whether educated or uneducated, rural or urban, possesses a body of traditions which may be called its folklore. Into these traditions enter many elements, individual, popular, and even 'literary,' but all are absorbed and assimilated through repetition and variation into a pattern which has value and continuity for the group as a whole" (Botkin, "Manual").

2. For further information and analysis, see my book, *Portrait of America*, which I draw on throughout this essay.

Works Cited

Botkin, B. A., ed. *A Treasury of American Folklore: Stories, Ballads, and Traditions of the People.* New York: Crown Publishers, 1944. Print.

_____. ed. *A Treasury of Western Folklore.* New York: Crown Publishers, 1951. Print.

_____. "The Folk and the Individual, Their Creative Reciprocity." *English Journal* 27 (1938): 121-135. Print.

_____. "The Folk in Literature: An Introduction to the New Regionalism." B.A. Botkin, ed. *Folk-Say, A Regional Miscellany.* Norman: University of Oklahoma Press, 1930. Print.

_____. "The Folkness of the Folk." *The English Journal* 26 (1937): 461-469. Print.

_____. *Folk-Say, A Regional Miscellany.* Norman: Oklahoma Folklore Society. University of Oklahoma Press, 1937. Print.

_____. "Living Lore on the New York City Writers' Project." *New York Folklore Quarterly,* 2 (1946): 252-263. Print.

_____.Botkin, "Manual For Folklore Studies," August 15, 1938, Box 69, Federal Writers' Project files, Works Progress Administration, Records Group 69, Federal Writers' Project, National Archives, Washington, D. C..

———. Papers, Personal and Business Correspondence, *Lay My Burden Down* files, University of Nebraska-Lincoln archives, Lincoln, Nebraska.

———. "Regionalism: Cult or Culture." *English Journal* 25 (1936): 181-185. Print.

———. "We Called it 'Living Lore.'" *New York Folklore Quarterly* 14 (1958): 189-201. Print.

———. "WPA and Folklore Research: Bread and Song." *Southern Folklore Quarterly* 3 (1940): 7-14. Print.

Bourne, Randolph. "Trans-National America." *Atlantic Monthly* 118 (1906): 86-97. Print.

Briggs, Charles L. "Disciplining Folkloristics." *Journal of Folklore Research* 45 (2008): 91-105. Print.

Brown, Sterling. "By the Rivers of Babylon." *Nation* 162 (1946): 574. Print.

Christman, Henry. "In the Slaves' Own Words." *Saturday Review of Literature* 28 (December 15, 1945): 21. Print.

Clifford, James. *Routes: Travel and Translation in the Late Twentieth Century*. Cambridge, Mass: Harvard UP, 1997. Print.

Conroy, Jack. "Brilliant Work on Slavery in U. S.: Fine Readability Plus Thoroughness Mark Folklorist's Account." *Chicago Sun* 9 Dec. 1945.

Denning, Michael. "'The Special American Conditions': Marxism and American Studies." *American Quarterly* 38 (1986): 356-380. Print.

"Have You Discovered America," Box 70, Federal Writers' Project files, Works Progress Administration records, Record Group 69, National Archives, Washington, D. C., n.d.

Federal Writers' Project. *These Are Our Lives, As Told By The People and Written By Members of the Federal Writers' Project of the Works Progress Administration in North Carolina, Tennessee, and Georgia*. Chapel Hill: University of North Carolina Press, 1939. Print.

Frisch, Michael. *A Shared Authority: Essays on the Craft and Meaning of Oral and Public History*. Albany: State University of New York Press, 1990. Print.

Hirsch, Jerrold. "Before Columbia: The FWP and American Oral History Research." *Oral History Review* 34 (2007): 1-16. Print.

———. "Folklore in the Making: B. A. Botkin." *The Journal of American Folklore* 100 (1987): 3-38. Print.

———. Foreword to the new edition of *Lay My Burden Down: A Folk History of Slavery*. Ed. B. A. Botkin. Athens: University of Georgia Press, [1945] 1989, ix-xxx; New York: Delta. 1994. Print.

———. *Portrait of America: A Cultural History of the Federal Writers' Project*. Chapel Hill: University of North Carolina Press, 2003. Print.

Kalin, Andrea, dir. *Soul of a People*. Infinity Entertainment/Hepcat, 2010. DVD.

Kallen, Horace. *Culture and Democracy in the United States: Studies in the Group Psychology of the American Peoples*. New York: Boni and Liveright, 1924. Print.

Lewis, Lloyd. "Uncle Tom's Cabin as it Really Was." *New York Times* 1 Jan. 1946: BR3. Print.

Nevins, Allen. *The Gateway to History*. Boston: Heath and Company, iv, 1934. Print.

Pogrebin, Robin. "Saving Federal Arts Funds: Selling Culture as an Economic Source," *New York Times* 15 Feb. 2009. Web.

Reynolds, Horace. *Yale Review* 35 (1945): 736. Print.

Royse, Morton W., Joseph S. Roucek, Caroline F. Ware. "Approaches to Studies of Nationality Groups in the United States: Summary of the Discussion." *The Cultural Approach to History*. Ed. Carolin Ware. New York: Columbia University Press, 1940. 85-89.

Wiebe, Robert. *The Segmented Society: An Introduction to The Meaning of America*. New York: Oxford University Press, 1973. Print.

Jerrold Hirsch is Professor of History at Truman State University, Kirksville, Missouri, author of *Portrait of America: A Cultural History of the Federal Writers' Project* and co-editor of *America's Folklorist: B.A. Botkin and American Culture*. He has published articles on the FWP, the history of American folklore studies, and disability history.

Informed, Passionate, and Disorderly: Uncivil Rhetoric in a New Gilded Age

Nancy Welch

Little known about the now celebrated 1912 Bread and Roses strike is that prominent Progressive-era reformers condemned the strikers as "uncivil" and "violent." An examination of Bread and Roses' controversies reveals how a ruling class enlists middle-class sentiments to oppose social-justice arguments and defend a civil order—not for the good of democracy but against it. The strikers' inspiring actions to push against civil boundaries and create democratic space can challenge today's teachers of public writing to question the construction of civility as an acontextual virtue and consider the class-struggle uses of unruly rhetoric for our new Gilded Age.

> Civility may well be a virtue. But it is probably not a virtue that will be of much help in deciding the political questions that ultimately matter.
>
> —James Schmidt, "Is Civility a Virtue?"

> It was the spirit of the workers that seemed dangerous. They were confident, gay, released, and they sang ... The gray tired crowds ebbing and flowing perpetually into the mills had waked and opened their mouths to sing, the different nationalities all speaking one language when they sang together.
>
> "Revolution!" screamed the conservative press.
>
> —Mary Heaton Vorse, "The Lawrence Strike" in *A Footnote to Folly: The Reminisces of Mary Heaton Vorse*

The Truthiness About Indian Point

Nuclear Regulatory Commission (NRC) officials were in for a shock when, not three months after the Fukushima catastrophe, they arrived in Cortlandt Manor, New York, to give their annual safety debriefing on the Indian Point nuclear power plant. The overflow crowd of more than four hundred—a startling turnout for the tiny town—carried signs imploring "Westchester Aglow—Where Do We Go?" They refused to sit still for the usual PowerPoint presentation. "Lap dogs!" and "Liars!" they shouted when officials claimed that the aging, accident-ridden plant had "operated in a manner that preserved public health and safety" (Clary; Williams). Finally the NRC officials gave the crowd what they had politely requested at the meeting's start: two minutes of silence for Fukushima's victims and suspension of the PowerPoint presentation, available online, so the meeting could proceed straight to Q&A. "Raucous" is how the local newspaper reporter summed up the open mic that followed. "Boisterous" and "confident" wrote environmental activist and Pace University professor Chris Williams. "[O]ne of the best public meetings I ever attended," declared local blogger Dawn Powell. The more than eighty people who stepped up to the microphone, she reported, were "informed, passionate, and empowering."

Less than three weeks later, however, this same meeting was roundly criticized by highly regarded anti-nuclear activist Raymond Shadis. In a public radio interview and on a Vermont news blog, Shadis decried the conduct of the Indian Point meeting attendees as "completely disorderly" (Dillon). Their rhetoric, he charged, had veered toward "irresponsible" incitement to "violence" (Shadis). Shadis' purpose in going public with this reprimand wasn't simply epideictic. Rather, it was deliberative, aiming to shape audience behavior at the NRC's next stop: Brattleboro, Vermont, in the shadow of the 39-year-old Vermont Yankee nuclear reactor. Coming on the eve of federal court hearings to determine whether to set aside the state senate's 26-to-4 decision to shutter the plant, the Vermont meeting promised to be fraught. Adding to the tension was the revelation that the NRC had taken sides, joining with Entergy, the corporation that also owns Indian Point, to argue for keeping Vermont Yankee open. This was the context in which Shadis urged "civility" and "calm" among Vermonters lest "violent language … stimulate violent action" (Dillon). To be sure, Shadis acknowledged, the NRC should cease advancing unconvincing claims about reactor safety that only serve to "insult and infuriate" the public (Shadis). Infuriating, for instance, has been the NRC's downplay of the partial collapse of a cooling tower at Yankee and the leakage of radioactive tritium into the groundwater from pipes Entergy disavowed any knowledge of (Zeller). But "upset members of the public too," Shadis concluded, "need to find better means to communicate" (Shadis).

Shadis' counsel, especially as it came in the aftermath of the appalling shooting of Congresswoman Gabrielle Giffords, has strong persuasive appeal. That appeal is further bolstered by his reputation as an effective activist—he led the successful movement to end nuclear power in his home state, Maine—and by his practical wisdom in advocating keeping communication channels open. Through ethos alone, Shadis' statements have a resounding ring of truth, and his plea for civility received wide broadcast, the story published under the headline "Nuclear Critic Urges Civility" on news websites nationwide. Undisclosed, however, is that Ray Shadis did not attend the Indian Point hearing. Instead, he was "contacted indirectly by members of [the] NRC" who were concerned about "the safe and civil conduct of NRC public meetings" because the "personal attacks" at the Indian Point meeting led "younger staffers" to fear for their "physical safety" and a possible repeat of "the Representative Giffords shooting" as a "mob mentality takes over" (Shadis). In his op-ed and radio interview, Shadis makes no mention of having contacted any of Indian Point's non-NRC meeting participants. He seems also not to have consulted the local newspaper, the handful of independent media outlets covering the meeting, and the shift reports of local police officers, none of which recorded violent language or threatening behavior. Compared with eye-witness accounts, Shadis' single-source and apparently corporate-spun message starts to ring not with truth but with what comedian Stephen Colbert dubs "truthiness."

But no matter. With the Indian Point hearing having received such limited coverage while the Shadis interview enjoyed wide circulation, the NRC's version of the event takes on its own reality. In place of Raging Grannies belting out "Indian Point / Is a dangerous joint" and a state assemblywoman reminding the NRC, "It's your job to protect the public, not the industry" ("Raging Grannies Against Indian Point"; Clary), we have the frightening prospect of "deranged individuals" overtaken by a "mob mentality." "Shut it down" becomes not the open demand of an informed and passionate public but the concealed goal of a private industry and its quasi-governmental defenders aiming to shut down audible protest—and to do so in the name of civility.

What's Wrong with Just Being Civil

"If you would civil your land, first you should civil speech": Auden's adage is at the heart of Wayne Booth's influential "rhetoric of assent" or "listening rhetoric," first formulated from his dismay at the civil unrest of the late 1960s and later offered as a remedy for a country that had just marched under false warrants into war (*Modern Dogma*; *Rhetoric*; "War Rhetoric"). Theresa Enos likewise turns to Auden as she recommends rhetorical restraint to create greater space for deliberation and deeper respect between contending parties. If "we can work toward more constructive, and civil, ways of expressing opposition," especially by "suspending urgency," she suggests, parties to a conflict can open themselves to the "spaciousness of rhetoric" and create "greater comity" between them (151). Many first-year composition courses, writes John Duffy in *Inside Higher Education*, are already engaged in the work of creating rhetorical spaciousness and generosity, offering their students Aristotelian lessons in argument and ethics that can counteract the "corrosive language of figures such as Rush Limbaugh" and move us toward "healthier, more productive, and more generous forms of public argument." Especially given the toxicity of what passes for public discourse on corporate radio and cable-news broadcasts, the projects of cultivating civility and opening rhetorical space appear interdependent. Hence the rekindled interest among compositionists in civic literacy and public rhetoric along with a pedagogical emphasis on rhetorical listening, balance, and civility.

The story of the Indian Point meeting, however, troubles the belief in civility's powers to create conditions and space needed for democratic deliberation and the power of well-reasoned, proof-backed claims alone to advance effective arguments for the public good. Consider: The Indian Point residents and activists arrived at this meeting equipped with meticulously researched arguments regarding the dangers of and alternatives to nuclear power. In this way, they were much like the members of a citizens group Jeff Grabill describes in "On Being Useful: Rhetoric and the Work of Engagement." Members of that group undertook painstaking research to challenge the U.S. Army Corps of Engineers' claim that a proposed dredging project would have no adverse environmental and health effects. Such rhetorical preparation—not the work of lone rhetors, Grabill emphasizes, but "coordinated and distributed" across many people—is necessary for groups without official credentials and backing to make arguments that can "open up" dredging a canal or relicensing a nuclear power plant as a "matter of concern" (203-4).

In the case of Indian Point, however, something more was also needed: the audience's ability and willingness, likewise coordinated and distributed, to rival the NRC's authority to relegate audience arguments to the meeting's end. By refusing to await the designated Q&A period, these audience members were indeed "uncivil" in two conventional senses of the term: incivility as indecorous behavior and incivility as refusal to subordinate one's grievances to the presumed greater good of maintaining order (Shils, *The Virtue of Civility* 4, 345). Yet in this case their incivility served to *make* rhetorical space in which more views could be heard. They sought to civil their land—or at least this meeting—by *unciviling* their speech.[1]

Why uncivil, even rude speech was necessary, a precondition for a democratic discussion, is captured by David Lochbaum of the Union of Concerned Scientists: "Absent dead bodies," he told the *New York Times*, "nothing seems to deter the NRC from sustaining reactor operation" (Zeller). In these circumstances, civility toward spokespersons for the nuclear industry may be a virtue—but not one in service to democracy. Instead civility functions to hold in check agitation against a social order that is undemocratic in access to decision-making voice and unequal in distribution of wealth. Indeed, a *neoliberalized* regulatory body like the NRC—one that understands its purpose not as regulating an industry to safeguard the public good but influencing public opinion to safeguard an industry (Associated Press; Gonzales and Goodman; Zeller)—*depends* on civility to *curtail* rhetorical spaciousness.[2] Faced with working- and middle-class individuals and groups joined to oppose a corporation's considerable political power and economic resources, NRC officials deployed the accusation of incivility and the specter of mob violence as a regulatory force, one aimed at discrediting meeting attendees and discouraging future audiences from pushing for a democratic agenda. Through its calls for calm, the NRC effectively shifted the focus and the topic: from Entergy's conduct to the audience's and from public rights to social manners.

Is This What Democracy Looks Like?

The use of civility as a bulwark against agitation for the expansion of democratic rights isn't unique to the neoliberal era. It was in the interest of polite peace, observes James Schmidt, that Congress adopted the infamous "gag rule" of 1836 against any discussion of slavery or abolition (36). In his classic *Civilities and Civil Rights*, William Chafe examines how the white progressives of 1960 Greensboro, North Carolina, prided themselves on "being hospitable to new ideas" so long as no actual move toward integration was required (7). Half a century later, Barack Obama presents himself as hospitable to discussion when it comes to LGBT marriage while at the same time he relies on the Jim Crow warrant of states' rights to justify federal inaction.[3] Although civility can smooth dialogue about contentious issues between people *already* meeting on a plane of equality and respect, in these examples we also see its history of enabling "timid acquiescence" to inequality to masquerade as "reasonable compromises in the name of the public good" (Schmidt 37).

This history of civil accommodation to injustice, argues Ellen Meiksins Wood, isn't incidental to but constituitive of liberal democracy with its elevation of private rights, especially property rights, above public. The "liberal" in liberal democracy is specifically *economic* liberalism where individual "liberty"—the freedom of the market, the right of owners to exploit the resources in their control for maximum profit—trumps "rule by the *demos*" (Chapter 7 *passim*). Even as historically excluded groups have won juridical recognition and political enfranchisement, Wood points out, the institutions and ideas of a liberal or capitalist democracy ensure that "many varieties of oppression and indignity" have been "left untouched by political equality" (224) and that "vast areas of our daily lives…are not subject to democratic accountability but governed by the powers of property and the 'laws' of the market, the imperatives of profit maximization" (234). Hence, while liberal democracy's celebrated tenets—the civil-liberties brake on state absolutism, for instance— appear to enable expansive democratic participation, at liberalism's historic heart is fortification from democratic interference. And while civility in manners and speech would appear to be a desirable precondition for democratic deliberation, civility also serves in a liberal democracy as a powerful ideological tool by a propertied class seeking to curtail the public participation that might also result in a more expansive conception of public rights. This participation-inhibiting civility is the "substantive civility" that the conservative Chicago School thinker Edward Shils championed as protecting liberal democracy from such threats as "collectivist liberalism," "emancipationism," "populism," and "egalitarianism" (Shils, *The Virtue of Civility* 4-5, 345).[4] Such civility, in service to preserving an unjust social order, is also what more than two centuries of collectivist, populist, and emancipatory movements have contested, resulting in measurable expansions of who is included in the political sphere and what democratic rights and social-justice oversight can be exercised in the economic.

What I'd like to turn to now is a chapter from one such movement for social and economic justice: the 1912 Bread and Roses strike. As a rhetorician concerned with how working-class and oppressed groups create space and means to exercise public voice, I'm drawn to the U.S. Progressive era because its conditions suggest how neoliberalism's diminished conception of democracy doesn't mark a brand-new development but instead a *restoration*, a return to the constricted conception of public rights and public good that likewise defined civil society in the first Gilded Age. For coming to terms with Indian Point's lessons for public rhetoric, a look back to Bread and Roses seems particularly instructive because unfettered corporate power and the civic institutions poised to protect that power are likewise what the immigrant workers of Lawrence, Massachusetts, were taking on. This they did with the scantest of means, making this strike a celebrated chapter in U.S. social history. What few of us learn in school, however, is that the strike also drew sharp rebuke—not just from the robber barons whose dominion the strikers challenged but also from prominent Progressive era reformers who accused the workers of using violence to press their argument. What was the danger to civil society this strike posed? What makes the assertion "We Want Bread and Roses Too" *violent*? A fuller story of this strike illustrates the unruly rhetoric that has been necessary to challenge civil boundaries of a civil society that would shield vast realms of injustice from democratic reckoning. A fuller examination of the strike's controversies, especially the Settlement Movement's condemnation of strikers for their "incivility," also reveals how a ruling class enlists middle-class sentiments to oppose social-justice arguments and defend a civil order not for the good of democracy but against it.

"A College for the Workers"

"People who have never seen an industrial struggle," observed labor journalist Mary Heaton Vorse, "think of a strike as a time of tumult, disorder and riot. Nothing could be less true. A good strike is a college for the workers" (*Footnote* 11-12). The strike to which she refers and which she covered as a young reporter for *Harper's Weekly* is the Lawrence textile strike during the bitterly cold winter of 1912. Sparked by a 30-cents-a-week pay cut to a workforce already living on starvation's edge, that now-fabled strike was carried out by some 25,000 workers, primarily women and teens, coming from more than two dozen ethnic groups speaking some 50 different languages—"all the peoples of the earth," Vorse told her *Harper's* readers, "of warring nations and warring creeds" ("Trouble" 32). The next nine weeks would demonstrate that the immigrant workers shunned by the American Federation of Labor (AFL) could unite against such daunting forces as the powerful Wool Trust monopoly and J.P. Morgan, whose American Woolen Company ran Lawrence's largest mills.

"Better to starve fighting than to starve working": This assertion by mill workers, whose average wage was less than $6 a week and whose life expectancy was half that for a Lawrence lawyer or minister, was no hyperbole (Vorse, "Trouble" 31; Tax 243). The strikers' desperate economic demands were also inseparable from a political demand for recognition by a society that regarded them, the mills where they worked, and the mill-owned tenements where they lived as the manufacturers' private property shielded from public interference. It wasn't only mill owners who viewed Lawrence's workers as little more than extensions of the looms they operated. A Lawrence minister and charity society official, for instance, denied any difference between "ball playing and bobbin tending, school work and mill work, as long as the child was occupied" (Dubofsky, *We Shall Be All* 231). When Vorse interviewed "the principal men of the town and all the ministers and several prominent women," they insisted that the workers were "pigs" who "preferred to live as they did to save money" (*Footnote* 18).

Against such ruling sentiments the strikers asserted, "We Want Bread and Roses Too." The nation would be made "to see that we are something more than mere textile workers, but are human beings," proclaimed Joseph Ettor of the Industrial Workers of the World (IWW), the radical new labor movement under whose banner the strike was waged (Palmer 1697). How the Lawrence workers with the IWW made a nation hear their arguments—making this strike a college for all students interested in learning how social justice arguments are pressed and won—is the subject of numerous histories and memoirs (e.g., Dubofsky, Flynn, Foner, Kornbluh, Tax, Vorse). Here I'll focus on the strikers' commitments to mass participation and strike democracy that *both* created the conditions for comity—recognition of Lawrence's workers and regard for their arguments—*and* unleashed backlash arguments equating their mass democratic action with riotous behavior and mob violence.

The strike's earliest hours did include window- and machinery-smashing by workers outraged to have been shorted "four loaves of bread" in their weekly pay (Palmer 1690). But as the city banned standing pickets and the state called in twenty-four infantry companies and cavalry troops—one filled with Harvard students reportedly happy to accept strike-suppression duty in exchange for Cs in their courses ("Harvard Men")—the strikers turned to mass participation coupled with the principle of "folded arms" or nonviolence as their most practical means to resist the city's and state's repressive forces. To foster across a multiethnic, multilingual workforce the unity needed for nonviolence to become a reckoning force, they set up a strike committee with 56 representatives from each of the ethnic groups; the biggest questions were decided through mass assemblies of all strikers. The commitment to full participation extended across gendered boundaries with women serving on the general strike committee, leading mass pickets, and confounding police who lamented that "'there were no leaders in the streets ... The crowds on the street were usually led by women and children'" (Tax 249).

As the strikers served together on committees and led mass pickets, they thus created rhetorical space to rival the hegemony of market logic *and* shake off such "age-old tyrannies" as nativist and sexist chauvinism (Vorse, *Footnote* 15). In mass meetings and mass marches, Vorse observed, they were "the antithesis of mob" as they "came together to create and build" and learned through the strike to "get up on platforms and speak with fire and with the eloquence of sincerity," "write articles and leaflets," or "invent new forms of demonstration" (*Footnote* 12-13). Those new forms included the mass moving picket line that the workers devised to circumvent the ban on standing pickets. With as many as 20,000 strikers circling the mill district, the workers visually demonstrated their resolve while also deterring strikebreakers. As they marched, they sang, and the sight of singing strikers stood in sharp contrast to the lethal violence meted out by the police and militia and the anti-strike propaganda painting the strikers as lawless dynamiters. "The public as a whole realized that the strikers are peacefully inclined although determined in their manner," the *Lawrence Evening Tribune*, no friend of the strikers, had to admit (Foner 332).

From strike democracy also came the action that brought the struggle's turning point. Facing a mounting need to protect the strikers' children—a Syrian boy had just been killed, bayoneted in the back by a soldier—Italian workers recommended sending the children away to sympathetic families, as was often done in European strikes. The widely publicized spectacle of scores of emaciated children arriving in New York drew mass public sympathy; the scandal of Lawrence police clubbing children and tossing women into paddy wagons to try to stop the exodus drew mass censure. In the *New York Times* incendiary headlines of the strike's early weeks—"Fear Dynamite in Lawrence Strike," "Revolutionary Socialists Incited Workers"—gave way to "More Strike Waifs to be Sent Here" and "Heads Broken Over Order to Prevent Strikers Shipping Their Children Away."

Newspapers did not retreat from their anti-strike editorializing: the *Times* scolded the strikers as "selfish" because the "demand that something be done instantly for these poor children ... ignores how much has already been done for their class" ("Children and Society") while the *Boston Morning Journal* continued to represent the strikers as an "angry mob" waging vicious "battle" against the militia ("Cavalry

Repulses Rioters' Attack"). But photographs of small children marching beneath banners proclaiming "They Asked For Bread. They Received Bayonets" drew both public sympathy *and* investigation. Government inspectors, journalists, the wife of President William Howard Taft, and many scores of heretofore absent reformers and trade unionists poured into Lawrence. In Washington, Congress convened hearings. By mid-March the mills capitulated with an agreement that included progressive wage increases of up to twenty-five percent; as a strike wave spread across New England, manufacturers extended wage increases to some quarter million textile workers region-wide (Tax 263-4).

What workers gained, Vorse reported in *Harper's*, went well beyond money for bread:

> Young girls have had executive positions. Men and women who have known nothing but work in the home and mill have developed a larger social consciousness. A strike like this makes people think. Almost every day for weeks people of every one of these nations have gone to their crowded meetings and listened to the speakers and have discussed these questions afterward, and in the morning the women have resumed their duty on the picket lines and the working together for what they believed was a common good. ("Trouble" 34-5)

Upon seeing the "six stores and seven soup kitchens" plus regular "mass demonstrations and mass amusements, huge picnics and concerts" that the workers had organized, Vorse gave up the assumption that the working class required the middle class's moral shepherding. "[A]ll laws made for the betterment of workers' lives," she argued, "have their origin with the workers. Hours are shortened, wages go up, conditions are better—*only* if the workers protest" (*Footnote* 14, emphasis added).

Bread and Roses on Trial

That Lawrence's social elites and textile barons did not share this enthusiasm is not surprising. Their vociferous condemnation, wrote Vorse, was "the inevitable reaction of the owning group protecting itself instinctively against any vital workers' movement" (Vorse, *Footnote* 18). But also troubled by and outright hostile to the strike were some of the Progressive era's most prominent reformers. Why would middle-class social workers, journalists, educators, and labor organizers waiver before or join mill owners and the press in denouncing a "vital workers' movement" that drew national attention and won some of the very reforms they had been advocating? The "trial" of Bread and Roses reveals how ruling ideas of civility can recruit even—or especially—those middle-class reformers working for social change to reinforce the very civil boundaries and social manners that allow injustice and inequality to perpetuate.

To read of Bread and Roses in *The Survey*, the journal of the Settlement movement, is to encounter an event almost entirely different from what Vorse described. Edward Devine set the tone for the April 1912 issue on "The Lawrence Strike from Various Angles" with an editorial explaining that while no one should "seek to keep alive" the strike's "bitter controversies" and "tragic incidental blunders," *The Survey* "as a journal of constructive philanthropy" had an obligation to assess these recent events "in an atmosphere far removed from the angry tumult of the labor conflict" (1). With few exceptions—Women's Trade Union League founder Mary O'Sullivan praised the strike's revival of the spirit of the early trade union movement and declared the IWW "the best possible thing that could happen to the labor unions of America" (72-3); also reprinted was Vida Scudder's speech of support to the strikers that nearly cost her job at Wellesley and became an early test of the idea of academic freedom—the issue's contributors focused on censure (of the strikers), guilt (of the IWW and also of reformers for allowing workers to fall prey to a radical union), and absolution (of the military and police). For example:

- The strike, argued Walter Weyl, who would later found *The New Republic*, did not open up a promising direction for achieving the reformers' heretofore thwarted agenda of ending child labor, improving factory safety, and ensuring a more equitable distribution of wealth. Instead, it marked the middle class's failure to stand as guardians of the immigrant poor, leaving Lawrence's workers to trade "oceans of public sympathy" for "an ounce of working class revolt" (65).
- The xenophobic Robert Woods, head of Boston's South End House and secretary of the National Federation of Settlements, who had during the strike called Lawrence's workers "the very clod of humanity" ("The Clod Stirs" 1932), declared that the strike victory under the IWW banner "represents an amount of harm which only years of aggressive educational effort can overcome" ("The Breadth and Depth" 68).
- About the police beating of women and children at the Lawrence train station, Carl Christian Carstens, head of the Massachusetts Society for the Prevention of Cruelty to Children, argued, "We must all agree that the removal of the children, even with the parents' consent, to a place where they might be brought up as thieves or prostitutes, would certainly be an offense" requiring the intervention of police who "are entitled to the credit of having acted with sincere good intentions" (71).

Their solutions varied—Weyl exhorting the middle class to greater vigilance; Harvard's James Ford favoring workers' cooperatives as an evolutionary road to prepare mentally unfit immigrants for democratic participation; Devine and Woods recommending restricted immigration; a mill overseer advocating the restoration of patient petition by workers and benevolent patronage from employers. Shared among these contributors, however, was the belief that Lawrence's problems required a remedy other than that devised by the workers themselves. At the core of their rejection of any worker-led remedy: the conviction that the mill workers' means, mass unity for a mass strike, were inherently violent.

The Survey's prominent characterization of the strikers and their union as violent is at first startling. After all, by now it had been widely acknowledged that Lawrence's workers—three dead, many hundreds wounded and beaten, at least one miscarriage resulting—had been victims, not perpetrators. By now the nation knew that it was a Lawrence school board member who, apparently at the behest of the American Woolen Company's president, had planted dynamite caches to fuel headline hysteria (Flynn 129-30; Dubofsky, *We Shall Be All* 247). As for the pillorying of the IWW as "'blood-stained Anarchists,'" it was the IWW, O'Sullivan reminded *Survey* readers, that brought to the strike "the policy of non-resistance to the aggressions of the police and the militia" (73). Yet from Devine's opening characterization of an "angry tumult" to sociologist John Graham Brooks' closing warning that the IWW aimed for "the immediate inclusion of the tramp and gutter bird" in respectable unions (82), most contributors gravitated to the truthy appeal that strike violence had been promulgated by "imported leaders" (Devine 1) who led astray Lawrence's "poor ignorant fellows" ("A Mill Overseer" 75) whose "[m]istakes of threats and violence" were "inevitable … within a large population so alien and mentally impoverished" (Ford 70).

Influencing their responses were, of course, the Settlement movement's currents of nativism and paternalism as well as the conservative drag of the AFL which had aggressively opposed the strike. Also evident is the pique of reformers at immigrant workers acting on their own authority, even marching in parades with signs insisting, "Give Us a Living Wage, Not Charity." Perhaps too, we might hear these responses as the expressions of what Barbara and John Ehrenreich would later term the "professional-managerial class" that, joining together "salaried mental workers" such as social workers and teachers, seeks the "reproduction of capitalist culture and capitalist class relations" for its own interests distinct from both labor and capital (45).[5] But in the wide agreement among reformers—present in *The Survey*'s discussion as well as in the progressive journal *The Outlook*—that the strike had been dismayingly violent and that responsibility lay with the workers for striking in the first place, I think we find something quite different from a group acting in its *own* class interests. We find the enlistment of the middle class in the corporate class's project to undo the strike victory and reassert a strict separation between the narrow sphere for practicing formal democracy (from which most mill workers were, in any case, excluded) and the vast sphere of free-market liberty into which democracy was never to encroach.

The rallying of these reformers to defend this existing undemocratic order in the name of civil ideals becomes most evident in their explanations of what precisely made the workers' actions violent. The workers and the IWW, wrote Devine, were not "frankly breaking out into lawless riot which we know well enough how to deal with"; instead, they relied on such "strange" forms of "violence" as "direct action" and "the general strike" which threatened "the fundamental idea of law and order" and the "sacredness of property" (1-2). The IWW's method of "folding the hands," warned Brooks, was intended to create a "riot of confusion" and revealed their "inveterate hostility toward society as it now exists" (82). Devine and Brooks weren't wrong in surmising that the aspirations of Lawrence's laboring majority went even beyond the crucial demands of higher pay and fewer hours. They were not wrong in suspecting that the workers had scant faith in the institutions of civil society—the mill-aligned press, the dismissive relief societies, the courts that arraigned strike leaders for deaths caused by police bullets. The strike had provided ample demonstrations that those institutions did not serve as impartial mediators providing open deliberative spaces but instead as custodians for ruling interests. The workers, who vowed in their statement accompanying the strike's settlement to continue seeking an "ever-increasing share of the value of the product of labor" and "increasing control of the machines that the workers operate" (Lawrence Textile Workers 79), were indeed arguing for "rule by the *demos*" that liberal democracy's foundational institutions and ideals—law and order, the sacredness of property—would hold in check. Whereas Vorse celebrated the new society workers were "coming together to build and create" (13), Devine, Brooks, and others defended the social order workers also sought to undo.

This isn't to say that these reformers were not deeply disturbed by the dire conditions the Lawrence strike had brought to light. "If textile workers are earning less than a living wage," Devine argued, "we should pay them more, not because they will follow strange doctrines and smash machinery if we do not, but because it is right and decent that they should have a living income" (2). Brought to light, too, were troubling questions about the very nature of U.S. democracy. "[W]hen we turn to the processes of industry, can we say that America is democratic?" was the question posed by an editorial in the leading progressive journal *The Outlook*:

> … Is there not something wrong in our industrial system itself, when thousands upon thousands among those who make the clothes of the Nation and produce the food of the Nation and help to supply the other wealth of the Nation are ill clad and on the edge of starvation? There is justice in the law, "Work or starve," but what justice is there in conditions that virtually say to thousands of workers, "Work and starve"? ("Violence and Democracy" 352-3)

Yet although *The Outlook* acknowledged that democracy should extend into the workplace—"substituting for industrial oligarchy a prevailing industrial democracy"—its editors argued that it could not happen through workers withholding their labor and thus refusing to subordinate their grievances for the good of civil peace: "It is right that the people through their representatives should use the bayonets of the militia and the clubs of the policemen to restore order whenever disorder arises" (353). Instead, economic justice would come, promised *Outlook* columnist Theodore Roosevelt, through management that is both "intelligent and sympathetic" and workers who "understand and sympathize with management" (353-4). With this assurance that civil speech and attitudes between enlightened employers and patient workers will bring, eventually, recognition and rights, Roosevelt sets aside the "work and starve" facts of the mill workers' relationship to mill managers. The rhetorical ideals of moderation and mutuality are put to work to reprivatize, as a matter best dealt with between employer and employee, the strike's public complaints.

Echoing this counsel is Jane Addams' never-before-published response to the 1894 Pullman strike, "A Modern Lear," which *The Survey* printed, with the added headnote contextualizing it as "a message for today" (Addams 131), near the end of 1912 just as silk workers in Paterson, New Jersey, had begun to stir. In casting the conflict between capital and labor as a family drama in which both father/owner and daughter/worker have forgotten their obligations to one another, Addams' parable can be read as an understandable expression of a middle-class woman's sidelined helplessness in a pitched battle between the railroad magnates and U.S. army on one side and workers and their union on the other. Given how Bread and Roses had released women from the home as well as the mill, opening up new identities as organizers, speakers, writers, and leaders, "A Modern Lear" also needs to be placed within the campaign—one that served, it soon become clear, the ruling class's agenda against *both* middle-class moderates and working-class radicals—to re-close the strike's openings and re-privatize, as a "family matter," its public arguments.

Indeed, by the time *The Survey*'s debate on Bread and Roses appeared, the mill owners' "God and Country" campaign to redivide workers and break their new union was well underway. By the decade's end, the Red Scare had decimated the IWW and had sought to shred the reputations of progressives like Jane Addams as well (McGerr 306-8). The claims of the AFL leadership to moderate respectability provided no cover; with the 1920s the corporate class unleashed an "open-shop" campaign on the AFL, reducing its membership by half. When Vorse looked back on Bread and Roses twenty-three years later—amid the great labor upsurge that would finally secure for the next half century much of the Progressive era's reform agenda—she saw that "the injustices in the textile industry which made that strike … are in broad outlines as true today as they were then …" What she also saw: "an indignation whose fire has never gone out" (*Footnote* 19, 21).

What Democracy Looks Like

When Walter Weyl fretted that mill workers had forfeited "oceans of public sympathy" for an "ounce of working-class revolt," he missed the Bread and Roses strike's fundamental appeal: *Because* the workers acted, creating a space in which they could be viewed and recognized as more than extensions of their looms, public sympathy followed. For these workers, the IWW's big-idea arguments—for instance, "Time for a four-hour day!"—were not "strange" as Devine had found them. Rather, the argument captured by such a slogan—that automation shouldn't bring speed-ups and layoffs but instead full employment and less work hours for all—made practical, virtuous sense. Between the IWW's founding in 1905 and the devastation of the Red Scare, more than a million workers participated in its radical strikes and actions (Dubofsky, "The IWW" 538).

In that period we have rich illustrations in a U.S. context of social class not as a *thing* but as a *relationship* and class consciousness not as something *given* but *made* (Thompson, *The Making* 9-11; Wood, Chapter 3 *passim*). The exploitation and antagonism workers experienced from New England mills and West Virginia mines to Midwest wheat fields and West Coast ports created in the first Gilded Age contexts for people within and across diverse workplaces to experience a new sense of relationship to one another and think in what E. P. Thompson terms "class ways" about the ruling ideas, including to varying degrees racism and nativism, that would divide them. The super-exploitative relations of production that marked the era did not automatically produce working-class solidarity and instigate mass action in all places in the same way and all at once. Instead, as Thompson emphasizes, *experience* figured as a "necessary middle term between social being [of exploitation and oppression] and social consciousness [of one's means with others to intervene]" (Thompson, *The Poverty of Theory* 98; see also Wood, Chapter 3 *passim*). The wealth of political ideas and agitational experiences brought by immigrant workers from their home countries, the class-struggle and solidarity arguments delivered by IWW soapboxers and balladeers, the legacies of the late 19th century's eight-hour day and Populist movements, and the Progressive era's myriad political campaigns—for women's and African American civil rights, against corporate monopolies, for consumer health and workplace safety—all created a rich experiential cultural environment in which U.S. workers, like those Thompson describes in his biography of England's working class, could "feel an identity of interests as between themselves, and as against their employers and rulers" (*The Making* 11).

For the journalists, labor organizers, women's suffrage advocates, and social reformers who stood in the middle of Lawrence's argument between the producers and appropriators of the region's wealth, class was likewise not a fixed position on a sociological scale. The ideas of Bread and Roses coupled with their experiences and observations drew strike witnesses like Vorse, O'Sullivan, and Scudder, as well as Helen Keller and Elizabeth Glendower Evans to the side of workers while Weyl, Devine, and the Settlement movement's most visible leaders lined up with employers. "If we stop history at any given point," observes Thompson,

> then there are no classes but simply a multitude of individuals with a multitude of experiences. But if we watch these men [and women] over an adequate period of social change, we observe patterns in their relationships, their ideas, their institutions. (*The Making* 11)

The pattern that emerges in Bread and Roses is one that repeats through the 20th century's social-justice flashpoints: the big-idea arguments and actions of exploited and oppressed groups testing society's boundaries and drawing ruling-class reprisal while a middle class is pulled in one direction—Weyl warning that to revolt against the social order means forfeiting public sympathy—or another—Vorse discerning that through a strike's upheaval "Harmony, not disorder, was being established … a collective harmony" (*Footnote* 13).

This difficulty—this class politics—of discernment is one compositionists, especially those concerned with public rhetoric for social change, need to draw out and also reassess in the work of some of our field's most celebrated thinkers. Like Weyl, for instance, Wayne Booth viewed radicalism and recognition, protest and sympathy as mutually exclusive. Consider the opening to his 1974 *Modern Dogma and the Rhetoric of Assent* where he expresses puzzlement over "the inability of *most* protest groups to get themselves heard" (xi, emphasis added). His case in point: a sixteen-day sit-in by University of Chicago students protesting the tenure denial of a popular professor. Here and throughout the book, Booth stresses his opposition to both the protest's method and substance, which he sums up as a "frantic and self-defeating multiplication and discarding of the issues" as the students advanced such further demands as voting rights on university committees, university-provided daycare centers, doubled salaries for service workers, and a democratic voice for Hyde Park residents in university appointments (8). Although it is for good reason that his subsequent life's work of seeking a "revitalized rhetoric" to rival the "warfare" of "lying, trickery, blackmail, and physical persuasion" (149-50) has had such influence, we need to trouble his founding premises: that the "protest groups" of the 1960s and early 1970s did not "get themselves heard"; that calls for university democratization are unreasonable; that such forms of "physical persuasion" as the sit-in are tantamount to blackmail, even warfare. Just as Addams' "A Modern Lear" needs to be read with critical attention to the conservative impetus for its first publication, we should place Booth's appeals for a rhetoric of assent in its historical context: a harassed dean defending a university's limited participatory sphere against a burgeoning rule-by-the-*demos* argument. By doing so, we can bring into view, and into our teaching, the wider field of rhetorical practice and the history of the rhetorical means that have won social change. Through that history we and our students can consider, against the seemingly common-sensical claim that audience unruliness always closes communicative channels, those instances where it has taken unruliness to create the conditions—"a rhetorical field," Booth writes, "… what [John] Dewey called 'a public'" (149-50)—within which communication and respect can actually flourish.

At stake in taking up such questions and engaging our students in a fuller appreciation of the rhetorical assets required—and the rhetorical controversies that ensue—in arguments for social change is the future of the very idea of a public good. The imperilment of the public good is what Raymond Shadis recognized when he called out the NRC for "infuriating" audiences by promoting nuclear-industry propaganda. In a revealing footnote near the end of *Modern Dogma and the Rhetoric of Assent*, Booth also anticipated the threat of the advancing neoliberal agenda to any rhetoric of mutual recognition and common ground. Despairing of the utter lack of comity at the core of capitalist democracy, he writes:

> It is … not just the advertising and political propaganda spawned by capitalism that must go: the whole 'liberal' assumption that men are not accountable to their fellows for how they acquire and spend their private fortunes is untenable … [I]t seems clearer and clearer that if we do not find some way to move beyond our inhumane economic system, we will lose what is left of our humane political traditions … as our present economic system induces viciousness, deception, and privatization to the point of psychosis. "Weak" forces like tradition, the church, the university, or natural altruism, if any, cannot combat this systematic destructiveness indefinitely. (201-2 n.32)

Those words not only point ahead to today's neoliberalized democracy, where state governors push legislation to privatize public resources for the profit of corporate donors and where regulatory agencies are staffed by former executives from the industries for which they are to serve as watchdogs. Booth's words also point back to the same problem of capitalist plutocracy that the IWW captured in an editorial cartoon for its journal *Solidarity* depicting a textile magnate standing on a map of the United States, wiping his feet on child labor laws and first-amendment protections while in the corner a cowering Uncle Sam bites his nails (Young).

Between then and now we have not only the past forty years of increasingly unrestrained economic destructiveness but also the previous sixty years of agitation for and the realization of indisputable, however incomplete and fragile, democratizing gains. Before we lose what is left of "our humane political traditions," we should consider and teach that what is humane and what is democratic in those traditions is owed to people, from the workers of Lawrence to the residents near Indian Point, who have been informed, passionate, *and*, when confronting an entrenched and unjust social order, frequently disorderly.

Endnotes

1. This essay began with invited talks for the Federation Rhetoric Symposium/Writing Democracy Conference at Texas A&M Commerce and the composition programs at the University of North Carolina-Charlotte and Syracuse University. I'm grateful for those opportunities to develop and discuss these ideas as well as to Shannon Carter and Deborah Mutnick for their insightful reading of an earlier draft of this article. My thinking in this essay is further influenced by the scholarship of Dana Cloud, Susan Herbst, Seth Kahn and JongHwa Lee, Paula Mathieu and Diana George, and Rolf Norgaard who likewise recommend historical, contextual, and political rather than normative approaches to the question of uncivil speech.

2. This argument about neoliberalism's dependence on civility might seem counterintuitive since most often it is associated, from Reagan's mass firing of striking air traffic controllers to the post-Katrina privatization of New Orleans' public schools, with shock-doctrine tactics and disaster opportunism. But day to day corporate privatization has also depended on a fuzzy language of consensus and compromise in service to privatizing goals (Lecercle 219-20; Welch). *Reforming* Social Security, for instance, appears as a *reasonable compromise* against the foil of Tea Party extremism. Dressed in appeals to fairness and sharing, neoliberalism's wooly rhetoric, argues Marxist linguist Jean-Jacques Lecercle, aims to avoid debate and deflect scrutiny away from policies that deepen inequality and threaten the environment (213-21).

3. At an LGBT fundraiser for the 2012 Obama campaign, a few audience members heckled the president with shouts of "Marriage!" That they also paid up to $35,800 a plate to be able to do so (Werner and Pace) illustrates the neoliberalization of protest itself—the ability to speak one's truth to power coming at a hefty price—to which the Madison capitol takeover and Occupy park encampments provide a welcome counterpoint. Welcome too is the president's recent, and long overdue, acknowledgment that same-sex couples should be able to marry. But by qualifying his statement as personal and emphasizing that the issue remains one for states, including North Carolina with its recently passed LGBT marriage ban, to decide, Obama gives us a further example of neoliberalism's wooly rhetoric: the packaging of states' rights as more democratic and just than a Constitutional right to equal protection under the law.

4. For Shils' elite conception of the "civil citizen," see also Shils "The Virtue of Civility," 304; for a survey of anti-democratic sentiment in Plato and Aristotle see Wood Chapter 6, *passim*.

5. See Erik Olin Wright's "Intellectuals and the Class Structure of Capitalist Society" for an incisive critique of the Ehrenreichs' conception of a professional-

managerial class that, with 20th-century middle-class professionalism, emerges as a social force that could rival both the working and capitalist classes.

Works Cited

Addams, Jane. "A Modern Lear." *The Survey: A Journal of Constructive Philanthropy* 29.5 (1912): 131-7. Print.

Associated Press. "AP Impact: Federal Nuclear Regulators Repeatedly Weaken or Fail to Enforce Safety Standards." *Washington Post*. Washington Post, 20 June 2011. Web. 23 June 2011.

Booth, Wayne C. "War Rhetoric, Defensible and Indefensible." *JAC* 25.2 (2005): 221-44. Print.

_____. *The Rhetoric of Rhetoric: The Quest for Effective Communication*. Malden, MA: Blackwell. 2004. Print.

_____. *Modern Dogma and the Rhetoric of Assent*. Chicago: U of Chicago P, 1974. Print.

Carstens, C. C. "The Children's Exodus from Lawrence." *The Survey: A Journal of Constructive Philanthropy* 28.1 (1912): 70-71. Print.

"Cavalry Repulses Rioters' Attack in Brisk Battle." *Boston Morning Journal* 26 February 1912. ProQuest Historical Newspapers. Web. 11 July 2011.

Chafe, William H. *Civilities and Civil Rights: Greensboro, North Carolina, and the Black Struggle for Freedom*. New York: Oxford UP, 1980. Print.

"Children and Society." *New York Times* 20 February 1912. ProQuest Historical Newspapers. Web. 11 July 2011.

Clary, Greg. "Indian Point Opponents Disrupt NRC Safety Forum." *Journal News* [White Plains, NY]. Gannett, 3 June 2011. Web. 22 June 2011.

Cloud, Dana. "In Defense of Unruliness." *Rhetoricians for Peace*. Rhetoricians for Peace listserv, 28 April 2005. Web. 24 June 2011.

Devine, Edward. "Social Forces." *The Survey: A Journal of Constructive Philanthropy* 28.1 (1912): 1-2. Print.

Dillon, John. "Nuclear Critic Urges Civility at Yankee Briefing." *Vermont Edition*. Vermont Public Radio. WVPS, Burlington. 21 June 2011. Radio.

Dubofsky, Melvyn. "The IWW at One Hundred: The Return of the Haunted Hall?" *Working USA: The Journal of Labor and Society* 8.5 (2005): 535-43. Print.

_____. *We Shall Be All: A History of the Industrial Workers of the World*. New York: Quadrangle/New York Times, 1969. Print.

Duffy, John. "Virtuous Arguments." *Inside Higher Ed*. Inside Higher Ed, 16 March 2012. Web. 17 March 2012.

Ehrenreich, Barbara and John Ehrenreich. "The Professional-Managerial Class." *Between Labor and Capital*. Ed. Pat Walker. Boston: South End Press, 1979. 5-45. Print.

Enos, Theresa. "A Call for Comity." *Beyond Postprocess and Postmodernism: Essays on the Spaciousness of Rhetoric*. Ed. Theresa Enos and Keith D. Miller. Mahway, NJ: Lawrence Erlbaum, 2003. 131-57. Print.

"Fear Dynamite in Lawrence Strike." *New York Times*. 18 January 1912. ProQuest Historical Newspapers. Web. 11 July 2011.

Flynn, Elizabeth Gurley. *The Rebel Girl: My First Life (1906-1926)*. 1955. New York: International Publishers, 1994. Print.

Foner, Philip S. *The Industrial Workers of the World 1905-1917*. 1965. History of the Labor Movement in the United States Vol. 4. New York: International Publishers, 1997. Print.

Ford, James. "The Co-Operative Franco-Belge of Lawrence." *The Survey: A Journal of Constructive Philanthropy* 28.1 (1912): 68-70. Print.

Gonzales, Juan and Amy Goodman. "New Exposé Reveals Nuclear Regulatory Commission Colluded with Industry to Weaken Safety Standards." *Democracy Now!* Democracy Now, 24 June 2011. Web. 5 July 2011.

Grabill, Jeff. "On Being Useful: Rhetoric and the Work of Engagement." *The Public Work of Rhetoric*. Ed. John Ackerman and David Coogan. Columbia: U of South Carolina P, 2010. 193-208. Print.

Kahn, Seth and JongHwa Lee, eds. Introduction. *Activism and Rhetoric: Theories and Contexts for Political Engagement*. New York: Routledge, 2011. 1-7. Print.

"Harvard Men on Guard." *New York Times* 1 February 1912. ProQuest Historical Newspapers. Web. 11 July 2011.

"Heads Broken Over an Order to Prevent Strikers Shipping Their Children Away." *New York Times* 25 Feb 1912. ProQuest Historical Newspapers. 11 July 2011.

Herbst, Susan. *Rude Democracy: Civility and Incivility in American Politics*. Philadelphia: Temple UP, 2010. Print.

Kornbluh, Joyce. *Rebel Voices: An IWW Anthology*. New and expanded edition. Chicago: Charles Kerr, 1988. Print.

Lawrence Textile Workers. "Lawrence and the Industrial Workers of the World." *The Survey: A Journal of Constructive Philanthropy* 28.1 (1912): 79-80. Print.

Lecercle, Jean-Jacques. *A Marxist Philosophy of Language*. Trans. Gregory Elliott. Chicago: Haymarket, 2009. Print.

McGerr, Michael. *A Fierce Discontent: The Rise and Fall of the Progressive Movement in America, 1870-1920*. New York: Free Press, 2003. Print.

"A Mill Overseer's View." *The Survey: A Journal of Constructive Philanthropy* 28.1 (1912): 75-6. Print.

"More Strike Waifs to be Sent Here." *New York Times*. 13 February 1912. ProQuest Historical Newspapers. Web. 11 July 2011.

Norgaard, Rolf. "The Rhetoric of Civility and the Fate of Argument." *Rhetoric, the Polis, and the Global Village: Selected Papers from the 1998 Thirtieth Anniversary Rhetoric Society of America Conference*. Ed. C. Jan Swearingen and Dave Pruett. Mahwah, NJ: Lawrence Erlbaum, 1999. 247-253. Print.

O'Sullivan, Mary K. "The Labor War at Lawrence." *The Survey: A Journal of Constructive Philanthropy* 28.1 (1912): 72-74. Print.

Palmer, Lewis E. "A Strike for Four Loaves of Bread." *The Survey: A Journal of Constructive Philanthropy* 27.18 (1912): 1690-97. Print.

Powell, Dawn. "Close Indian Point." *Points*. dawnpowell.wordpress.com, 7 June 2011. Web. 22 June 2011.

"Raging Grannies Against Indian Point." *Indian Point Miscellany*. Indianpointmiscellany.blogspot.com, 15 June 2011. Web. 22 June 2011.

"Revolutionary Socialists Incited Workers." *New York Times* 8 February 1912. ProQuest Historical Newspapers. Web. 11 July 2011.

Roosevelt, Theodore. "A Phase of Industrial Justice." *The Outlook* 11.7 (1912): 353-6. Print.

Schmidt, James. "Is Civility a Virtue?" in *Civility*. Ed. Leroy S. Rouner. Notre Dame: Notre Dame UP, 2000. 17-39. Print.

Shadis, Raymond. "NRC: Manners, Methods, Messages." *VTDigger*. VTDigger.org, 21 June 2011. Web. 22 June 2011.

Shils, Edward. *The Virtue of Civility*. Indianapolis: Liberty Fund, 1997. Print.

_____. "The Virtue of Civility." In *The Civil Society Reader*. Ed. Virginia A. Hodgkinson and Michael W. Foley. Lebanon, NH: Tufts UP / UP of New England, 2003. 292-305. Print.

Tax, Meredith. *The Rising of the Women: Feminist Solidarity and Class Conflict 1880-1917*. Urbana: U of Illinois P, 2001. Print.

Thompson, E. P. *The Making of the English Working Class*. New York: Pantheon, 1963. Print.

_____. *The Poverty of Theory & Other Essays*. New York: Monthly Review Press, 1978. Print.

"Violence and Democracy." *The Outlook* 11.7 (1912): 352-3. Print.

Vorse, Mary Heaton. 1912. "The Trouble at Lawrence." In *Rebel Pen: The Writings of Mary Heaton Vorse*. Ed. Dee Garrison. New York: Monthly Review P 1985. 29-35. Print.

_____. *A Footnote to Folly: Reminisces of Mary Heaton Vorse*. New York: Farrar and Rineheart, 1935. 1-20. Print.

Welch, Nancy. "La Langue de Coton: How Neoliberal Language Pulls the Wool Over Faculty Governance." *Pedagogy* 11.3 (2011): 571-579. Print.

Werner, Erica and Julie Pace. "Obama Again Stops Short of Backing Gay Marriage." *MSNBC*. Msnbc.msn.com. 24 June 2011. Web. 6 July 2011.

Weyl, Walter E. "It Is Time to Know." *The Survey: A Journal of Constructive Philanthropy* 28.1 (1912): 65-67. Print.

Williams, Chris. "No Fukushima-on-the-Hudson." *Indypendent*. Indypendent, 6 June 2011. Web. 22 June 2011.

Wood, Ellen Meiksins. *Democracy Against Capitalism: Renewing Historical Materialism*. Cambridge: Cambridge UP 1995.

Woods, Robert A. "The Breadth and Depth of the Lawrence Outcome." *The Survey: A Journal of Constructive Philanthropy* 28.1 (1912): 67-68. Print.

_____. "The Clod Stirs." *The Survey: A Journal of Constructive Philanthropy* 27.24 (1912): 1929-1932. Print.

Wright, Erik Olin. "Intellectuals and the Class Structure of Capitalist Society." *Between Labor and Capital*. Ed. Pat Walker. Boston: South End P, 1979. 191–212. Print.

Young, Art. "Uncle Sam Ruled Out." Image. *Solidarity* 7 June 1913. Reprinted by Labor Arts. Web. 13 June 2011.

Zeller, Tom, Jr. "Nuclear Agency Is Criticized as Too Close to Its Industry." *New York Times*. New York Times, 7 May 2011. Web. 23 June 2011.

Nancy Welch is Professor of English at the University of Vermont where she teaches courses in composition, rhetoric, women's studies, and fiction writing. Her articles have appeared in *College English*, *JAC*, *College Composition and Communication*, and *Pedagogy*, and her short stories have appeared in such journals as *Prairie Schooner* and *Threepenny Review* as well as in her collection *The Road from Prosperity* (Southern Methodist University Press). She is a recipient of College English's Richard Ohmann award for "'We're Here and We're Not Going Anywhere: Why Working-Class Rhetorical Traditions *Still* Matter," and her most recent book, *Living Room: Teaching Public Writing in a Privatized World*, was published by Boynton/Cook.

Gambian-American College Writers Flip the Script on Aid-to-Africa Discourse

Elenore Long, Nyillan Fye, and John Jarvis

This article analyzes a group of Gambian-American college writers creating an alternative public to challenge the patronizing norms operating in prevailing "aid-to-Africa" rhetorics. These young rhetors evoked performative genres and hybrid discourses so that members of their local public (the African nationals, African American professionals, white educators, fellow students, Muslim elders, conservative Christian community leaders) might themselves embody more productive self-other relations as they considered together the issue that drew them together publicly: the often hidden and insidious ways that cultural gender norms limit young African women's ability to thrive, whether in the U.S. or in the Gambia.

Efforts to yoke writing and democracy bear witness to our personal and professional commitments to participate in democratic discourses and practices. The contested relationship between writing and democracy highlights not only that "writing democracy" merits our best thinking to date, but also that, as Leo Panitch notes, no one has "a foolproof blueprint for a new type of political and economic democracy" (43). Rather, this project calls for our disciplined imagination, "an imagination which is"—as Noah De Lissovoy and Peter McLaren see it—"synthetic and philosophical, responsible to the particularities of its immediate surroundings yet intent on elaborating a vision of a common project beyond those particularities" (176).[1]

As much that stands to be imagined here, one thing is clear: *writing democracy* involves rewriting the power-laden terms of what Michael Warner calls stranger-relationality (76)—the self-other logics that govern how we relate to one another in public. That power circulates in self-other relations is perhaps inevitable (cf. Young 41); yet, contrary to prevailing scripts, these self-other power dynamics need not reinforce the rigid binary of unearned privilege. So in writing this piece, we join scholars whose research has named and interrogated the self-other norms of public life, whether those are norms that structure welfare reform debates (Flower, "Intercultural"; Higgins and Brush); urban renewal projects (Coogan; Swann); risk communications (Grabill and Simmons; Sauer); gatekeeping encounters (Cushman; Long, "Educating"); or college writing classrooms—"fashion[ing]" as rhetorical education does "the souls required for a public life" (Greene 434). Further, we argue that nowhere is the need to flip the script on stranger-relationality perhaps more important than in the United States' cultural imaginary of global citizenship where patronizing norms hold such sway that it is almost impossible to imagine and enact more humanizing alternatives so that citizens, in a spirit of mutuality, listen and learn from one another. In this study, we ask, *How do rhetors call together a public to address issues of shared concern when the prevailing norms for public deliberation thwart rhetorical engagement by undercutting the agency and expertise of those most affected by the practices under question?*

Under the leadership of co-author Nyillan Fye, a loosely organized group of Gambian-American students has come together for the past four years to script and to host annual public events advocating girls' secondary and tertiary education in the Gambia and access to schooling, including college, here in the U.S. The dozen students that came together for the 2009 action-research project featured in this article were at that time enrolled in various colleges and universities up and down the New England seaboard and positioned in a whole host of different ways to lives "back in Gambia." Additionally, they had organized the event over the Internet and had come together for a very brief interval—a handful for a full weekend, but most just for the evening. Thus, the entirely student-run annual event, held in the multipurpose room of a suburban Catholic high school, was an impressive organizational feat in its own right.

As we will elaborate below, the event called on writing teachers and other college educators—including the other authors of this piece, John Jarvis and Elenore Long—to circulate what resources they could. However, the script and other plans for the event were not developed in a college classroom or through a single community-university collaborative project. Rather, these students came together in the spirit of what Jenn Fishman et al. in Stanford's longitudinal writing study refer to as performative "out-of-class [...] self-sponsored" literacies (244). Thus, in a special issue of *Community Literacy Journal* focused on writing democracy, our argument does not pertain to the work of a given university writing program *per se* or even a given set of rhetorical interventions, as important as such scholarship is (cf. Ackerman and Coogan; Flower, *Community*; Goldblatt, *Because*; Kells). Rather, our point here is that college writers like Fye have a lot to teach those of us who teach rhetoric about this highly inventive public discourse that is taking place with or without us.

The rhetors in this study co-constructed a complex rhetorical stance—the dynamics of which can be understood in terms of what Linda Flower calls "scripts of empowerment": *speaking up*, *speaking against*, and *speaking with* (*Community* 123-49). On the one hand, they were "*up to*" a great deal (Flower, *Community* 130). That is, they were "*speaking up about*" education for women at the same time that they called audience members to enact and to imagine with them gendered ways in the world capable of significant cultural work in our transnational age (Flower 130). In addition to speaking with Gambian young people for their personal and collective well-being, these rhetors were also "*speaking against*" the social conditions that limit the life chances of many Gambian children to thrive (Flower, *Community* 127-31). They themselves were also "*up against*" a great deal—including norms of public life that would cast them as recipients of international aid rather than as actively engaged public rhetors. Finally, the student rhetors also modeled how people in "*relative institutional privilege*" can speak wisely and persuasively for social change (Flower, *Community* 149). Especially because of the relative privilege they are negotiating, these rhetors have a great deal to teach us as they disrupted reductive self-other norms toward international aid and activism even as they negotiated—as must we all—the noise (Gee, Hull and Lankshear 27), greed (Wood 230-31), and existential anomie (Crawford 186) of transnational new capitalism. These rhetors called for more inventive, playful and imaginative ways of relating to one another publicly. They suggested that in this inventive play may well reside not only the material fabric of the here and now, as well as relationships that need to continue to span generations and geographies, but also glimpses of yet unrealized futures.

Available Means of Persuasion

The event itself—cast as a beauty pageant—highlights what a tenuous rhetorical enterprise Fye and her colleagues had undertaken. If they were going to disrupt aid-to-Africa discourses, they'd have to begin by flipping the script attached to the very venue that organized the participants and attendees.

Of course, beauty pageants are often criticized, and for good reason. The United States has a relatively long history of college-age women protesting pageants on the basis that one would think might matter most to a group like Fye's, promoting as it does girls' and women's empowerment: that such pageants objectify women and cast them in passive roles for the benefit of male voyeurs. Additionally, internationally cultural critics have exposed the colonizing logic behind some pageants—for example, those that make speaking English a measure of beauty and, thus, of worth (Billings; McAllister). One might reasonably ask, then, if the pageant is so controversial, why invoke its trappings anyway? Why take these risks? Why knowingly agree to walk into such a symbolic mine field?

These may be the questions that come to mind for us as readers, but actually another set of contextual conditions were more pressing to Fye and her colleagues. In planning the event, the question before Fye was less, *Is the pageant appropriate?* And more, *What's an available cultural form? A form, that is, that's at once capable of drawing an audience and flexible enough to be adapted to our purposes?* That is, as rhetors, Fye and her colleagues had to invent an occasion to which others would likely come—in fact, one for which people would travel great distances by car and even plane to attend. Further, she needed a venue that would likely invite the participation of both women and men—behind the scenes, on stage and in the audience; an event that could be organized inexpensively and at a distance with other people investing all different levels of time and commitment. In the context that Fye knew firsthand, other venues—such as a symposium or town meeting—were far less likely to create such a draw. This was an argument Fye herself was accustomed to making, for no one approached the pageant with greater scrutiny than some of the contestants' Muslim parents who blessed their daughters' participation only in light of what Fye and her colleagues were doing with the pageant.

In the end, the pageant that Fye and her colleagues hosted that evening was undeniably hybrid. Sure, the playful contest among the contestants created a plot line. Further, this pageant invoked the precedence of other political projects across the continent of Africa, such as the Stigma-Free Miss HIV Pageant, that use the beauty pageant to accomplish significant critical cultural work (Luginaah, Yiridoe, and Taabazuing; Wolfe, Weiser, Leiter et al.). For Fye's purposes, the pageant proved a flexible enough genre to incorporate prayer, feast, talent show, and the call-and-response of audience engagement. That is, the pageant could support Fye's purposes of casting imagination among all the disparate strangers to be together for the evening in this highly inventive way. And as bell hooks reminds us, that cultural work is often most effectively cultivated not within more formal institutional spaces but within the hospitality of a public homeplace. Toward this end, the pageant fit the bill.

But this is not to say that readers aren't right to be concerned. As global citizens, we are right to watch vigilantly for the ways discourse affects how we relate to one another in public. Carolyn Miller writes: "[W]e need a rhetoric that helps build social trust" (33). If anything, the Miss-Gambia-USA pageant speaks to the risks rhetors often take to go public: in this case, the risk of hosting a poorly attended event; the risk of unintended consequences; the risk of being misunderstood. Yet for Fye and her colleagues, these were risks that had to be negotiated in real time if they were ever going to take on the larger challenge of disrupting prevailing self-other norms of aid-to-Africa discourse. This challenge was not something Fye and her colleagues could address entirely preemptively—as a precondition to their public work. Rather, as Miller concludes: "[S]uch a project cannot be a global or programmatic one: it must be risked one situation at a time" (33).

Stranger-Relationality in Aid-to-Africa Discourse

The problem space in which these Gambian-American college students worked is highly charged, for a crisis of public imagination limits how Americans tend to relate to Africans "in need." In talk and in practice, aid to Africa most commonly invokes the stranger-relationality of *noblesse oblige*, celebrity refeudalism or neoliberal economics. Here's the most maddening thing: on the one hand, these discourses thread within and around one another—binding them to one another and strengthening their resolve on the public imaginary. On the other, they push out or appropriate other discourses from which it would be easier to cast more humane and inventive self-other relations. Mutually reinforcing one another as they do, these discourses inscribe a dehumanizing doer/done-to relationship between those giving and those receiving the aid.[2]

Noblesse Oblige

The generous benevolence of *noblesse oblige* refers to a social code obligating the wealthy or noble to perform service for others (Goldblatt, "Van Rides"). Though this stance dates back to the noble princes depicted in Homeric myths, *noblesse oblige* still holds sway today, perhaps nowhere as dramatically as in aid-to-Africa discourse. Consider, for instance, *American Idol's* recent "Event to Benefit American and African Children in Poverty." Referring to the wealth accrued through the show's popularity, the show's host, Ryan Seacrest, celebrated the benefit event as an opportunity "to give something back" (Rocchio n.p.). Evidence of his benevolence, the prominent talent scout Simon Cowell, whose own career was catapulted into the far reaches of the tele-sphere by the show's commercial success, told his television viewers with uncharacteristic humility: "[Traveling to Africa] was something I'll never ever forget. Seeing some of the most appalling conditions I've ever seen in my life, and then we met some of the nicest people I've ever met. So mixed emotions, *but I'm glad that we can do something to help these guys*" (Rocchio emphasis added).

As Eli Goldblatt elaborates, *noblesse oblige* is a familiar trope for structuring stranger relationality within any kind of outreach, emphasizing as it does unequal exchange: "the fortunate give assistance to the dispossessed in exchange for a feeling of righteous accomplishment" ("Van Rides" 79). In relation to the tenacious, structural issues of poverty, illiteracy, and social fragmentation that have brought colleges and communities together, colleges and universities have often assumed their expertise, research agendas, and curricula could be readily exported to the community. As Flower explains, past or present, what often foils such partnerships are the logics motivating them. For instance, the logic of cultural mission puts patronizing distance between the learnéd "doer" and the community "receiver" or "done to"; the logic of technical expertise assumes the tools of academic research are the only viable ways to frame solutions and structure relationships; and the logic of compassion fosters an "intensely individual consciousness" quite separate from "public action" ("Partners" 97-100). It's not that colleges and universities aren't sites of useful expertise and technological resources. Instead, the challenge is figuring out how to get these resources into circulation in ways that are responsive to community needs (Mathieu 20-22), supportive of their own interests (Goldblatt, *Because* 128), and grounded in inquiry (Flower, "Partners" 100; Peck, Flower and Higgins 205) and mutual learning (Long, "Rhetoric" 303). Our point here is that if rhetors are going to flip the script of *noblesse oblige*, they have to flip the self-other relationality that drives it.

Celebrity Refeudalism
Another discourse that the rhetors in this study were up against was celebrity refeudalism. In "Rogue Cops," Susan Wells observes that prominent models for going public tend to focus upon large-scale, media-driven public arenas where the only real movers and shakers are either celebrities or politicians, *not* the likes of "you" and "me." As a result, ordinary people get cast as a mere prop in a politician's speech. Recall the typical state of the union address in which a president's speech writers have planted in the audience a "representative citizen" who waves during a quick camera scan (Wells 329). The president's speech sketches a bit of this citizen's biographical information to represent his or her endorsement of the president's political policy, whether it be on health care reform or homeland security measures. But it is the politician's agenda, not the citizen's situated knowledge, that's the focus of attention (Wells 329).

Jürgen Habermas called the worst of this phenomena *celebrity refeudalism*, those "modern forms of mediated publicness, where the powerful parade once again their power before a communicatively emasculated [sic] audience" (Cottle 412). If *noblesse oblige* casts stranger relationality in terms of the benevolent giver and grateful receiver, celebrity refeudalism turns on an even more insidious relationship among the politician-celebrity, mediated spectacle, and the consuming public (Habermas 175).

Under celebrity refeudalism in aid-to-Africa discourse, "consumption, trade and aid wed dying Africans with designer goods" (Richey and Ponte 711).

Celebrity refeudalism allows, for instance, for George Clooney to travel to Darfur as a humanitarian and return to the U.S. "the sexiest man alive" (*People*). Worse yet, in prevailing aid-to-Africa discourse, the mediated spectacle of this public display objectifies the passive needy and casts them as the backdrop against which the celebrity acts, as demonstrated in the photo op that Brad Pitt and Angelina Jolie staged for their newborn recently to turn America's attention to poverty and disease in Namibia (Smith 61). Sure, celebrities sharing their wealth and leveraging their social capital is not all bad. What is problematic, however, is that such versions of publicity tend to depict global citizens not as listeners or learners but as zealous consumers of publicity stunts and other "staged display[s]" of public life (Habermas 206).

The discourse of celebrity refeudalism posed additional challenges for the rhetors in this study. This discourse suggests that since there's no better alternative than celebrities shaping the direction of international aid discussions, there's no legitimate way to publicly point to or question the implications that follow from it. One scholar who has tried is Dambiso Moyo, the Zambian-born, Oxford- and Harvard-educated author of *Dead Aid: Why Aid is Not Working and How There is a Better Way for Africa*. A critic of "Western aid to Africa and its recent glamorization by celebrities," she argues that "Western aid to Africa has not only perpetuated poverty but also worsened it" (Solomon n.p.). As Moyo explained in a recent interview: "I object to this situation as it is right now where [...] celebrity rock stars [...] have inadvertently or manipulatively become the spokespeople for the African continent" (qtd. in Solomon n.p.). Moyo contends that celebrity-led aid to Africa has led to corruption, waste, and a debilitating sense of agency.

Public reception of Moyo reflects the sway of celebrity refeudalism. Some background is in order here. Moyo is a free-market economist; she conceives of a global free market where rock stars aren't shaping foreign aid policy. Now, as we would expect, critics of her book criticize her faith in the free market. What's ironic, however, is that critiques of her economics aren't framed primarily in relation to other economic models but rather in defense of the stranger relationality that Moyo finds so abhorrent: celebrity refeudalism as epitomized by the Irish rock musician and activist Bono, who launched Project (RED)™ to "rebrand Africa" as a site where "companies selling the RED products [could ...] make a profit by helping the poor" (Richey and Ponte 713).[3] Take, for instance, the final line in Niall Ferguson's foreword to *Dead Aid*. Ferguson writes: "This reader was left wanting a lot more Moyo, and a lot less Bono." Regardless of Ferguson's intent, that choice between Moyo and Bono has served as the central trope in subsequent reviews of *Dead Aid* as analysts debate the relative merits and flaws of Moyo's scholarship (cf. Hamm; Solomon; Watkins). As a consequence, Moyo's urgings to rethink the stranger relationality behind foreign aid have been silenced or worse yet even turned against her, as evidenced in Kevin Watkins' "Why Dead Aid is Dead Wrong." Watkins concludes his piece: "'More Moyo and a lot less Bono?' Thanks but no thanks"—as if celebrity refeudalism were both the only viable solution to poverty in Africa and, because of the shroud of glory that surrounds it, in a league of its own, protected from the rigors of critical scrutiny.

Neoliberal Economics

The rhetors in this study were also up against the sway of neoliberal economics. Neoliberal economics seriously reduces the complex and often contradictory relationship between democracy and global capitalism. Here, stranger-relationality turns on the generosity of citizens from "developed" countries to extend resources to the "developing" poor. In public life, neoliberalism trumps other ways of conceiving public engagement and how people would configure themselves for such engagement. It assumes when people gather publicly, their interests are primarily monetary, so the main reason for getting together in public is to promote, pump up, and stage the transfer of funds. Thus, this economic transfer creates both the plot for the event and the stranger-relationality among participants. If *noblesse oblige* obligates the wealthy to give back and if celebrity refeudalism markets a corporate Cool Factor to those who do, then the stranger-relationality of neoliberal economics extends the glorification of the humanitarian celebrity to the United States Everyman. And what is it that this Everyman bequeaths onto others by offering capitalist charity or by micro-financing entrepreneurial efforts? Empowerment.

In rhetoric and composition, empowerment is largely understood as a complex dynamic that can be manifested in numerous ways under various if daunting constraints and conditions. Consider, for instance, Michelle Hall Kells, Valerie Balester, and Victor Villanueva's *Latino/a Discourses: On Language, Identity and Literacy Education*. Essays throughout the volume dramatize versions of empowerment that re-imagine relationality to honor the linguistic diversity Latino/a students bring to writing classrooms and to challenge the linguistic racism that still permeates mainstream culture. In the name of such empowerment, Villanueva celebrates the capacity of discourse to bear witness to diverse cultural legacies. Recognizing the multiplicity of differences across Latino/a discourses, he urges readers not only to honor differences but also to bear witness to shared experiences of struggle, exile, displacement, and servitude. In coming together to understand their Latino/a discourses, Villanueva argues that he and other readers of Latino/a Discourses can receive the respect that is rightly theirs.

But neoliberalism has a voracious appetite. It gets its fill by co-opting the values we care about—such as empowerment—for its own gain. James Gee, Glynda Hull and Colin Lankshear explain this phenomenon in relation to the fast capitalist economic theory that promotes neoliberalism:

> [P]art of the way in which fast capitalism texts "grab us" is that they use words that name things which nearly all of us like but which, on reflection, are seen to mean slightly (and sometimes *very*) different things in fast capitalism texts than they might mean to many of us: words like "liberation", "empowerment", "trust", "vision", "collaboration" [...]. (29)

With this slight of hand, current economic conditions go unquestioned. Behind the scenes, however, those conditions not only support the system that glorifies financial generosity but also intensify the need for its display.[4] Worse yet, neoliberalism threatens the dignity of everyone positioned on the spectrum from the wealthy few who benefit from it to the increasing number of poor people it presses down on and often downright exploits. As Gee, Hull and Lankshear point out, neoliberalism is inherently insulting; instead of paying people what they're worth, it offers membership in a club where the privilege of membership is the honor of working harder for less. Rather than live with the recognition of how insulting this logic is, the tendency is to accept the allure of neoliberalism's magnetism. Neoliberalism insists we must agree to both the new meanings accorded our core values and to the loyalty it demands of us; otherwise, we are all fools. The siren song of neoliberalism is that to have any dignity, we must keep re-inscribing the neoliberal script.

We can glimpse the bankrupt stranger relationality of neoliberalism through the work of transnational feminists who offer careful analyses of foreign aid to poor women. Their deepest critique is that this neoliberal discourse foregrounds and glorifies the agency of those giving the aid without recognizing the numerous material and intangible ways women already contribute to the health of their communities, often under the most dire of circumstances. For instance, in *Networking Arguments: Rhetoric, Transnational Feminism, and Public Policy Writing*, Rebecca Dingo explains that such aid tends:

- to be top-down, welfare-based and basic-needs oriented
- to focus on individual women and their choices as agents for economic change
- to make standard particular gendered ways of acting and to homogenize women's experiences
- to frame the empowerment of women as a means toward an end—particularly a nation's economic stability, well-being, and global contribution
- to be linear in concept whereby technological advancement, industrial development, and formal labor participation mark a nation's success. (cf. Rowlands 12-13)

Neoliberal economic policies tend to put women in "developing" countries in a double bind, responsible for both preserving the integrity of the family unit and for gaining employment outside the home to secure the family's economic independence (Dingo, "Linking" 491). In this context, neoliberalism fails to recognize that efforts to integrate women into the local and global economics do not always alleviate women's oppression. It also overlooks the fact that women's well-being is affected by a complex and nuanced relationship among development practices, local culture, geopolitical factors, gender relationships, and resources (Grewal 23).

And yet the stranger-relationality that neoliberal foreign aid invokes is popular and alluring. It appears, for instance, on our campuses when universities sponsor and then promote students' social entrepreneurial ventures where the deepest purple robe of agency is clearly wrapped around generous and concerned students who have reached out and made possible the initiative of individual enterprising others. For instance, at one of our schools this past fall, the administration circulated a Sharepoint slideshow as an exemplar for student groups to follow when submitting their ideas for a social entrepreneurial contest. In this exemplar, the innovative students were individuated if highly stylized as urban, successful movers and shakers: the young women in short skirts and long flowing hair, the young men in Miami-Vice haircuts and deep pocketed suit jackets. The students' plan offered to "inoculate Africa" against meningitis—the population of which was represented not as people let alone as individual persons with experiences and expertise, but rather invoked repeatedly through a map of the entire continent.

Neoliberalism supports the free market fiction that drives privatization, sidestepping the fact that this very model is in worldwide crisis (cf. Solomon; Stiglitz 295). The cultural workers that matter to this discourse are—as Wells points out—celebrity politicians whom we, as global citizens, are asked to consume or mimic, as an alternative to seeking out and listening to the people most affected by the international policies and transnational practices under discussion.

In sum, then, the student rhetors in this study had to contend with how *noblesse oblige*, celebrity refeudalism, and neoliberal economics mutually reinforce the distinctive self-other relationship that circulates in aid-to-Africa discourse. In this script, the liveliest actors are the benevolent givers of the aid. The script masks the givers' own power and privilege by casting it—even glorifying it—as benevolence. In order for these givers to remain benevolent, the hierarchy that structures this relationality has to remain in place. Thus, the giver of aid may say and write things that speak to the underlying issues that the aid is meant to assuage, but only in ways that reinforce the self-other relationship and preserve the hierarchical structure that holds that relationship in place. Exemplifying this dynamic was the July 2007 issue of *Vanity Fair* that Bono guest-edited, "unapologetically promot[ing] status, capitalism and conspicuous consumption in the name of 'helping'" (Richey and Ponte 713-14). Lisa Ann Richey and Stephano Ponte explicate the fallacious logic behind this stance:

> Given the legacy of slavery and colonialism and the history of extraction of resources and supply of armaments to the continent, it is difficult to imagine a time when the rich have not been interested in Africa. Assuming that Africa is far from the minds, lives, and income-sources of the rich readers of *Vanity Fair* contributes to the myth that there is no real linkage between the rich and the poor, between the entrepreneurs and Africa, or between capitalism and disease. (713)

Such discourse "mask[s...] the social and environmental relations of trade and product that underpin poverty, inequality and disease" (711).

Within this rhetorical vortex, the underlying structures that perpetuate injustices do not change. This is Amarpal Dwaliwal's argument: "The inability of radical democratic inclusion politics to deal with inclusion retaining peripheralization is a key limitation, especially given that, in many liberal democratic societies, many subordinated groups have been 'included' by being accorded certain formal rights like the right to vote" (44). Such a limitation also lurks in international aid. For such aid may profess inclusion—hopes of bringing more people to the center—and, in fact, this desire to be inclusive may be a genuine sentiment. But this version of inclusion is an invitation that those at the margins conform to norms, values, and practices that maintain the pre-existing privileges, deprivations, and power relations. Dwaliwal continues:

> If inclusionary attempts often reaffirm "a hegemonic core to which the margins are added without any significant destabilization of that core"

> or continue to valorize the very center that is problematic to begin with, it is clear that the motivation to include needs questioning. The governing assumptions or conceptual logic guiding gestures to include must be interrogated in order to grapple with oppression in the form of appropriation, commodification, fetishization, and exoticization, to name a few. (44)

Thus, these norms of stranger-relationality that circulate in discourses of *noblesse oblige*, celebrity refeudalism, and neoliberal economics pose a serious challenge for the rhetors in this study.

The Miss-Gambia Action-Research Project

In June of 2009, a group of Gambian-American college writers hosted the fourth annual Miss Gambia-USA Pageant. The event was attended by a loosely organized network of strangers. The African American attorney from Harlem who sat next to Jarvis and Long, for instance, had read about the event on Facebook and had come to check it out. In the audience of just under eighty people, some of the African nationals had come to the U.S. not by way of Gambia but Nigeria or Senegal. That evening in June—a few weeks after finals week for some and graduation for others—was also a reunion of sorts for college friends offering an excuse to get together.

As is clear from its motto—crown a miss, educate a child—the 2009 Miss Gambia-USA Pageant focused public attention and resources on educational opportunities for young women in Gambia, a small Muslim country in West Africa that runs in the middle of Senegal along the Gambia River.[5] Fye and her Gambian siblings and cousins who participated in the event in various ways are Muslim, as is 90% of the Gambian population. Public primary and secondary schools in Gambia are largely Muslim; typically, even small village schools will have their own leading imam. Although traditionally families could afford only to educate their sons, since the late 1980s the government has subsidized the education of girls through the primary grades. And yet, even though it is subsidized, primary education is not to be taken for granted, especially among girls whose traditional roles keep them at home. Traditional roles aside, affording daughters' schooling beyond these years taxes many poor families (Perfect 430). In the rural region of the Gambia called Barra, some of the madrassas for orphan boys make daily stints of begging a condition for enrollment. In real and persistent ways, drug and sex trades threaten the exploitation of poor children. We are not suggesting the education of girls is politically neutral or uncomplicated, but it does defy the commodification of them. As a contestant, who finished high school here in the U.S. after doing most of her schooling in Gambia, announced during the pageant, finishing high school was her "most noteworthy accomplishment."

The Miss-Gambia USA organization promotes the education of girls by raising money for students' tuition, by providing school supplies and books for a community library, and by sending the winner of the Miss Gambia pageant each December or January of her "reigning year" to a set of schools in the Barra region to talk to students about her education and to encourage them in theirs.

We do not contend that this 2009 Miss Gambia-USA Pageant did or could expunge from its event all consumer-driven impulses toward international aid. Discourse doesn't work that way. Nor do we mean to suggest that the pageant is entirely free from prevailing inclinations toward aid, or that it set out to exemplify some radical brand of neo-Marxist politics. But the pageant did actively negotiate these norms of relationality as it invented discursive space where global citizens could venture together to name—to co-construct—some of the terms of a yet uncharted future.

Turning *Noblesse Oblige* on its Head

If *noblesse oblige* makes benevolent, honorable generosity the responsibility of persons of high birth or rank, then the Miss Gambia USA pageant began subverting this self-other norm the moment the event's project manager, Sutaye Jarju,[6] launched into his invocation. Jarju's epideictic rhetoric turned on the theme of nobility. His remarks acknowledged that nobility was accessible not only to everyone in the room but also to the people on whose behalf they had gathered. Jarju framed the pageant as an "auspicious occasion," one that "stands against oppression and injustice" in his home country by standing for the education of girls. He continued:

> There is nothing more noble than helping young people to turn their dreams into realities. There's nothing nobler than trying to inspire young people to become great future leaders. And that is what makes this program very unique, as it is run by young people ourselves.

Echoing Martin Luther King and John F. Kennedy, Jarju concluded: "We must live together as brothers or we will all perish as fools. [...] Each time a man stands up for an ideal that improves the lives of others or strikes out against injustice and oppression, he stands for hope. And this is what the Miss Gambia pageant stands for."

In conventional aid-to-Africa discourse, participants are included under the aura of nobility as long as the celebrity is there bestowing empowerment onto others. This is false or cheap inclusion Dhaliwal criticizes in her analysis of the "relationships between discourses of race, rights, representation, and democracy" (43). Such inclusion is temporary and contingent on the glorification of the capital-S Self acting against the backdrop of the passive other. But the nobility Jarju referred to changes the very criterion of nobility. Participants are noble not because there was a celebrity among us but because of the ways we enact our concern for the well-being of others. This is driven home when, toward the end of his remarks, Jarju quoted the remarks of a young girl in the Gambia whose education has been underwritten by the Miss Gambia-USA organization. He drew attention to this young girl's comments in the context of a slideshow he introduced:

> You will hear young people speaking. What those young people are speaking about is what they want to become after they finish school. Gratefully, I was not surprised when one of them said that "I want to become Miss Gambia." She said she wanted to become Miss Gambia to

help other young people like them. That personally brought so much joy to me because I came to understand, Oh, young people understand exactly what we are trying to do [...] and they want to do that for other young people. And I believe that is a trend that each of us must take.

The mutuality the girl expresses here humanizes givers and recipients as it interrogates the division between the two.

Currency and Capital

According to the logic of global capitalism that governs international aid, "work produces the value that is itself the sense and substance of this system (i.e., capital) and by which alone the system is reproduced" (De Lissovoy and McLaren 163). Aid to Africa participates in this reproduction when it masks "the social and environmental relations of trade and production that underpin poverty" (Richey and Ponte 711) by selling to consumers the allure of the Bono-fide "cool quotient" (711). As a corporate strategy, "celebrities and consumer-citizens unite [...] to do good by dressing well" (712), whereby "perpetuat[ing] the disengagement of 'needy' recipients in order for us to become benefactors with bling" (726). Thus, in marketing an antidote to Western white-collar workers' alienation under the guise of "heroic shopping" (713), the logic driving this discourse further "alienates [...] imaginative potentiality from the subject and shuts the latter down into a finished and singular positivity" (De Lissovoy and McLaren 163).

In contrast, the Miss Gambia USA pageant circulates a relationship among labor, meaningful work, and cultural capital that is marked not by the transcendent "'hard commerce' sex appeal" of Project (RED)™ (Richey and Ponte 725), but by the situated accounts of ordinary people building meaningful and purposeful lives with and for others (Wood 230). Consider, for instance, the introduction that the Mistress of Ceremonies, Yahar Ceesay, extended to one of the pageant's judges, Mr. Wilson, a professor at a nearby college. Wilson was honored with the opportunity to serve as a judge not because he himself is such a snappy dresser or has some distinctive fashion sense that would qualify him to somehow evaluate the contestants' performances. Rather, as Ceesay explained, he was selected for the pageant because of his track record working—over the course of his "thirty seven years" a college professor—to put young Gambian-Americans in touch with educational programs and other resources that they have found genuinely beneficial. Ceesay announced: "He is actually my mentor, so I'm very proud to have him here tonight." She crafted Wilson's introduction in terms of these programs and resources, and made information about them available orally over the course of the evening and in print through the flyers distributed at the pageant's end.

Likewise, before announcing the pageant's winner, Miss District of Columbia Sarena Royce explained her involvement, as an American college student, in the Gambia where both she and Fye had served as field researchers. Royce served as a researcher for a community assessment project sponsored by the International Red Cross; Fye as fieldworker for a research project sponsored by the Sajuka School to investigate child- and drug abuse in the Gambia and its relationships to children not going to school, the results of which were submitted to Save the Children Representatives in the Gambia. Royce used her time on stage to refer to this research project and the ways in which the information the children provided is shaping the design and delivery of a new community hospital.

Against the backdrop of the Western slave trade with deep roots in the Gambia—home to the ancestral heritage that Alex Haley retraces in his epic book *Roots*—this move merges "experiential understandings" with information about at least some of the "historical [and economic] forces" that perpetuate poverty in the Gambia (Scatamburlo-D'Annibale and McLaren 147). By circulating such information, Royce identified publicly some of the mechanisms that perpetuate the conditions of poverty in which so many young girls go to school. There was nothing sanctimonious about her delivery. In her remaining seconds on stage before turning the microphone over to the newly crowned Miss Gambia USA, she asked us all: "Anyone have the recipe for chicken yassa?"—the chicken-and-rice dish served to everyone who gathered that evening for the pageant.

Interspersed throughout the pageant, such speeches described in material terms ways that real people are building full adult lives that include professional and personal commitments and projects in the Gambia—even as they maintain close ties and projects here in the U.S. So doing, participants modeled how people in relative institutional privilege can speak wisely and persuasively for social change (Flower, *Community* 135). Moreover, these speeches challenge the static binary of more conventional aid-based self-other norms by charting reciprocal movement between the cities in the U.S. where pageant participants and members of the audience now live for much if not all of a given year and "back home in Gambia." So it's not that— as in *Blind Side*—the Sandra Bullock character rescues a poor misunderstood young Black man from an urban waste land by drawing him into her nuclear family values and practices, nor that capital-O Others are the ones held responsible for staying behind to make said improvements. Instead, this reciprocal movement manifests itself in ways imaginable only in the peculiar climate of transnationalism (Dingo, "Securing" 178).

Disrupting the Hegemonic Core

The rigid self-other norms that prevail in international aid discourse are met in traditional Gambian culture by equally fixed gender roles and expectations—roles and expectations that are, rather ironically, both fixed under long-established custom and under siege by neoliberal economic-development rhetoric (Dingo, "Linking" 492). Of the pageant's most important rhetorical work disrupting this intersection of aid and custom, two acts are particularly significant: a hip-hop dance and the contestants' skit.

The hip-hop dance. Four Gambian-American young men known collectively as the Ndaga Boys performed a dance in which Jarju, playing a village leader, or *alkali*, in the Gambia, comes across the young men dancing in the street. In the performance, the *alkali* vehemently objects to the men's American-style of hip hop for being too sexually suggestive and threatens to shut down the performance altogether. The young men reply—in dance, of course—that traditional dance can be just as suggestive and proceed to illustrate just how suggestive these traditional dances moves can be. To the dancers' highly stylized kicks and thrusts, the audience erupts in laughter, and for a while the music can't be heard over the din of applause. In the end, the young men's skill at performing traditional dance steps succeeds in winning over the *alkali*.

The contestants' skit. Four young women performed a play—also set in a village in the Gambia. The dramatization begins with the first daughter calling her mother into a discussion about the daughter attending secondary school. At first, the mother resists—demonstratively—insisting that what's needed is not her daughter attending more schooling but the daughter showing up at market each day to sell the family's farm produce. The mother and daughter's disagreement escalates. But the daughter invokes her rights to education under UNICEF, and she insists that her mother's plan for her could leave her destitute should she, after marriage, be widowed or her husband fall ill. In the end the daughter's argument is so persuasive that the mother then takes her daughter's argument and uses it to engage the a second mother-character in a dialogue about *her* daughter's education.

The performative rhetoric here works less according to the propositional logic associated with deliberation and more according to the logic of disruption that, for instance, Gwendolyn Pough associates with hip hop and "wrecking." For Pough wrecking is that instance of hip hop that connotes "fighting, recreation, skill, or boasting" (65). In *Check it While I Wreck it*, she observes that wrecking has been frequently used to call attention to the work African American rhetors have traditionally had to accomplish before public deliberation even becomes possible.[7] Were the pageant orchestrated primarily to promote access to education, it might be said to have worked according to the democratic-lite model that Dhaliwal associates with cultural appropriation, drawing previously excluded people into its hegemonic core. But these performances did more than accommodate difference by arguing to extend education to previously excluded girls; rather, these performances disrupted simultaneously the status quo of both international aid and traditional custom. They did so through the careful interplay of what in the study of radical street theater goes under the name of "authenticating" and "rhetorical" conventions.

The orchestrated tension between "authenticating" and "rhetorical conventions" is theorized by Baz Kershaw in *The Politics of Performance: Radical Theater as Cultural Intervention*. Drawing on the work of Elizabeth Burns, Kershaw explains that *rhetorical conventions* "secure an agreement to conjure up a fictitious world [...]; the means by which the audience is persuaded to accept characters and situations whose validity is ephemeral and bounded to the theater"; *authenticating conventions* "imply a connection to the world of human action of which the theater is only a part. [...] Their function is, therefore, to authenticate the play" (25).

Within these two pageant performances, the authenticating conventions were affiliated with Gambian culture: traditional dress in both performances; traditional dance for the Ndaga Boys, a script in Wolof language for the contestants' skit. In both performances, the rhetorical conventions were those that conjured up worlds where young people could engage elders in sustained and focused conversations about cultural norms and institutional practices that have limited women's options. In both cases dramatic tension had to be achieved within the tenor of the pageant.

Kershaw's point is not simply that political street theater often makes use of authenticating and rhetorical conventions or that street theater regularly puts these conventions in circulation together, but rather that the interventional technique *per se* is a rhetorical move—a logic, if you will—that deliberately strives to limit the interpretations available to the audience by orchestrating the interplay of the two sets of conventions to the point of "rupture" (Kershaw 33-35). The point of disruption is to perform a new way in the world—an invention—that otherwise would not have seemed possible. This is the premise on which Kershaw assigns efficacy to radical street theater: "For the 'possible worlds' encountered in the performance are carried back by the audience into the 'real' socio-political world in ways which may influence subsequent action" (37).

For the Ndaga Boys, disruption allowed invoking a world where young men can speak back to biases they find hypocritical and unfounded (cf. Cintron 92); a world where men actively support the education of girls and young women without either taking over or feeling emasculated. If—as the transnational feminists' Gender and Development movement suggests—men have important yet under-elaborated roles to play in enfranchisement of women in developing countries, the Ngada Boys' hearty participation in the pageant enacts a kind of sharing of responsibility for the current and future well being of sisters, daughters, cousins, and female friends.

For the pageant's contestants, the skit's disruption allowed them to invoke a world where women of different generations engage together in the shared use of reason (cf. Habermas 24); a world where daughters are so persuasive that their mothers use the arguments they hear their daughters making to appeal to and persuade other mothers (cf. Fraser 123; Young 52). Some readers may wonder whether the skit, by virtue of being staged on a kitchen floor back in Gambia, didn't re-inscribe women to the most limited of traditional roles. But this reading would enormously reduce both the possibility that "the home" can serve as a site of political resistance (hooks 32) and the rhetorical power the skit recognizes in the authenticating conventions of the lively Wolof of ordinary Gambian women (cf. Young 71).

Conclusion

This study asked: *How do rhetors call together a public to address issues of shared concern when the prevailing norms for public deliberation thwart rhetorical engagement by undercutting the agency and expertise of those most affected by the practices under question?* We've contended that the pageant reconfigured the norms for stranger-relationality in aid-to-Africa discourse itself. We've tried to show how the rhetors evoked and enacted pageantry, prayer, theatrics, traditional tribal dance, hip-hop, and call-and-response, and moved among Wolof, Arabic, and English to expose and to interrogate both Islamic and Western cultural gender expectations and to embody some of the hidden and under-acknowledged ways that these expectations limit options for girls and women. The intensely hybrid discourse that resulted is distinctly multivocal and performative, one that reconfigured norms of stranger-relationality as it transformed women's daily experiences into grist for inquiry and action.

As we've tried to understand what these rhetors were up against, we've sought also to underscore the significance of these students' cultural work. Of course, such work does not and cannot flip the script on aid to Africa once and for all. Rather, such rhetorical performance works with tenacious persistence that does—at the same time—have a ripple effect on real bodies. For as M. M. Bakhtin reminds us: "The living utterance, having taken meaning and shape at a particular historical moment in a socially specific environment, can not fail to brush up against thousands of living dialogic threads, woven by socio-ideological consciousness around the given object of utterance; it cannot fail to become an active participant in social dialogue" (276).

The most immediate ripple effect of the pageant was the assembly and care of what John Dewey might call the collective, public We. Dewey writes: "But 'we' and 'our' exist only when the consequences of combined action are perceived and become an object of desire and effort" (151). Consider that this event lasted for five and a half hours—long into the evening, and most of us had long drives ahead of us still that night. After the performance, when people perhaps more typically would have eagerly packed up and gone home, another public configuration emerged. Members of what had been "the audience" for the pageant reconfigured themselves to seek out people whose comments over dinner or whose questions during the Q-and-A portion of the pageant had piqued one another's interests. This public discourse was distinctly multivocal, just as the pageant itself had been. To someone arriving late to the event, the mix of Wolof, French, and various World Englishes under the acoustical constraints of a high school multipurpose room may have seemed cacophonous. However, a local public is under no obligation to subscribe to the terms of even the best normative theories. We believe the din instantiated on empirical grounds the "untidy communicative practices" that shape local vernacular public life (Hauser 275) under transnationalism—that is, a publicity that Gee, Hull and Lankshear called for in *The New Work Order*:

> This new Discourse would disavow the consumer determinism of the new capitalism. It would argue for the reinvigoration of the local as against the "*faux*" local of the new capitalism. It would see critique as necessary to real learning and thus as part and parcel of critical thinking and the empowerment of workers. Most importantly, it would envision a new "global citizenship" in terms of which we all begin to care about the members of the cooperative in Nicaragua and about the poor in our own communities—as being linked to each other and ourselves—if only to avoid degradation of all our spaces and lives. (166)

In the moments immediately following the pageant, a young man grabbed a microphone and created a stage area for himself on the gymnasium floor. He performed a raucous, impromptu hip-hop tribute to his home country located just north of the Gambia: Senegal. Between stanzas of his song, several people stopped to talk to him about his boyhood there. Another circle formed around Royce, asking her to elaborate on the findings she had earlier mentioned from her research in the Gambia; an elderly woman slipped her a half sheet of paper where she had jotted the recipe for chicken yassa. Fye and Ceesay were joined by ever-growing circles of aunts, mothers, cousins, African American college friends, and African nationals, teachers and friends to hear about what was next for them as they mapped their young adult lives between the Gambia or other west African countries, and New England. This discussion had a distinctive theme: transnational womanhood; and, more specifically, how we could be together in charting and supporting those new paths and projects. For each such path or project entails new risks and puts existing relationships under new kinds of pressure—as well as opens up new possibilities. These conversations were lively and engaging, and came to a close only when the night janitor jingled his keys and flicked the lights to signal that the multipurpose room was now his to reclaim.

The pageant also reconfigured real bodies by offering further form and function to the young Gambian-American men's interest in the well-being of their sisters, nieces, cousins, and neighbors. The Ngada Boys' participation, for instance, included not only dancing at the pageant but also producing the video of the event, burning it to DVDs that they have then circulated, and maintaining the organization's Web presence. These latter projects have helped to scaffold the commitment and imagination of an increasing number of young people. For Fye, this reconfiguration has been one of the most significant effects of the pageant—one proving to have some of the greatest staying power.

Further discursive ripples inspired the administration at Jarvis's college to offer scholarships to twelve girls at the Sajuka School each year for the foreseeable future and to extend those scholarships to their college after the recipients' high school graduations.[8] Within this framework, Jarvis and Fye have since launched a program to take a dozen to fifteen college students to the Gambia in January or May of each subsequent year to work for the Sajuka School and to produce jointly directed documentaries featuring lives of Sajuka School students.[9] (For the method and curriculum shaping these documentary projects, see Long, Jarvis, and Deerheart Raymond.) Significantly, as a result of the pageant and the work it did to challenge norms of stranger relationality, the educational training for students preparing to go to the Gambia to work with Fye and Jarvis has been reconceptualized. Along with reading more familiar texts on humanitarian aid such as *Three Cups of Tea: One Man's Mission To Fight Terrorism And Build Nations . . . One School At A Time* and *Half the Sky: Turning Oppression into Opportunity for Women Worldwide* and others available through UNESCO and Red Cross, students read together this essay, as well as many of the sources cited in this piece—texts like those by Dingo and by Richey and Ponte—to help college students and faculty members name, evaluate, and negotiate their own motivations, stances, and identities as members of a globally situated, locally positioned, public We.

Endnotes

1. We'd like to thank Linda Flower, Jennifer Clifton, Shannon Carter, and Deborah Mutnick for responding to previous versions of this essay. We are grateful to Tim Dawson for helping us see and articulate the play of authenticating and rhetorical conventions at work in the Ngada Boys' hip-hop performance and the contestants' skit.

2. Martin Luther King Jr., bell hooks, and Cornel West belong to what Keith Gilyard terms a "prophetic tradition" in deep democracy—a tradition both insisting that structural injustices perpetuate attitudes and practices that dehumanize all involved, and also demanding engaged efforts to hold the structures accountable to the people who experience daily violations (Gilyard 59).

3. Bono's less celebrated name is Paul David Hewson.

4. Gee, Hull, and Lankshear explicitly treat the relationship between global privatization and the exploitation of the poor. See pages 35, 67, 150.

5. In the 11th century, Islam was superimposed on a dynamic matriarchal culture. In 1816, the Gambia became a British colony—thus, English is still its official language—and has had a turbulent political history, gaining independence from Britain in 1965.

6. Pseudonyms are used throughout this analysis.

7. Because in the U.S. Black people have historically been invisible "in the eyes of the governing body and society at large," Pough notes, "spectacle becomes key; [… s]pectacle and cultural representation are the first steps in bringing a disruption, the first steps in bringing wreck" (21). Harkening back to the Black Panther Party, Pough calls attention to the ways that they and other Black groups used spectacle to "renegotiate the public sphere in order to claim power for themselves" (22).

8. The 2009 Miss-Gambia USA pageant helped launch several scholarship programs and fund a library at the Sajuka Elementary School in the Barra region, the only non-madrassa school in its region that enrolls girls as well as boys. The pageant was also instrumental in Fye's and Jarvis's efforts to create the Sajuka Community Development Project, an exchange program and partnership between Fye's undergraduate college, Bay Path College, and the Sajuka Elementary School in Barra.

9. Fye has since graduated from college. For her current job, she travels regularly between Nigeria and New England. She's been able to organize her work for the months of January and May so she can join Jarvis and the college students in Barra, the Gambia, for weeks at a time.

Works Cited

Ackerman, John and David Coogan, eds. *The Public Work of Rhetoric: Citizen-Scholars and Civic Engagement.* Columbia: U of South Carolina P, 2010. Print.

Bakhtin, M. M. *The Dialogic Imagination: Four Essays.* Ed. Michael Holquist. Trans. Caryl Emerson and Michael Holquist. Austin: U Texas P, 1981. Print.

Billings, Sabrina. "'Education is the Key of Life': Language, Schooling, and Gender in Tanzanian Beauty Pageants." *Language & Communication* 31.4 (2011): 295-309.

Burns, Elizabeth. *Theatricality: A Study of Convention in the Theater and in Social Life.* London: Longman, 1972. Print.

Cintron, Ralph. *Angels' Town: Chero Ways, Gang Life, and Rhetorics of the Everyday.* Boston: Beacon P, 1997. Print.

Coogan, David. "Sophists for Social Change." *The Public Work of Rhetoric: Citizen-Scholars and Civic Engagement.* Eds. John Ackerman and David Coogan. Columbia: U of South Carolina P, 2010. 157-74. Print.

Cottle, Simon. "Mediatized Rituals: Beyond Manufacturing Consent." *Media Culture Society* 28.3 (2006): 411-32. Web.

Crawford, Matthew. *Shop Class as Soulcraft: An Inquiry into the Value of Work*. New York: Penguin, 2009. Print.

Cushman, Ellen. *The Struggle and the Tools: Oral and Literate Strategies in an Inner City Community*. New York: SUNY P, 1998. Print.

De Lissovoy, Noah and Peter McLaren. "Toward a Contemporary Philosophy of Praxis." *Radical Relevance: Toward a Scholarship of the Whole Left*. Ed. Laura Gray-Rosendale and Steven Rosendale. SUNY P, 2005. 156-79. Print.

Dewey, John. *The Public and Its Problems: An Essay in Political Inquiry*. Chicago: Gateway Books, 1945. Print.

Dhaliwal, Amarpal. "Can the Subaltern Vote? Radical Democracy, Discourses of Representation and Rights, and the Question of Race." *Radical Democracy*. Ed. David Trend. New York: Routledge, 1996. 42-61. Print.

Dingo, Rebecca. "Linking Transnational Logics: A Feminist Rhetorical Analysis of Public Policy Networks." *College English* 70.5 (2008): 490-505. Print.

⎯⎯⎯. *Networking Arguments: Rhetoric, Transnational Feminism, and Public Policy Writing*. U Pittsburgh P, 2012.

⎯⎯⎯. "Securing the Nation: Neoliberalism's US Family Values in a Transnational Gendered Economy." *Journal of Women's History* 16.3 (2004): 173-86. Print.

Feguson, Niall. Foreword. Dambisa Moyo. *Dead Aid. Why Aid is Not Working and How There is a Better Way for Africa*. New York: Farrar, Straus and Giroux, 2009. ix-xii. Print.

Fishman, Jenn, Andrea Lunsford, Beth McGregor, and Mark Otuteye. "Performing Writing, Performing Identity." *College Composition and Communication* 52.2 (2005): 224–52. Print.

Flower, Linda. *Community Literacy and the Rhetoric of Public Engagement*. Southern Illinois UP, 2008. Print.

⎯⎯⎯. "Intercultural Knowledge Building: The Literate Action of a Community Think Tank." *Writing Selves, Writing Societies: Research from Activity Perspectives*. Ed. Charles Bazerman and David Russell. 239–70. Fort Collins: WAC. Web.

⎯⎯⎯. "Partners in Inquiry: A Logic for Community Outreach." *Writing the Community: Concepts and Models for Service-Learning in Composition*. Ed. Linda Adler-Kassner, Robert Crooks, and Ann Watters. Washington, DC: American Association for Higher Education, 1997. 95–111. Print.

Fraser, Nancy. "Rethinking the Public Sphere: A Contribution to the Critique of Actually Existing Democracy." *Habermas and the Public Sphere*. Ed. Craig Calhoun. Cambridge, MA: MIT P, 1993. 109–42. Print.

Gee, James, Glynda Hull and Colin Lankshear. *The New Work Order*. Westview P, 1996. Print.

"George Clooney Named PEOPLE's Sexiest Man Alive." *People* 15 Nov. 2006. Web.

Gerson, Michael. "Dambisa Moyo's Wrongheaded 'Dead Aid.'" *Washington Post* 3 April 2009. Web.

Gilyard, Keith. *Composition and Cornel West: Notes Toward a Deep Democracy*. Carbondale: Southern Illinois UP, 2008. Print.

Goldblatt, Eli. *Because We Live Here: Sponsoring Literacy Beyond the College Curriculum*. Cresskill: Hampton P, 2007. Print.

———. "Van Rides in the Dark: Literacy as Involvement." *Journal for Peace and Justice Studies* 6.1 (1994): 77–94. Print.

Grabill, Jeffery T., and Michele Simmons. "Toward a Critical Rhetoric of Risk Communication: Producing Citizens and the Role of Technical Communicators." *Technical Communication Quarterly* 7.2 (1998): 415–41. Print.

Greene, Ronald Walter. "Rhetorical Pedagogy as a Postal System: Circulating Subjects through Michael Warner's 'Publics and Counterpublics.'" *Quarterly Journal of Speech* 88.1 (2002): 434–43. Print.

Grewal, Inderpal. *Transnational America*. Durham: Duke UP, 2005. Print.

Habermas, Jürgen. *The Structural Transformation of the Public Sphere: An Inquiry into a Category of Bourgeois Society*. Trans. Thomas Burger and Frederick Lawrence. Cambridge: MIT P, 1989. Print.

Haley, Alex. *Roots: The Saga of an American Family*. New York: Doubleday, 1976.

Hamm, Steve. "It's Bono vs Moyo on Aid." *Business Week*. 27 March 2009. Web.

Hauser, Gerard. *Vernacular Voices: The Rhetoric of Public and Public Spheres*. Columbia: U South Carolina P, 1999. Print.

Higgins, Lorraine, and Lisa D. Brush. "Personal Experience Narrative and Public Debate: Writing the Wrongs of Welfare." *College Composition and Communication* 57.4 (2006): 694–729. Print.

hooks, bell. *Yearning: Race, Gender and Cultural Politics*. Boston: South End Press, 1990. Print.

Kells, Michelle Hall. "Writing Across Communities: Deliberation and the Discursive Possibilities of WAC." *Reflections: A Journal of Writing, Community Literacy, and Service-Learning* 6 (2007): 87-108. Web.

Kells, Michelle Hall, Valerie Balester, and Victor Villanueva. *Latino/a Discourses: On Language, Identity and Literacy Education*. Portsmouth: Boynton/Cook, 2004. Print.

Kershaw, Baz. *The Politics of Performance: Radical Theater as Cultural Intervention*. New York: Routledge, 2005. Print.

Kristof, Nicholas D. and Sheryl WuDunn. *Half the Sky: Turning Oppression into Opportunity for Women Worldwide*. New York: Knopf, 2009. Print.

Long, Elenore. "Educating Future Public Workers: Can We Make Inquiry Professional?" *Teaching Peace: The Frontlines of Non-Violence,* spec. issue of *Reflections: A Journal of Writing, Community Literacy and Service-Learning* 8.1 (2008): 22-49.

———. "The Rhetoric of Literate Social Action." *Inventing a Discipline, Rhetoric and Composition in Action: Essays in Honor of Richard E. Young*. Ed. Maureen Daly Goggin. Urbana: NCTE, 2000. 289-313. Print.

Long, Elenore, John Jarvis, and Diane Deerheart Raymond. "The Nipmuck Chaubunagungamaug People *Do* Exist: Imagining *the What Next*—An Experimental Alternative to Evidentiary Legal Discourse." *Texts of Consequence: Composing Rhetorics of Social Activism for the Writing Classroom*. Ed. Christopher Wilkey and Nick Mauriello. Cresskill: Hampton P, 2012. 317-48. Print.

Luginaah, Isaac N., Emmanuel K. Yiridoe, and Mary-Margaret Taabazuing. "From Mandatory to Voluntary Testing: Balancing Human Rights, Religious and Cultural values, and HIV/AIDS Prevention in Ghana." *Social Science & Medicine* 61.8 (2005): 1689-1700. Print.

Mathieu, Paula. *Tactics of Hope: The Public Turn in English Composition.* Portsmouth: Boynton/Cook, 2005. Print.

McAllister, C. "Authenticity and Guatemala's Maya Queen." *Beauty Queens on the Global Stage: Gender, Contests, and Power.* Ed. Heather Jordan, Ballerino Cohen, R. Wilk, and B. Stoeltje. Routledge, New York and London, 1996. 105–24. Print.

McIntosh, C. Alison and Jason L. Finkle. "The Cairo Conference on Population and Development: A New Paradigm?" *Population and Development Review* 21.2 (1995): 223-60. Print.

Miller, Carolyn. "Should We Name the Tools? Concealing and Revealing the Art of Rhetoric." *The Public Work of Rhetoric: Citizen Scholars and Civic Engagement.* Ed. John Ackerman and David Coogan. Columbia: U of South Carolina P, 2010. 19-38. Print.

Mortenson, Greg and David Oliver Relin. *Three Cups Of Tea - One Man's Mission To Fight Terrorism And Build Nations . . . One School At A Time.* New York: Penguin, 2007. Print.

Moyo, Dambisa. *Dead Aid: Why Aid is Not Working and How there is a Better Way for Africa.* New York: Farrar, Straus and Giroux, 2009. Print.

Panitch, Leo. "Renewing Socialism." *Monthly Review* 53.9 (2002): 37-47. Print.

Peck, Wayne, Linda Flower, and Lorraine Higgins. "Community Literacy." *College Composition and Communication* 46.2 (1995): 199–222. Print.

Perfect, David. "Politics and Society in The Gambia since Independence." *History Compass* 6.2 (2008): 426-38. Print.

Pough, Gwendolyn. *Check it While I Wreck it: Black Womanhood, Hip-Hop Culture, and the Public Sphere.* New York: Northeaster, 2004. Print.

Richey, Lisa Ann and Stefano Ponte. "Better (Red)™ than Dead? Celebrities, Consumption and International Aid." *Third World Quarterly* 29.4 (2008): 711-29. Print.

Rocchio, Christopher. "'Idol' Launching 'Idol Gives Back' African and American Charity Benefit." *RealityTVWorld.com* 09 Mar. 2007. Web.

Rowlands, Jo. "A Word of the Times, but What Does it Mean? Empowerment in the Discourse and Practice of Development." *Women and Empowerment: Illustrations from the Third World.* Ed. Haleh Afshar. New York: St. Martins P, 1998. 11-34. Print.

Sauer, Beverly. *The Rhetoric of Risk: Technical Documentation in Hazardous Environments.* Mahweh: Lawrence Erlbaum Associates, 2003. Print.

Scatamburlo-D'Annibale, Valerie and Peter McLaren. "Class Dismissed? Historical Materialism and the Politics of 'Difference.'" *Critical Pedagogy and Race.* Ed. Zues Leonardo. Malden: Blackwell, 2005. 141-58. Print.

Smith, Sean. "The Celebrity: Brad Pitt." *Newsweek.* 10 July 2006: 59–61. Web.

Solomon, Deborah. "Questions for Dambisa Moyo: The Anti-Bono." *New York Times* 19 Feb. 2009. Web.

Stiglitz, Joseph. *Freefall: America, Free Markets, and the Sinking of the World Economy.* Norton, 2010. Print.

Swan, Susan. "Rhetoric, Service, and Social Justice." *Written Communication* 19.1 (2002): 76–108. Print.

Warner, Michael. *Publics and Counterpublics.* New York: Zone Books, 2005. Print.

Watkins, Kevin. "Why Dead Aid is Dead Wrong." *Prospect Magazine* 4 May 2009. Web.

Wells, Susan. "Rogue Cops and Health Care: What Do We Want from Public Writing." *College Composition and Communication* 47.3 (1996): 325–41. Print.

Wolfe, William R., Sheri Weiser, Karen Leiter et al. "The Impact of Universal Access to Antiretroviral Therapy on the HIV Stigma in Botswana." *American Journal of Public Health* 98.10 (2008): 1865-71. Print.

Wood, Mark. "Another World is Possible." *Radical Relevance: Toward a Scholarship of the Whole Left.* Ed. Laura Gray-Rosendale and Steven Rosendale. SUNY P, 2005. 211-31. Print.

Young, Iris Marion. *Intersecting Voices: Dilemmas of Gender, Political Philosophy, and Policy.* Princeton: Princeton UP, 1997. Print.

Elenore Long is an associate professor of community literacy in the Department of English at Arizona State University. With Linda Flower and Lorraine Higgins, she published *Learning to Rival: A Literate Practice for Intercultural Inquiry.* They published the lead article—a fifteen-year retrospective—for the inaugural issue of *Community Literacy Journal.* Her book, *Community Literacy and the Rhetoric of Local Publics,* offers a comparative analysis of local publics and the exuberant ways people go public within them. With John Jarvis and Diane Deerheart Raymond, she has recently written "The Nipmuck Chaubunagungamaug People *Do* Exist: Imagining *the What Next*—An Experimental Alternative to Evidentiary Legal Discourse" for Christopher Wilkey and Nick Mauriello's collection of essays entitled *Texts of Consequence: Composing Rhetorics of Social Activism for the Writing Classroom.*

Nyillan Fye came to the U.S. from the Gambia, West Africa, at age 12. She earned a Bachelor's Degree in Health and Human Services Management from Bay Path College in Massachusetts in 2010, and recently completed her Master's Degree in Non-Profit Management and Philanthropy, also at Bay Path. In addition to launching the annual Miss Gambia USA Pageant treated in this article, she continues to work closely with partners in the U. S., Sweden, and Switzerland to keep the Sajuka School running for 300 children in her family village on the banks of the Gambia River near the site to which American author Alex Haley traced his family roots in the generational saga *Roots* that appeared in print and in film in the 1980s. Her life mission is to provide quality education to children through non-profit efforts.

John Jarvis is a professor of English and Cultural Studies at Bay Path College in Longmeadow, Massachusetts. He and Fye recently launched the Sajuka Community Development Project, a partnership between Bay Path College and the Sajuka Elementary School in Barra, the Gambia. This initiative was recognized in 2010 as a Top Program by the Higher Education Task Force and the U.S. Center for Citizen Diplomacy and during the U.S. Summit for Global Citizen Diplomacy under the Obama Administration.

Shakespeare and the Cultural Capital Tension: Advancing Literacy in Rural Arkansas

David A. Jolliffe

University of Arkansas at Fayetteville

A multi-faceted Shakespeare festival in a small town in rural east central Arkansas, part of a larger Community Literacy Advocacy Project, represents a concerted effort to alter the discourse of decline in this economically troubled region, but it also raises some challenging issues about how such projects distribute social and cultural capital among their participants.

As I do my job, trying to sponsor and support reading and writing practices that will ideally enrich lives and communities throughout Arkansas, I'm always tempted to rewrite the American Declaration of Independence so that its second paragraph begins this way: "We hold these truths to be self-evident, that all men are created equal, that they are endowed by their creator with certain unalienable rights, that among those rights are Life, Liberty, Literacy, and the pursuit of Happiness." As I reflect on this minor emendation, I always recognize the original sentence as one of the most evocative assumptions ever penned by humankind. It's the clearest example I know of an enthymeme with the major premise explicitly expressed, not suppressed, as would be the case in most arguments. Would that it were true. Jefferson and his fellow Deists certainly assumed that all people were *created* equal; I wonder if they believed, as we now must concede, that, even though people are created equal, the inequitable social structures that persist—the inequality of access to life, liberty, literacy, and the pursuit of happiness—begin to materialize about one second out of the womb. I see a major part of my job as working to equalize people's chances to live freely and pursue happiness, however they define it, by understanding the roles that literacy plays in those endeavors. In what follows, I describe the most recent project of an ongoing initiative in rural, east central Arkansas to foster literacy throughout a small community, and I unpack some thorny ideas about how the concept of *capital* figures in this specific project, as well as in the overall initiative.

Let me offer two specific scenes that set the stage for these ideas to come to life. Here's the first scene: It's a Saturday morning in early April 2011 in tiny Augusta, Arkansas, population 2400. While other tenth-, eleventh-, and twelfth-graders from Augusta High and two neighboring schools, McCrory High and Newport High are sleeping in, or getting up to help with family obligations, or going to work, or resting their sore muscles from Friday night athletic pursuits, a dozen kids from these three schools are spending the day improvising, drumming, chanting, reciting, writing, running, chasing--all activities toward the goal of learning William Shakespeare's enormous and challenging romance *The Tempest*. This troupe's goal, to be achieved some six weeks later after several of these day-long sessions, is to perform a forty-five-minute remixed version of the play, combining Shakespeare's scenes with their own text, music, and choreography. The student performance, *The Tempest Tossed*, is the curtain raiser to a full-length production of the play, cast with professional actors from Northwest Arkansas and talented amateurs from rural Arkansas, performed on an outdoor stage on the banks of the White River in Augusta on May 28. The student performance, the full-length play, a brief concert of original art songs based on themes in *The Tempest*, and an early-spring statewide tour of lectures and discussions about the play all collectively comprise the first of what is hoped to be the annual ARCare Shakespeare Festival, an event that brings reading, writing, and the arts to life in rural Arkansas in ways that the region has never experienced before.

Here's the other scene: It's November 2006, and I'm sitting in a conference room at the Augusta headquarters of White River Rural Health, an organization that operates clinics and supports development in twenty-two small towns throughout east central Arkansas. I have been invited by Dr. Steven Collier, executive director of White River Rural Health, to meet with a group called the Augusta Recovery Initiative, convened in response to the closing of a plant in the town that took dozens of jobs out of the economy. Seated around the conference table is this group of everyday citizens, determined to keep their town from going under:

- Katina Biscoe, a nurse practitioner for White River who graduated from Augusta High School in 1991 and has children there now and who serves on both the Augusta School Board and the Woodruff County Literacy Council.
- Raymond Bowen, a teacher who retired from Augusta High School after thirty-five years but who still pinch-hits as a teacher of algebra II and advanced math.
- Regina Burkett, the Community Development Coordinator for White River and a licensed practical nurse.
- Evelyn Coles, a farm owner, mother, and grandmother whose husband serves on the Augusta School Board.
- Brenda Collins, longtime resident of Augusta whose children and grandchildren have gone to school there and who serves on both the town council and the Woodruff County Literacy Council.
- Craig Meredith, a graduate of Augusta High School who, having served in the U. S. Navy, has returned to the region to work as a computer technician for White River Rural Health.
- Jimmy Rhodes, a longtime resident of Augusta who runs the funeral home ("I'm burying too many young people," he says), serves on town council, and plans to run for mayor.
- Donny Shields, the postmaster in Augusta whose wife and son teach in the district's schools
- Janice Turner, an ordained minister who recently moved to her husband's hometown, Augusta, after he retired and who now runs a Christian bookstore called "The J Spot" and serves as president of the Woodruff County Literacy Council.

Of course, presiding at the meeting is Dr. Collier, who graduated from Augusta High School, took a degree in history from Baylor University, and after completing his

M.D. at the University of Arkansas Medical Center and his residency in Pine Bluff returned to Augusta as CEO of White River.

The committee had been meeting, I learned, for about eighteen months, having been convened initially to address the economic downturn in the town and the county, Woodruff, of which Augusta is the seat. As Dr. Collier told me then--and I've heard him repeat the point several times in other gatherings—the group decided about a year into its existence that the problem wasn't economic, it was "educational." As the Initiative's notes from its October 2006 session put it, "Last year we started an Augusta improvement plan with brainstorming sessions. The topic of education kept coming up. We are now putting it on the front burner." In other words, Dr. Collier and the others realized that, unless Augusta could responsibly convey the impression that its schools were top-notch and that its graduates went on to college, graduated, and got decent jobs, the town would stand a slim chance of not only finding a company to fill the deserted space from the shuttered plant but also of urging new businesses and industries to locate in Augusta and Woodruff County and thereby create jobs, a stronger tax base, and so on.

This was where the Initiative expected me, I think, to pitch in. As an educator who grew up in small-town America and had accrued thirty-five years in the trenches at the secondary and post-secondary level, I was a fresh face in Arkansas, where I had recently moved to become the initial occupant of an endowed chair in literacy studies at the state's flagship university.

A thought occurred to me. Seated around this table were representatives of all sorts of "constituencies" in this small town: education, health care, small business, government, religion, agriculture. Each was interested in helping to save Augusta. Each had come with the notion that improving "education" could play a central role in the recovery initiative. Each was completely open to my argument that improving literacy—improving all citizens' abilities to read and write to the extent that they can live a rich, fulfilling personal life and participate in a changing economy[1]—was *the* most vital aspect of the educational improvement plan.

To make this plan work, I proposed to the group, we couldn't simply focus solely on the schools and hope that they "fix" the literacy problem. Without wanting to endorse any political candidate, I argued that "it takes a village" to raise the profile of reading and writing and to improve education. Consider, I asked them, all the organizations and entities in Augusta that might say, if asked, that they were interested in helping folks read and write more fully and effectively: not only the schools, but also the churches, the library, the local literacy council, the local economic development council, the health clinics. Why not launch, I asked them, a project that would have a designated person at its helm who would actively seek out individuals and groups in Augusta who wanted to read and write in fuller, richer ways than they had in the past and who would forge "literacy liaisons" between and among all the constituencies who wanted to raise the profile of literacy in Augusta but who had not known about one another or worked together in the past.

Thus was born the idea for the Augusta Community Literacy Advocacy Project. After a quick marshaling of resources by White River Rural Health and the Office of the Brown Chair in English Literacy, Collier identified the miraculous Joy Lynn Bowen, a former teacher in Augusta Public Schools who knows and is trusted by nearly every person in Augusta, and he placed her on the staff of White River as the Community Literacy Advocate.

What we have accomplished since the fall of 2006—in other words, between the second and the first scenarios above—is substantial. We have run two events, a single-day workshop and a multi-session class, for parents and childcare providers on how to make homes more literacy-conducive for pre-school children. For the elementary school, we have sponsored family reading of the principal's "book of the month." For the high school, we have involved the students in the Arkansas Delta Oral History Project (Jolliffe, "The Arkansas Delta Oral History Project"; Goering, Jolliffe, Riley, Swanton, and Gates), a semester-long endeavor that connects University of Arkansas undergraduates with students from small, rural high schools in eastern Arkansas as they collaboratively develop essays, stories, plays, poems, and websites that capture the unwritten history of the region. In addition, at the high school, we have run regular sessions to help students score better on the ACT examination, and we even recruited a young playwright whose work was performed as part of the Arkansas New Play Festival sponsored by TheatreSquared, a professional company based in Fayetteville. The general citizenry in the town has gotten involved in two ways. First, many of them wrote stories and essays about military service, their own and that of family members, for a commemorative volume that my office published to coincide with the unveiling of a new veterans' monument outside the courthouse on Memorial Day 2012. Second, many folks have been involved in an evolving effort to write about the "pillars" of the churches in Augusta: We've been trying to link up young people and senior citizens in the churches and get them to write, collaboratively, the stories that capture how long the older generation has been attending the church, what changes they've seen over the decades, how the church has served the community, and so on. Our goal is a volume of pieces published for each of five or six churches in the town.

Each time we've had a major accomplishment with the Augusta Community Literacy Advocacy Project, the folks at White River Rural Health (which has changed its name to ARCare to reflect a new statewide presence) have sponsored some kind of public celebration—a lunch, a reception, a dinner—to honor the participants. Elsewhere, I have appropriated a term from the work of communication theorist David Procter and described these celebrations as "civic communions" ("The Community Literacy Advocacy Project"). Indeed, just as the communion service in Christian churches celebrates the life of the church with bread and wine, so do civic communions epideicticly commemorate the spirit of a the town's citizens, their accomplishments, their initiative.

Have we made a difference in Augusta? I think so. The year before we started the Community Literacy Advocacy Project, of the forty-eight students who graduated from Augusta High School, only twenty-two even took the ACT and only six went to college. Four years into the project, twenty-nine students graduated, twenty-three took the ACT, and twenty-two went to college, many with scholarships. The town is changing. Store fronts on the old main street are being renovated, and small businesses, many related to the health-care industry that ARCare anchors, are moving in. ARCare has also opened its new Community Health and Education Center, which provides high-quality preventive programming and offers the first substantial preschool day-care in the region.

Bowen, the community literacy advocate, and I continue to look for ways that reading and writing can enrich the quality of life in Augusta and Woodruff County, and the Team Shakespeare project emerged from our opportunistic searching. The project actually was sparked by a comment from Dr. Collier: "David, I remember a time when we used to do Shakespeare plays in Augusta." A little further digging revealed the existence, until the 1950s, of a Shakespeare club in the town. The game was on: We would create the ARCare Shakespeare Festival with four components. First, since I have a substantial background as an actor and a director, I knew right away that I wanted to direct a production involving both professional actors from the outstanding theatre community in Northwest Arkansas[2] and good amateur actors from near Augusta. I selected *The Tempest* because (a) I love it; (b) we would be performing it on an outdoor stage on the banks of the White River in Augusta[3], a very tempest-conducive setting; and (c) I would be able to fill the roles of the "main" cast—Prospero, Ariel, Caliban, Ferdinand, Miranda, Stefano, and Trinculo—with Northwest Arkansas actors and the roles of the "usurper" cast—Antonio, Sebastian, Gonzolo, and Alonzo—with actors from Augusta and nearby Beebe. We rehearsed scenes from the play in two separate locations—Fayetteville and Beebe—for five weeks, only putting the two casts and the entire play together the night before we performed it in Augusta.[4]

We capitalized on an Augusta connection to forge the second part of the ARCare Shakespeare Festival. Beth Gregory, who grew up in Augusta in a family that has lived there for generations, is married to Professor Peter Smith, a prominent Shakespeare scholar, critic, and dramaturge based at the University of Nottingham. We prevailed upon Smith, during his and Beth's visit to Augusta in late winter, to give a series of wonderful public lectures about *The Tempest* at five locations throughout Arkansas, sort of "priming the pump" for audiences who we hoped would travel to Augusta in May to see the play.

The third component came from an old personal connection of mine. The composer in residence at the University of Arkansas at Little Rock, Dr. Bob Boury, is from Wheeling, West Virginia, near my hometown of New Martinsville. I had met Bob in 1976 when, as part of Wheeling's bicentennial celebration, he had written the score for a new musical called *Time Steals Softly* about, of all things, the love match between Henry Clay and his secret paramour who lived in Wheeling. I had reconnected with Bob in Little Rock shortly after I moved to Arkansas in 2005, and I knew he had written a series of art songs based on *The Tempest*. It took little to convince Bob to rehearse the songs with two outstanding singers, a baritone and a mezzo-soprano, who agreed to come to Augusta and sing the pieces as people were coming in for the curtain-raiser and the full production.

The fourth component was *The Tempest Tossed*. Before describing the process and production, let me focus solely on this aspect of the ARCare Shakespeare Festival as the most visible "hot spot" in this relatively thorny issue about literacy outreach and cultural capital. A snapshot preview: Sponsoring a project like Team Shakespeare's production of *The Tempest Tossed* forces one to walk a dialectical tightrope over the chasm of capital, with Louise Rosenblatt's rosy terrain on one side and Pierre Bourdieu's briar patch on the other.

On the one hand, I know that as people read and write, they don't simply decode and encode, but instead, in Rosenblatt's terms, they transact with the text by tapping into their "linguistic-experiential reservoir," a phenomenal entity that she describes as "[t]he residue of the individual's past transactions," his or her "funded assumptions, attitudes, and expectations about language and about the world," an embodiment of "*inner capital* . . . that is all each of us has to draw on in speaking, listening, writing, or reading." As Rosenblatt puts it, "We 'make sense' of a new situation or transaction and make new meanings by applying, reorganizing, revising, or extending public and private elements selected from our personal linguistic-experiential reservoirs" ("Transactional" 5, italics added). Or, as she writes in her influential book, *The Reader, the Text, and the Poem*, "The reader's attention to the text activates certain elements in his [sic] past experience . . . that have become linked with the verbal symbols" (11). The reader doesn't "understand" the meaning but instead actively constructs it. The reader selectively attends to clues in the emerging text and to responses he or she evokes by connecting the emerging text to elements of the linguistic-experiential reservoir (10-11 and *passim*). In other words, according to Rosenblatt, people never actually learn anything completely *new* while reading; instead, they *construct* the new by connecting to what they have already learned and experienced. This Rosenblattian principle is evoked in reading comprehension instruction in its initial dictum: "Activate prior knowledge." The principle finds a home in common parlance as well: The more you know, the more you can learn.

Our goal with Team Shakespeare's *The Tempest Tossed*, and other similar projects that the Brown Chair has sponsored, is to deepen the participants' linguistic-experiential reservoir, to enrich this "inner capital." It's not that I believe the folks in rural Arkansas don't know anything and therefore have a difficult time learning more. But having grown up in a small town in a rural region, I understand that "the new" is often not a completely welcome visitor in these locales, and the linguistic-experiential reservoirs of folks in this type of location can be relatively shallow. Manifesting an admirable aspect of their culture, people in small town/rural America often recount stories from the past—achievements of high school sports teams, memories of times when famous personages visited the area, accounts of community pageants and parades that marked historical moments, such as centennials and the like. It's important in these locales for people to know their roots, their heritage. It's rare in small town/rural America that one encounters forms of art—theatre, the visual arts, dance, esoteric music—that transcend the boundaries of the expected, the traditional. In other words, it's difficult to encounter—live—art that offers the salutary, educational shock of the unfamiliar, the unknown.

But if one believes Rosenblatt's theory, one can only hope to become more literate—to become a more effective transactional reader—by encountering the unfamiliar and the unknown, making it the familiar and the known, and then connecting to it in later encounters with more, new "unfamiliars" and "unknowns." Nothing in Rosenblatt's work suggests that she had the slightest political or ethical qualms about educators' roles in enriching the "inner capital" of readers to support and fuel the transactional process.

Reading the French sociologist Bourdieu, on the other hand, brings political and ethical issues rapidly to the forefront. Developed by Bourdieu and his colleagues, the concept of cultural capital refers to the "cultural habits and . . . dispositions inherited from" the family that are fundamentally important to school success" (Bourdieu and Passeron 8). Bourdieu emphasizes that cultural capital comprises "competences" that conduce an appropriation of a society's "cultural heritage," but that are unequally distributed and lead to "exclusive advantages" for their bearers, especially in countries with highly differentiated social class structures, including educational systems that institutionalize the criteria of evaluation so that the competences held by children from a particular class are deemed elite and preferable (Bourdieu). In their tidy book, *The Elements of Literacy*, Julie Lindquist and David Seitz define the term simply: "Cultural capital refers to inherited cultural habits and competencies that can be transferred first into social capital (membership in social groups and networks with power and access) and then into economic access—real money" (104).

Given this dialectical tension—acknowledging that people's literacy can be enhanced by strengthening their inner capital, yet acknowledging that cultural capital is socio-politically loaded—I have tried to sponsor literacy-enrichment opportunities in rural Arkansas that manifest the trope, frequently invoked in educational practice, of mirrors and windows. On the one hand, I try to provide opportunities for people to read and write in ways that mirror their existence and in ways that open windows to new experiences. For example, the Brown Chair has sponsored two major "mirrors" experiences, the Arkansas Delta Oral History Project and the Augusta Veterans' Stories Project. On the other hand, I try to sponsor reading and writing activities that offer windows, operating under the assumption that these experiences will help, especially for young people, to deepen linguistic-experiential reservoirs and foster connections to new ideas, new perspectives, new language. The Team Shakespeare project was, I believe, the boldest of these windows experiences, and in initiating it, I gulped and admitted, as least to myself, that I was trying to provide the dozen young participants with a helping of cultural capital.

The Team Shakespeare Project in Augusta in May 2011 was actually the third such project my office has undertaken in collaboration with Trike Theatre, an innovative enterprise led by Kassie Misiewicz that produces professional theatre for children and provides professional development activities for teachers at all grade levels who would like to integrate the performing arts in their curriculums and pedagogies. The first two iterations of Team Shakespeare involved gifted and talented middle school students who spent all morning with us for three consecutive weeks studying, rewriting, remixing, writing about, and ultimately performing *A Midsummer Night's Dream* in 2008 and *Much Ado About Nothing* in 2009. The 2011 project in Augusta was a bit of a departure. Rather than working with us three hours on fifteen consecutive days, the Augusta group devoted all day for five Saturdays between the first of April and the end of May. In the earlier projects, we had worked primarily with eighth- and ninth-graders. In this project, we were working with sophomores, juniors, and seniors. While they all volunteered for the project, we had no idea—nor did we actually need to know—whether they were designated as "gifted" or "talented" in any way.

Here's how the Team Shakespeare process works. First of all, there are three instructors: a "Shakespeare" person who introduces the play to the students and helps them understand it; a "theatre" person who works via improvisation and tableaux, the latter a brilliant technique that gets participants to physicalize moments in scenes and kinesthetically understand them; and a creative writer, who periodically pulls the students away from the study and performance and leads them in exercises to write poems or short fiction about the themes and issues raised in the play. In the Augusta project, Erika Wilhite was the Shakespeare person, Kassie Misiewicz was the theatre person (although Erika's and Kassie's roles blended a good bit in practice), and Erika's husband, Rodney Wilhite, was the creative writing person.

Whether spread over three weeks of daily sessions or five weeks of Saturday sessions, the Team Shakespeare process is essentially the same. From the outset, the young participants learn how to do Short Shakes scenes, ten- to fifteen-minute chunks of the plays, with cue cards provided by the leaders. In Augusta, Erika and Kassie would provide lots of context about what's happening in the play prior to this scene and what comes after it, but the students begin simply by getting Shakespeare's words in their mouths.

Once they've had the Short Shakes experience with several of the scenes, the leaders and the students take the scenes one at a time, reading the script carefully and then paraphrasing the lines. Invariably, the students want to put Shakespeare into formal, academic language. That's not the goal. Team Shakespeare very soon wants to get them up on their feet, doing the scenes in their own language, thereby inviting scene analysis: Who are the characters? What kind of relationship do they have with one another? With others not on the stage? What do the characters want to do, to achieve? What's standing in their way?

After a substantial amount of scene analysis work, the participants move from acting to writing. As part of the process of paraphrasing, performing, and analyzing, the leaders and the students have been discovering literary techniques that Shakespeare employs: for example, metaphor, parallelism and antithesis, alliteration and assonance, and so on. Rodney, the creative writing specialist, sets the students to work by showing them models of poetry and short fiction and then helping them as they write in one of those modes about a theme or issue raised in the play, using a particular literary technique they've learned about.

By this time, the process is becoming recursive. In the midst of a scene, being done in either Shakespeare's language or the students' paraphrase, Erika will shout out, for example, "emphasize the antithesis." The students do so, and then immediately sit with Rodney and write something that embodies an antithesis.

As the sessions proceed, thus, each student is assembling a substantial packet: the play itself, their paraphrased scenes, their snippets of writing craft, their poems and stories. About three-quarters of the way through the total experience, the leaders and students begin to think about crafting a final performance. They discover a rhetorical situation, an exigence that will lead them to present their version of the play, in this case *The Tempest*, to an audience. They take everything they've done, divide it into moments, and then work to craft these moments for presentation.

In Augusta, *The Tempest Tossed* embodied this conceit: A random collective of students is trying to *explain The Tempest* to their friends who didn't participate in

Team Shakespeare, but the participants are getting the play all wrong and everyone is getting confused. So, one of them, a young woman, appears as Ariel and tells them (duh), "Let's not tell them about the play! Let's show them the play!" There follows, then, a forty-minute version of *The Tempest*, in the students' own words, with their poetry and prose interspersed, supplemented by their own singing, drumming, and dancing.[5] My words don't do just to *The Tempest Tossed*. It rocked.

Did the Team Shakespeare Project improve the participating students' literacy abilities? I employed no pretest/posttest assessment to see if students could score higher on some kind of test as a result of the Team Shakespeare experience. I can assert, however, that the students' experience deepened their connection with a significant literary work. The students connected with *The Tempest* emotionally, intellectually, and kinesthetically. As the five weeks of the Team Shakespeare project proceeded, Erika, Kassie, and Rodney were able to engage the high school students in challenging conversations about the issues and themes raised in the play because the students had experienced it fully as art.

The work of two educational theorists helps to support the proposition that the Team Shakespeare experience ultimately helped the students become stronger readers. Richard Marzano makes a strong case for the role of vocabulary enrichment in literacy development. The more extensive and deep a young person's vocabulary is, Marzano argues, the more he or she can develop comprehension and fluency skills. Marzano describes eight characteristics of effective vocabulary instruction:

1. Effective vocabulary instruction does not rely on memorizing definitions.
2. Students must represent their knowledge of words in both linguistic and non-linguistic ways.
3. Effective vocabulary instruction involves the gradual reshaping of word meanings through multiple exposures.
4. Teaching word parts enhances students' understanding of terms.
5. Different types of words require different types of instruction.
6. Students should discuss the terms they are learning.
7. Students should play with words.
8. Instruction should focus on terms that have a high probability of enhancing academic success. (62-90)

The Team Shakespeare project capitalized on all of Marzano's points except numbers 4 and 5. For the participants, definitions of complicated terms came experientially as they paraphrased, reorganized, and redefined Shakespeare's lexicon. They represented their knowledge of new terms kinesthetically, via improvisation and tableaux. They reshaped word meanings by making metaphors for difficult terms with their bodies. They discussed the terms they learned by collaboratively writing scenes. They played constantly, not only with the words of the play but also by inventing dances based on the punctuation in *The Tempest* and in their evolving scenes. They internalized definitions of "terms that have a high probability of enhancing academic success"--terms like metaphor, parallelism, antithesis, and climax--by experiencing them in their study, their improvisation, and their creative writing.

Donna Alverman extends her consideration of literacy achievement beyond the vocabulary-literacy connection, organizing her overview of "Effective Literacy Instruction for Adolescents" around five central principles:

1. Adolescents' perception of how competent they are as readers and writers, generally speaking, will affect how motivated they are to learn in their subject area classes (e.g., the sciences, social studies, mathematics, and literature). Thus, if academic literacy instruction is to be effective, it must address issues of self-efficacy and engagement (191).
2. Adolescents respond to the literacy demands of their subject area classes when they have appropriate background knowledge and strategies for reading a variety of texts. Effective instruction develops students' abilities to comprehend, discuss, study, and write about multiple forms of text (print, visual, and oral) by taking into account what they are capable of doing as everyday users of language and literacy (193).
3. Adolescents who struggle to read in subject area classrooms deserve instruction that is developmentally, culturally, and linguistically responsive to their needs. To be effective, such instruction must be embedded in the regular curriculum and address differences in their abilities to read, write, and communicate orally as strengths, not as deficits (195).
4. Adolescents' interests in the Internet, hypermedia, and various interactive communication technologies (e.g., chat rooms where people can take on various identities unbeknown to others) suggest the need to teach reading with a critical eye toward how writers, illustrators, and the like represent people and their ideas—in short, how individuals who create texts make those texts work. At the same time, it suggests teaching adolescents that all texts, including textbooks, routinely promote or silence particular views (198).
5. Adolescents' evolving expertise in navigating routine school literacy tasks suggests the need to involve them in higher-level thinking about what they read and write than is currently possible in the transmission model of teaching, with its emphasis on skill and drill, teacher-centered instruction, and passive learning. Effective alternatives to this model include participatory approaches that actively engage students in their own learning (individually and in small groups) and that treat texts as tools for learning rather than repositories of information to be memorized (and then all too quickly forgotten) (201).

Alvermann's ideas resonate soundly throughout the Team Shakespeare Project. The dozen students, early in the five weeks' work, quickly developed a keen sense of self-efficacy and engagement. The project capitalized on their "everyday uses" of language as it led them to create scenes they understand in terms that they use to comprehend Shakespeare's complex work. *The Tempest Tossed* captured beautifully the dialects of the multi-racial cast. With their bodies and their choreography, the participants created pictures and tableaux to depict the emotions, the tensions of the play kinesthetically and graphically. And, of course, the whole experience was, I'd argue, an exemplar of participatory education.

The ARCare Shakespeare Festival, especially the Team Shakespeare component, in short, was a highly satisfying mirrors and windows experience, enriching students with new inner, cultural capital, by infusing something radically new in their minds and words by connecting it to a mirror of their own lives.

Endnotes

1. This is a rough paraphrase of the definition of literacy promulgated by the National Assessment of Adult Literacy: Literacy is the ability to use printed and written information to function in society, to achieve one's goals, and to develop one's knowledge and potential.
2. The University of Arkansas' MFA program in acting provides an excellent training ground for local actors. Fayetteville's professional theatre company, TheatreSquared, recently received substantial award from the American Theatre Wing, sponsor of the Tony awards, as one ten outstanding, emerging regional theatres.
3. Coincidentally, central Arkansas was victimized by strong storms and flooding during the spring of 2011, when we were rehearsing *The Tempest*. Nature cooperated with our choice of plays.
4. We later moved the production and performed the play in Fayetteville.
5. Coincidentally, I was so impressed by one of the students' scenes in *The Tempest Tossed* that I stole some of their percussion and choreography for the opening scene of *The Tempest*.

Works Cited

Bourdieu, Pierre, and Jean-Claude Passeron, *Reproduction in Education, Society and Culture*. tr. Richard Nice. London: Sage, 1977.
Alvermann, Donna E. "Effective Literacy Instruction for Adolescents." *Journal of Literacy Research* 34.2 (2002): 189-208.
Arkansas Delta Made. 2010. Rural Heritage Development Institute. 12 December 2011. www.arkansasdeltamade.com.
Delta Bridge Project. *Phillips County, Arkansas, 2010-2020 Community Strategic Plan*. Helena/West Helena, AR: Southern Banccorp, 2010.
Gatewood, Willard B. "The Arkansas Delta: The Deepest of the Deep South." *The Arkansas Delta: Land of Paradox*. Ed. Jeannie Whayne and Willard B. Gatewood. Fayetteville, AR: U of Arkansas P, 1993. 3-29.
Goering, Christian. Z., David A. Jolliffe, Kelly Riley, Hilary Swanton, and Laine Gates. "The Arkansas Delta Oral History Project: Understanding ⊠Poverty in a Literacy Outreach Project." *Reclaiming Rural Literacies*. Ed. Kim Donehower, Charlotte Hogg, and Eileen Schell. Carbondale, IL: Southern Illinois UP, 2011. 285-309.
Jolliffe, David A. "The Community Literacy Advocacy Project: Civic Revival through Rhetorical Action in Rural Arkansas." *The Public Work of Rhetoric*. Ed. John Martin Ackerman and David Coogan. Columbia, SC: U of South Carolina P, 2010. 267-282.
_____. "The Arkansas Delta Oral History Project: A Hands-On, Experiential Course on School-College Articulation." *Going Public: What Writing Programs Learn From Engagement*. Ed. Shirley K. Rose and Irwin Weiser. Logan, UT: Utah S U P, 2010. 50-67.

Levine, Lawrence W. "William Shakespeare and the American People: A Study in Cultural Transformation." *American Historical Review* 89.1 (1984): 34-66.

Lindquist, Julie, and David Seitz. *The Elements of Literacy*. New York: Longman, 2009.

Marzano, Robert. *Building Background Knowledge for Academic Achievement: Research on What Works in Schools.* Alexandria, VA: American Society for Curriculum Development, 2004. 91-103.

Procter, David E. *Civic Communion: The Rhetoric of Community Building.* Lanham, MD: Rowman and Littlefield, 2005.

Rosenblatt, Louise. *The Reader, the Text, and the Poem: The Transactional Theory of the Literary Work*. Carbondale, IL: Southern Illinois U P, 2004.

_____. "The Transactional Theory of Reading and Writing." *Making Meaning With Texts: Selected Essays*. Portsmouth, NH: Heinemann, 2005. 1-38.

What is Main Street? 2010. West Memphis Main Street. 12 December 2011. www.broadwaywestmemphis.com.

David A. Jolliffe is Professor of English and Curriculum and Instruction at the University of Arkansas at Fayetteville, where he holds the Brown Chair in English Literacy.

What's Writing Got to Do with It?: Citizen Wisdom, Civil Rights Activism, and 21st Century Community Literacy

Michelle Hall Kells

This article examines what a pedagogy of public rhetoric and community literacy might look like based on an understanding of twentieth century Mexican American civil rights rhetoric. The inductive process of examining archival materials and conducting oral histories informs this discussion on the processes and challenges of gaining civic inclusion. I argue that writing can be both a healing process and an occasion for exercising agency in a world of contingency and uncertainty. To illustrate, I describe several key events shaping the evolution of the post-World War II Mexican American civil rights movement in New Mexico. Taking a case study approach, I begin this chapter by examining the civic discourses of one prominent New Mexico leader in the post-World War II civil rights movement: Vicente Ximenes. As a leader, Ximenes confronted critical civil rights issues about culture and belonging for over fifty years beginning in Albuquerque, New Mexico. It is a historical moment worth revisiting. First, I set the stage for this examination about writing, citizenship, and civic literacy by analyzing two critical rhetorical moments in the life of this post World War II civil rights activist. Secondly, I connect the Ximenes legacy to a growing movement at the University of New Mexico and the ways that we are making critical responses to current issues facing our local communities in New Mexico. By triangulating social acts of literacy, currently and historically, this article offers organizing principles for Composition teachers and advocates of community literacy serving vulnerable communities in their various spheres of practice.

Marking the ten year anniversary of 9/11, the Albuquerque Cultural Conference recently took as its theme: "Cultural Survival in Difficult Times" to signal the stark reality that our vulnerable communities (locally and nationally) are becoming increasingly fragile economically, culturally, and politically. This post 9/11 kairotic moment calls to mind the concept of *solastalgia* or what Glen Albrecht terms human ecosystem distress. Albrecht defines *solastalgia* as the embodied effects of isolation and the inability to exercise agency over place. *Solastalgia* can be mapped to such endemic social conditions as drug abuse, physical illness, mental illness, and suicide. I believe that we as a nation have been trying to resolve a kind of collective *solastalgia* or post-traumatic stress syndrome for the past decade. Moreover, the kind of border tensions that we are facing today, the current anti-immigration hysteria, and the omnipresent English Only movement are historically connected and politically relevant to the current work in public writing and community literacy education (Kells, Balester, and Villanueva; Kells "Mapping"). Writing can be both a healing process and an occasion for exercising agency in a world of contingency and uncertainty.

Literacy and civic engagement figure prominently in issues of agency as do issues of higher education access and Composition Studies as a gateway to enfranchisement. If the past twenty-five years of scholarship in Rhetoric and Composition has taught us anything, it is that there is no panacea, no single prescription for teaching literacy practice. Composition Studies is not a science. And I don't say that disparagingly. I do not mean to negate the kind of work that calls for the use of scientific and quantitative methods. It just seems that research on literacy practice and communicative action resists absolute predictability and generalizability. Language leaks. My own earliest language attitude studies adopted empirical research methods and applied a quantitative interpretative frame to issues related to ethnolinguistic identity (Kells, "Leveling;" "Linguistic Contact Zones"). And much to my surprise, I have found those early fragments of discovery circulated and cited in our field. The key word here is surprise. The consequences of writing myself into and out of dissonance never cease to surprise me (Kells and Balester, "Voices of the Wild Horse Desert"). The hermeneutics of research can help position us as scholars and teachers to attend to phenomena otherwise invisible to us. Moreover, research and writing can take us by surprise. Cultivating literacy practice is not about prescription-writing but making discoveries, sometimes and often by accident.

It is with that same kind of inquisitive wonder and interrogative impulse that I have applied another set of questions and interpretive frames to issues related to ethnolinguistic identity and civic engagement. For the past ten years, I have been asking: what a pedagogy of public rhetoric and community literacy might look like based on an understanding of twentieth century Mexican American civil rights rhetoric. The inductive process of examining archival materials and conducting oral histories has helped me to pay attention to the processes and challenges of gaining civic inclusion. As a result, I have been imagining a program, a national consortium that examines different civic discourses and the premises of rhetorical agency embedded in them (Kells "Rhetorical Imagination"; Rose and Paine). Why don't we, why haven't we, why couldn't we cultivate think tanks for civic engagement and help students analyze and generate texts that represent their spheres of belonging? Language is how we transmit culture—the implicit codes and expectations that hold us together as families, as neighborhoods, as institutions. Recently Marilyn A. Martinez, a self-published writer in Albuquerque, New Mexico reminded me of the intrinsic, humanizing value of language and the role of literacy in communities beyond the university. Our meeting was nothing less than serendipitous; the lessons learned were far deeper than expected.

Disabling Fictions and Community Literacy

I have been troubled by disabling fictions within literacy education for a number of years. I am reminded in the most unlikely places why this particular intellectual pre-occupation, this predilection for confronting "disabling fictions," has a place in academe. The story begins on a Southwest Airlines flight from Austin, Texas to Albuquerque in late August 2010, the tail-end of a year-long sabbatical nibbled away by the demands of my department and university. I was returning home from a trip to the Lyndon B. Johnson Presidential Library to complete archival research on my current book project, *Vicente Ximenes & LBJ's Great Society: The Rhetoric of Mexican American Civil Rights Reform*. It was the proverbial eleventh hour. Packing in what I had hoped to do at the beginning of my sabbatical at the very end. It was what I wanted to do *before* New Mexico's State Secretary of Higher Education called me at home a year ago as I was just beginning to settle into the lovely calm of my sabbatical. The State Secretary of Higher Education wanted me to help him revamp the state's core curriculum because of the role I had played at the University of New Mexico mobilizing the Writing Across Communities initiative for the previous five years. It was a rare opportunity—a worthy risk.

The first six months of my sabbatical were spent scrambling as chair of the UNM Core Curriculum Task Force. We finally put a bow on the final task force report in May 2010; then I promptly jumped into writing the Ximenes book over the summer. When I left for Texas in August, I had five working chapters under construction and needed just one last sweep through the LBJ Presidential Library archives to wrap up the primary research. I was feeling pretty single-minded when I met the person who would unequivocally re-affirm my commitment to the nebulous notion of "Writing Across Communities."

I sat in the aisle seat on my return flight to Albuquerque, the middle seat between the woman at the window and me was empty. We both sat quietly for the duration of the flight, both of us writing in notebooks with pencils. I was reflecting on my findings at the LBJ Library. We both ordered ginger ales to drink. I passed her the glass from the flight attendant and noticed the fingers of my fellow passenger that made grasping the flimsy plastic cup awkward and difficult. Precarious.

The descent into Albuquerque was bumpy as it always is during the summer monsoon season. The turbulence flying over the Sandia Mountains was especially troubling this day. I closed up my things as the woman's notebook slipped off her table onto the floor between us. I reached down and handed it back to her. She thanked me graciously. It was then that I noticed that her speech was slightly halting which she corrected by repeating her sentences deliberately, slowly for my benefit. As the plane pitched over the mountains, we slipped into a casual conversation. "I like to write," she confided. "I write all the time." And it was at that point that I became very interested and wanted to hear her story. "I wrote a book," she told me. "My name is Marilyn Martinez." I thought I heard her say, "The title of my book is 'Battling Debasement.'"

I have to admit that I had difficulty hearing and understanding the words over the engine noise, and I struggled to string together the details. I did realize, however, that Marilyn was talking about battling the stigma of developmental disabilities. I also realized that Marilyn was managing multiple developmental challenges indexed by her speech as well as large and small motor skills. I wasn't sure which disabilities that Marilyn was living with but within some deep intuitive place of my consciousness, I knew they were serious. With the engine noise and the soft modulation of her voice, I couldn't catch everything. I remember this though. Marilyn invited me to attend her book signing during the following week. "We're going to have cantaloupe, and strawberries, and watermelon," she explained. "I love watermelon, do you like watermelon? The director of the Disabilities Center says we can have watermelon because this will be my special day." I had to make a snap decision at this moment. Accept or politely decline this invitation. I took my UNM business card from my purse and handed it to Marilyn. "Please email me and send me the details for your book signing."

On Monday morning, an email message from Marilyn was waiting for me with the details of her book release celebration. In between meetings and classes of that first week of the semester, I attended the book signing for Marilyn Martinez's, *Battling the Basement*, a chronicle of her journey with Cerebral Palsy. And I ate watermelon and strawberries with Marilyn and her friends at the UNM Center for Development and Disability. There was joy. And after nearly fifteen years in the field of Rhetoric & Composition, I learned a lot about writing and agency that day. I will let Marilyn speak for herself. In the preface of her book, she explains:

> Basement Mentality is when people don't want you to grow in the world. You want to get out of the Basement by going one step higher, but some people want to keep you there in the comfort zone. They don't want you out of that box. You are only allowed to be on the one level where they can protect you—and no higher. But the Basement isn't for me. I have always wanted to get out and go higher, to live my own independent life.[1]

In a word, this is what education is all about: self-authorization. This is the key idea behind the Writing Across Communities initiative at the University of New Mexico: invigorating the public sphere, cultivating civic literacy on behalf of our most vulnerable communities—creating discursive spaces for historically excluded student populations.

And so it is language, community literacy, civil rights, citizenship, and belonging that will frame this article. Literacy can be a generative act of resistance to the indignities and despair of marginalization. In this post-9/11 America, Marilyn Martinez reminds us that there are many different groups assigned to many different kinds of civic "basements." There are entire communities literally and metaphorically kept underground, under-served, and under-represented. So the thorny questions around which I hang all these ideas are: what role does the rhetoric of disputation play in resolving the persistent question of who belongs in America (Beasley)? How might we engage the dissonances of (intellectual, geographical, linguistic) border-crossing in the hermeneutics of citizenship?

To illustrate, I wish to describe several key events shaping the evolution of the post-World War II Mexican American civil rights movement in New Mexico. Taking a case study approach, I begin this article by examining the civic discourses of one prominent New Mexico leader in the post-war movement: Vicente Ximenes. As a leader, Ximenes confronted critical civil rights issues about culture and belonging over fifty years ago beginning in Albuquerque, New Mexico. It is a historical moment worth revisiting.

First, I begin setting the stage for this examination about writing, citizenship, and civic literacy by analyzing two critical rhetorical moments in the life of this post- World War II civil rights activist. Secondly, I connect the Ximenes legacy to a growing movement at the University of New Mexico and the ways that we are making critical responses to current issues facing our local communities in New Mexico. By triangulating social acts of literacy, currently and historically, I offer some organizing principles for Composition teachers and advocates of community literacy serving vulnerable communities in their spheres of practice. The liminal spaces and geo-political borders in and beyond the Composition classroom are the literacy sites that most concern me here in New Mexico where I teach.

Immigration and the National Imaginary

Border anxieties continue to ignite across the country. Perturbations in the national imaginary were dramatically illustrated in May 2010 when several California high school students wore American flag t-shirts to *cinco de mayo* celebrations. In a strange post-9/11 American patriotic reversal, the students were expelled from school for promoting incendiary rhetorical statements. Wearing the American flag was grounds for expulsion as their Latino classmates donned the colors of the Mexican flag. The rogue demonstrators violated not only good taste but the boundaries of political tolerance at Live Oak High School. Against the backdrop of the recent immigration law SB 1070 enacted by the state of Arizona, this act of public rhetoric takes on multiple layers of significance.

What is particularly rich about the Live Oak, California incident is that the young men wearing the offending American symbol were both Mexican American and Anglo American students. This is not too surprising, however. Ambivalence toward immigrants has been a litmus test of belonging among many social groups for centuries. But I have to agree with syndicated columnist Leonard Pitts that the decision by the Live Oak High School administration to take a disciplinary response rather than use the moment for collective deliberation was a grave mistake. Certainly, there is a teachable moment here—not only for the students of Live Oak High School but for us as nation as the immigration debate once again unravels us at our seams (Pitts). To help us understand the nuances of these current political statements, we need to revisit the 1950s Cold War Mexican American civil rights movement.

There are a few still with us reading the national sign posts, those who took the long view and offered a hand to draft the larger map of US civil rights reform. There are a few whose voices provide contour and dimension to the flat, linear surface of history-making. Vicente Ximenes is one of those rare historical figures. Ximenes' style of leadership resonated with the post-war Mexican American generation and eventually bridged the World War II generation reformers of the 1950s with the Chicano activists of the 1960s. Ximenes's political impulse and rhetorical imagination rested upon four dimensions of democratic practice. Dissent, deliberation, dissonance, and disputation—these framed the guideposts of Ximenes's earliest activist work as a community organizer.

Vicente Ximenes and I met for the first time in November 2002 in Corpus Christi, Texas at the premiere release of the PBS film "Justice for My People," documenting the life and work of Vicente's friend and partner, Dr. Héctor P. García. Vicente told me his own story:

> From the time I was a grade school student in the 1920s until today the subjects of discrimination, race, color, national origin, and human rights have been a part of my life. From the first grade in a Mexican American segregated school in Texas until I received a Master's degree at the University of New Mexico, I had a preponderant majority of teachers that did not value my culture, language, custom, national origin, music, or food. Even my mother's tasty bean burritos and tortillas were ridiculed in school. I never had a Mexican American or Hispanic teacher during my formal education.

After the past eight years examining archival materials, conducting oral histories, and listening to the stories of Vicente Ximenes, I discovered that this generation of civil rights activists acquired citizen wisdom and civic literacy through the everyday experiences of growing up on the borders of American citizenship, in the liminal spaces of literacy practice.

Civic action for Vicente Ximenes and the World War II generation of reformers reflects many of the qualities identified by Hannah Arendt in her work, *The Promise of Politics*. Political action, as such, represents: "venturing forth in speech and deed in the company of one's peers—beginning something new whose end cannot be known in advance; founding a public realm; promising and forgiving one another. None of these actions can be realized alone, but always and only by people in their plurality." What Hannah Arendt describes in the work of restorative justice in the aftermath of World War II, reflects the same principles advanced by Desmond Tutu in the wake of South Africa apartheid. The gift-giving economy of democracy is, first and foremost, a discursive process.[2] Civic literacy is our capacity to read and respond to the world through language, symbol, and art. It is our ability to construct our experience together and to reinvent the public sphere. Civic literacy is our collective need to fabricate the narratives of history, and to construct imaginative fictions for the future, and to reconcile ourselves with one another.[3]

Twentieth-century Mexican American civil rights history suggests that in order for social movements to affect enduring institutional change, they must get into the sinew of governing organizations. They must shape and exercise the muscle and connective tissue of policy and practice from the inside out. It is not enough to stir a movement for social change. Activists must mentor advocates to implement and administer institutional transformation. The influence of a social activist is enhanced, and is best measured, by the effective and strategic placement of representatives within the dominant social structure.

Ximenes and the post-war Mexican American activists advanced a social movement that did not passively wait for justice and an invitation into the national conversation. Rather, they operated on the assumption that change was possible and stirred their own exigences for rhetorical access. They cultivated the rhetorical resources and literacy practices necessary to engage the inevitable dissonance of resistance and promote the requisite disputation toward social reform. This approach informed Ximenes's leadership style for over seven decades, including his tenure as Commissioner for President Lyndon B. Johnson's Equal Employment Opportunity Commission, Chairman of the Inter Agency of Mexican American Affairs, and coordinator of the landmark 1967 Presidential Cabinet Committee Hearings on Mexican American Affairs in El Paso, Texas.

It is important to note the anti-communist hysteria of the McCarthy age shaped the political situation of this twenty-year period of the postwar civil rights era from 1948-1968. The xenophobia and "redbaiting" discourses of the McCarthy age shaped the rhetorical situation of the twenty-year period of the postwar civil rights era. As Ellen Schrecker notes in *The Age of McCarthyism*, Cold War liberals of all ilk found themselves precariously aligned in the struggle against communism at home and overseas. Bobby Kennedy joined the ranks of anti-communist McCarthy democrats through the 1950s. He was in good company. Many Cold War liberals, like Minnesota Senator and future Vice President Hubert H. Humphrey, wanted to expand the welfare state and eliminate racial segregation to protect the world from the expansion of communism.[4]

Albert O. Hirschman in *The Rhetoric of Reaction: Perversity, Futility, Jeopardy* calls this tactic the "imminent-danger thesis" (153). Deployed throughout the Cold War era, social progressives argued for transferring resources from wealthier groups to poorer populations as a safeguard against the advances of communism. These advocates asserted that civil rights reform and welfare state programs were "imperatively needed to stave off some threatening disaster." The rhetorical resources available to Ximenes and his cadre of American GI Forum organizers were replete with the inconsistencies and fluencies of the Cold War rhetorical situation within which he exercised agency as a grassroots leader.

The peculiar problem facing Ximenes as new community organizer in Albuquerque sixty years ago was how to structure his arguments for Mexican American civil rights reform out of the hostile strands of rhetoric circulating within the Cold War cultural context. Ximenes responded to the local political climate by helping to organize Mexican American veterans in New Mexico around civil rights issues under the umbrella of the American GI Forum. This veterans' rights organization had been originally established in Corpus Christi, Texas by Dr. Hector P. Garcia just three years earlier (Kells, *Héctor P. García*). Ximenes adapted the vision and mission of the American GI Forum for the New Mexico situation. While the name "American GI Forum" hardly sounds radical to us today, it was sufficiently subversive enough to warrant persistent observation by the FBI. Vicente remembers:

> The organizational meeting of the Albuquerque GI Forum was held in the basement of the Sacred Heart Church. Eight persons came together and I was elected chairman of the GI Forum in 1951. Two months after the first meeting I received a frantic call from Monsignor García. The FBI had been by to ask him questions that the Monsignor could not answer about the GI Forum. If word got out in public that the FBI had questioned the Monsignor, the GI Forum would be doomed. I was scared because I had brought together friends to join the GI Forum and I knew the McCarthy Communist scare tactics had ruined the lives of many people. My professor of government had been literally run out of his job by the adherents of Senator McCarthy and for a few hours after the Monsignor's call I was frozen with fear of what might happen. Then I

> picked up the GI Forum constitution and by-laws and headed for the FBI office. I presented myself to FBI officials and told them I could answer any questions they had about the GI Forum. Our membership was open to anyone who would swear allegiance to the U.S. flag. The FBI person listened to all I had to say without any response to my statements. I then satisfied the Monsignor as to the legitimacy of the GI Forum.[5]

This is the backdrop that ultimately informed the choices Ximenes exercised on behalf of his constituencies.

Ximenes conceptualized his leadership style from a practical perspective rather than an abstract, theoretical model. He employed a pragmatic approach to civil rights reform, using grassroots community organizing strategies. Ximenes looked to the social realities of New Mexico and the Southwest to construct his understanding of civil rights reform and human rights activism. He believed that giving voice to the personal realities of citizens was the first step to promoting social change. The impetus for literacy practice for Ximenes and his contemporaries rested in the collective as well as the personal.

Civic Literacy and Mexican American Civil Rights Rhetoric

On December 20, 1951 Vicente Ximenes circulated one of his first acts of public rhetoric in the form of a letter to the editor of the *Albuquerque Journal*. The message embedded within this 300 word statement thoughtfully identifies the major issues and Cold War themes motivating the formation of the American GI Forum in Albuquerque that same year. Ximenes opens his letter with this declaration: "This is a letter about death." He then constructs a contrast between "death in New Mexico" and "death in Korea." The illustrative narrative that follows describes a recent event in Lovington, New Mexico. Ximenes delineates:

> On November 16, the Hobbs Daily News-Sun reported the death of two Mexican children from starvation. I assume that they meant that the children were American citizens of Mexican extraction, since it was reported that their legal residence was Yoakum, Texas. It seems no welfare funds were available for these American citizens because the law prevented disposition of funds to non-state residents. Furthermore, it seems that a nurse could not help the children because the nurse could not speak Spanish. Since when does a nurse have to speak Spanish in order to detect malnutrition. I always thought malnutrition was a health condition, not a language.[6]

Ximenes charges the state welfare system and then Senator Clint Anderson for his neglect of local conditions and for the consequent deaths of these two children. Ximenes contrasts the deaths of the two children in New Mexico with the deaths of one hundred and eight US Hispanic soldiers in Korea who gave their lives as American citizens.

This alignment seeks to establish a moral distinction between the noble and honorable Mexican American soldiers killed fighting in battle overseas and the disgraceful and dishonorable deaths of two innocent Mexican American children starved to death in the U.S. homeland. Ximenes deals with the particular classes, not general categories. Ximenes closes his letter of protest with a critique of New Mexico lawmakers and candidates campaigning for election and promoting various economic programs in the state. Ximenes argues:

> Not one single law-maker or would-be law-maker uttered a word about solving New Mexico's situation with reference to the two children that starved in Lovington, New Mexico. Perhaps silence means consent.[7]

Significantly, Ximenes signs his letter as "chairman" of the newly founded American GI Forum in New Mexico. Representing this new civic advocacy organization, Ximenes declares a new public presence in the region. The claims delineated in his letter are far-reaching. Ximenes tackles Cold War liberal issues alongside Mexican American civil rights questions related to national citizenship, regional identity, economic disparities, heritage language, and political representation. He would take up these very same themes for public action six years later in 1957.

Phronesis, Resistance, and American Democratic Practice

Ximenes conceptualized his leadership style from the perspective of particular cases rather than theoretical models. He employed a pragmatic epistemic approach to the construction of knowledge, using inductive and deliberative processes. *Phronesis*, according to Aristotle's *Nichomachean Ethics*, inextricably connects the dimensions of ethos, deliberation, and praxis—or purposeful choice. Or as Mary Whitlock Blundell argues, "Phronesis guides the process of deliberation and hence plays an essential role in purposeful choice, which in turn is the moving cause of praxis (action)."[8] Consistent with these characteristics of *phronesis*, Ximenes looked to the social realities of New Mexico and the Southwest to construct his understanding of civil rights reform and human rights activism.

Dramatically illustrating the contradictions of inclusion for Mexican American citizens, this second civil rights incident involved one of the institutions of Constitutional era US culture: the Daughters of the American Revolution. In February 1957, Art Tafoya, chairman of the Denver American GI Forum, along with José Ontiveros and Molly Galván of the Pueblo chapter, reported a racist incident in Colorado to Ximenes. Their reports indicated that the local chapter of the Daughters of the American Revolution had refused to allow a Mexican-origin boy to carry the American flag at a President Lincoln Day ceremony for the Colorado Industrial School for Boys in Golden, Colorado scheduled for February 12, 1957. The correctional institution was populated largely by Mexican-origin boys, many of whom were born in the United States to parents who were immigrant Mexican nationals. Questions of race, national identity, and cultural belonging were at the center of the controversy.

As national chairman of the American GI Forum, Vicente took the lead on the issue and expressed outrage to the local and national press. He immediately fired off a telegram to DAR National President Frederíc Graves and all chapters of the American GI Forum.[9] Within twenty-four hours, thousands of responses poured out in protest. Senator Dennis Chávez of New Mexico sent a telegram in rebuke, reminding public officials in Colorado that Mexican Americans had carried the US flag at Bataan in World War II. Governor McNichols of Colorado, in response, suspended all pending DAR activities in the state.

The symbolic value of this incident was clear to Ximenes. The American flag was a powerful symbol for his civic group; the colors were woven into the official emblem for the American GI Forum. The denial by the DAR of a Mexican-origin child to carry the US flag was a civil rights violation in Ximenes's mind, potentially as incendiary as the catalyzing event that propelled Dr. Héctor García and the American GI Forum into the national limelight in 1949. The refusal of a funeral director in Three Rivers, Texas to bury Mexican American soldier, Private Félix Longoria, had successfully cemented the reputation of the American GI Forum as a civil rights organization nearly a decade before (Kells, *Héctor P. García* 72). Ximenes did not waste any time to act on the infraction. He stirred public debate and demanded immediate redress.

The *Denver Star* and *Amarillo Globe-Times* noted that the Lincoln Day flag-carrying pageant had been immediately cancelled following Ximenes's complaint. Charlotte C. Bush, chair of the Denver Chapter of the DAR Patriotic Education Committee, publically defended her position: "I wouldn't want a Mexican to carry 'Old Glory,' would you?"[10] This offensive rhetorical question was advanced by Charlotte Bush in her capacity as a DAR official. Her statement not only revealed the character and attitudes of the speaker but the expressed goals of the organization. The premises of Charlotte Bush's assertion include: first, Mexican-origin people are not American citizens; second, only American citizens are entitled to carry the flag. The assertion was sufficiently damaging to DAR that it called for immediate action from the national headquarters.

DAR National President Frederíc Graves responded immediately by pulling the charter from the local Denver DAR chapter. She contacted Ximenes and offered to travel to Albuquerque to exchange flags with the American GI Forum as an act of reconciliation. Ximenes had to decide how much more negative press he wanted to promote, heaping political coals on the head of the DAR. However, Ximenes chose to take a restorative justice approach to the conflict, engaging in negotiations with DAR President Frederíc Graves. The flag exchange ceremony was promptly staged in front of the American GI Forum building in Albuquerque. The U.S. flag was carried by Roberto Durán, son of New Mexico American GI Forum organizer, Zeke Durán. President Graves delivered a statement regretting the incident and delineating the action she took to punish the Colorado DAR chapter and person who had refused to allow a Mexican American boy to carry the American flag. Ximenes formally accepted the apology and the National DAR's presentation of the American flag.

Symbolically, the American GI Forum raised the gift of the American flag in front of the newly constructed building that would become the permanent national headquarters of the American GI Forum in Albuquerque.[11] Equally important, the event signaled the authority of Ximenes as an emerging national leader, demonstrated his prudent exercise of citizen wisdom, and publically resisted the second class status of Mexican Americans in Cold War America. In effect, Ximenes asserted a new trajectory for Mexican American civil rights activism.

Ximenes exploited the flag-raising occasion toward a productive and peaceful outcome. He promoted an act of resolution through which both parties could recover honor and esteem. The flag exchange ceremony in Albuquerque provided a public occasion within which the American GI Forum, representative of Mexican American citizens, and the DAR, representative of Constitutional era America, could regain honor. Reverence and ceremony transformed drama and discord. Most importantly, the public event restored the dignity of the community.

Community Literacy and Cultivating Citizen Wisdom

Why are these stories important today? The current historical moment of healing national division and international polarization calls for models of democratic practice that promote dissent, engage difference, cultivate debate, and negotiate the noise of dissonance. As Hannah Arendt reminds, the promise of human freedom is realized through community—by plural human beings, "when and only when we act politically."

In brief, this is what democratized education is all about: cultivating conditions for self-governance and citizen wisdom (Woodruff). And this is the key idea behind the Writing Across Communities initiative at the University of New Mexico. My students and I have envisioned Writing Across Communities as a platform for invigorating the public sphere and cultivating civic literacy among our most vulnerable communities—creating spaces for historically excluded peoples.

Who constitutes our historically-excluded student populations? At the University of New Mexico, our vulnerable communities include a broad range of student groups: First generation college students, economically-vulnerable citizens, linguistically-diverse students, international students, Native American, Mexican American, African American student groups, non-traditional (re-entry) student populations, the unemployed, economically-disadvantaged students, physically and mentally disabled students, returning veterans and their families, political refugees, former prisoners (most of whom are disproportionately male students of color), LGBT students and survivors of hate crimes, sexual abuse, and domestic violence. In other words, I mean nearly the entire student population of the University of New Mexico constitute the intended beneficiaries of the Writing Across Communities initiative.

The impetus for Writing Across Communities at UNM began with some nagging questions about language and diversity. The most significant outcome of these past seven years is that Writing Across Communities continues to complicate the culture of writing at UNM with questions centering on issues of language, literacy, identity, and social justice. In a nutshell: the vision of the UNM Writing Across Communities initiative is to help students cultivate authority and alacrity across multiple contexts in order to develop the knowledge, understanding, and ethical habits of mind for citizenship in intellectually and culturally diverse academic, professional, and civic communities.

Let me code shift here for a moment. The Spanish term *bien estar* or wellbeing sums it nicely, I think. There are two different verbs of "being" in the Spanish linguistic system: *ser* (a stable, intrinsic state of being) and *estar* (a process of being). Writing Across Communities calls attention to the processes of being, of becoming literate members and citizens of our multiple diverse communities.

What I offer is a set of principles. I need to be honest about the organic and evolutionary nature of Writing Across Communities. There is no "blueprint" for Writing Across Communities. I have invited a number of my colleagues locally and nationally to help create this story. *Mi compadre* Juan Guerra from the University of Washington likens the UNM Writing Across Communities to "rhizomes:" he says that we are growing a forest of social activists from a single root. In reality, we are a work-in-progress. This provisional nature of Writing Across Communities is not only appropriate; it is intentional (Kells, "Writing Across Communities"). Literacy is a fluid, organic process. In other words, literacy is a human process. The notion that mastering any single literacy practice or writing genre is sufficient to becoming an educated and engaged citizen in the 21st century is a flawed notion.

The intellectual engine and the political operating space of Writing Across Communities begin and end with our students—not faculty, not administrators, not curriculum, per se). Our graduate and undergraduate students are the mobilizing force keeping the conversation going. When folks ask me where I find inspiration for this embattled initiative I respond that without a doubt, the story of the post-war Mexican American civil right movement and Vicente Ximenes provides me with the necessary "invisible means of support."

I would like to report, at the end of these past seven years of persistent mobilization, that the UNM administration recognizes, supports, and promotes Writing Across Communities university-wide. This is not the case. Infrastructure support remains limited and largely symbolic with annual small grants. We have no budget, no director, no staff, no office, no formal support whatsoever. We do have a WAC logo though, a website, and letterhead. Nonetheless, Writing Across Communities programs and events have served thousands of undergraduate students, included numerous community groups, supported graduate students from across the disciplines, and engaged hundreds of faculty members across the curriculum.

On the one hand, we have been called "an annoying insurgent movement" by administrators. Some would like the messy work of Writing Across Communities to just go away. A few would like a more traditional WAC program in its place "without all the political stuff." On the other hand, we have generated close to ninety-thousand dollars in cross-departmental grant support over the past seven years of mobilization, keeping our programs and events open and free to the public. We have our allies and beneficiaries.

My role as program chair, has been largely as a behind-the-scenes organizer. In practice, I am more of a network operator than an administrator. This protean role has required finding new ways to mobilize diverse constituencies toward a collective re-evaluation of how we teach writing across the university. In this ever changing game of role-shifting, I have also served as chair for the UNM Civil

Rights Symposia series for over five years. We have foregrounded African American, Mexican American, and Native American civil rights issues as well as sexual justice issues. Our 2011 Civil Rights Symposium was focused on Mental Health and Social Justice. My graduate students and I have coordinated these university-wide events to mark significant moments in U.S. civil rights reform as well as to call attention to current social justice issues. The response for 2007, 2008, 2009, and 2011 events exceeded our imagination. Hundreds have filled our sessions. We have practiced the deliberative ethics of peaceful social engagement. I have seen meeting rooms flowing over with students from high school to graduate school. Building on this history, our Spring 2012 Writing the World Symposium featured invited speakers, Paul Matsuda (Arizona State University) on second language writing issues and Michelle Eodice (University of Oklahoma) on writing center pedagogies. One young undergraduate student commented to me at the close of our 2012 Writing the World Symposium, "This is even better than a TED Talk."

Writing Across Communities: Changing the Culture of Writing

I have faith in deliberative processes and the possibilities of community engagement that promote healing, justice, and social connection. Our experience through Writing Across Communities suggests that it is possible to influence cultures of writing within and beyond the university, if we more fully represent and respond to the range of literacy practices associated with the civic, cultural, professional, and academic experiences of our students. Equally important, I have faith in the legacy of civil rights activists like Vicente Ximenes who resist the notion that civil rights reform is a once-done-always-done exercise. I am inspired by leaders like Marilyn Martinez who continue to call attention to the injustices and inconsistencies in our national terms of belonging. And I am especially concerned about the implicit racism embedded in literacy education programs nation-wide. As Leonard Pitts argues in his editorial essay following the Live Oak High School t-shirt ban, "The challenge for schools is to balance kids' impetuousness against their right of free speech" (A8). Pitts's recommendations for alternative responses to the Live Oak High School controversy that promote deliberative action and democratic practice reflects the kind of discursive public sphere that educational institutions (K-16) need to be cultivating. Pitt suggests:

> Imagine if [the principal of Live Oak High School] had corralled the most articulate of the T-shirt boys and the *cinco de mayo* celebrators and required them to research and represent their points of view in a formal debate before the entire school. The T-shirt kid could have challenged his classmates to explain why he felt the need, if he is an American, to celebrate a foreign holiday. The classmate could have pressed the T-shirt kid on why he felt threatened by a simple acknowledgment of heritage and cultural origin" (Pitts A8).

Regretfully, punitive action and silencing the ruptures in the democratic public imaginary continue to obscure and truncate these kinds of deliberative processes necessary for political inclusion and national transformation. Civic literacy must be as central to public education (K-16) as alphabetic and numerical literacy are to the national core curriculum (Guerra, "Nomadic Consciousness;" "Transcultural Citizenship"). Multiculturalism or "diversity" courses as isolated add-on requirements rather than embedded across-the-curriculum obfuscate the intrinsic value of pluralism woven into the national fabric of democracy.

Our nation has subscribed to racial and linguistic purity myths since the Constitutional era when the first naturalization laws were drafted (Kells, "Questions of Race;" López). The legalistic discourse of racial difference continues to inform our social institutions, our attitudes, our uneven distribution of resources and justice. In a country where people of color are disproportionately represented on the front lines of our military operations and in the jail cells of our prisons, we need to admit that our nation is seriously out of whack. When one of the greatest human rights tragedies in our history is being played out on our southernmost borders we need to acknowledge that racism is alive and well. When we fail to consider the impact of our economic, political, and immigration policies on the vulnerable communities whose transnational ties and connective tissue endure beyond the geopolitical divisions that separate them from their families—whose economic conditions leave them subsisting at our nation's edges, I need to say, in spite of the landmark moment when this nation elected a black man to the White House, we are not living in a post-racial world.

There is a subtext to my title here: "What's writing got to do with it?: Citizen Wisdom, Civil Rights Activism and Community Literacy." I have to admit, I keep hearing Tina Turner belting out the words: "What's love got to do with it?" Honestly. I think love and writing have a lot to do with it. Certainly, that is a thematic thread weaving throughout *Battling the Basement: The Trials and Triumphs of Marilyn A. Martinez*. Similarly, Juan Guerra in his book, *Close to Home: Oral and Literate Practices in a Transnational Mexicano Community*, examines the connective tissue of literacy (and writing) and its importance in sustaining and supporting families and their communities on both sides of the US border. What is so profound about Guerra's work is that his ethnographic study illustrates that writing is not only a personal skill, it is a social good, a community resource. Both Marilyn Martinez and Juan Guerra illustrate a common insight: giving voice to the personal realities of marginalized citizens represents the first step to promoting social change.

Writing Programs and Pedagogies of Leadership

So how can we respond? I believe that we each need to exercise the power of public rhetoric—moving between our spheres of concern and exercising authority (citizen wisdom, if you will) within our spheres of influence. Events like those offered through the Writing Across Communities initiative help us as a community protect the public sphere and promote dissent, deliberation, dissonance, and disputation. We need more opportunities and conduits for the cultural arts of resistance, disputation, difference, and debate. Our educational system (K-16) needs to move beyond passive models of literacy education that fail to critique and engage citizens as active "authors" of democracy. The enduring problem of public education is not rankings and test scores but intellectual and political passivity. Well-intentioned literacy programs stop short of cultivating active citizens when they stop short of promoting the full range of literacy practices—writing as well as reading. Teaching reading without cultivating writing (productive responsiveness) is like inviting guests to a party and not letting them speak. Those of us teaching undergraduate and graduate students in university settings have tremendous access to cultivating new leaders in community literacy.

My Spring 2012 graduate seminar, ENGL 640: Ideologies of Literacy, recently served as a deliberative space to examine the embedded assumptions and beliefs informing writing program administration at the University of New Mexico.[13] The exigence for this course was the growing momentum toward institutionalizing Writing Across Communities at UNM and the establishment of the new ABQ Community Writing Center by our graduate students. Additionally, we needed a reflective space for designing the new proposed ENGL 102 (WAC) Writing Intensive Course and cultivating our cross-institutional partnerships through the ABQ Community Writing Center. The messy work of democratizing literacy education is here to stay at UNM as long as we have engaged graduate students troubling the system. The issues of disparity and inequitable distribution of wealth and resources in New Mexico are historical and are not just going to go away. Literacy and social justice are inextricably connected in our local and national Constitutional-based system of governance.

The problem of the transparency of literacy is illustrated across academic, professional, and civic contexts. The value of literacy is so embedded in our social system we cannot see it even as educators. We simply take it for granted. That transparency is not a problem, so to speak, for educators and strategic planners in elite, exclusive institutions that mystify access and the practices of intellectual authority. In fact, the invisibility of literacy actually serves to maintain limited access and retain authority and exclusivity to an elite group of intellectuals. However, the invisibility of literacy is a real problem for diverse, open access institutions like the University of New Mexico and other two-year and four-year colleges across the nation where we are seeking to distribute knowledge and authority to historically-excluded social groups. Transparency of literacy is a problem for our students who do not have the culturally-prescribed literacies of elite, privileged social groups (see Appendix).

The new ABQ Community Writing Center is the heart and soul of the Writing Across Communities initiative. The pilot project is now located in the Albuquerque Public Main Library downtown as a drop-in center to assist local citizens with whatever writing task they want: a work-in-progress poem, a job application, a letter to the editor, a campaign flyer. Writing is and has always been a community endeavor. Admittedly, Plato was very suspicious about the lethal potential of writing. But the architects of the US Constitution were less reticent to wed writing to self-governance, more optimistic about the potential dimensions of literacy and democracy through the written codification of democratic principles. For the American democratic experiment civic literacy and democracy are inextricably intertwined. As the emerging community literacy scholarship suggests, the scope of writing education cannot be limited to the classroom and cannot be approached in a one-size-fits-all model. In *Writing and Community Engagement: A Critical Sourcebook*, Thomas Deans, Barbara Roswell, and Adrian J. Wurr observe, "One key insight proffered by nearly every community-engaged scholar is that each university/community partnership is shaped by local opportunities and limitations, local people and priorities" (5). We need to attend to difference.

Thanks to a dedicated team of graduate student social activists what once was a vague vision is now a reality for the citizens of Albuquerque.[14] Expanding on the community writing center model instituted by Tiffany Rousculp with the Salt Lake Community Writing Center in 2001, the ABQ Community Writing Center is extending the vision and principles of Writing Across Communities to the larger New Mexico community (Rousculp). While we commemorate the losses and travesty of 9/11 as a nation, we also need to recognize the generative responses and healing endeavors like the work of Rousculp in Salt Lake City launched a decade ago. We at the University of New Mexico are building this vision on the belief that writing can be a healing balm as well as a catalyst for change. Writing can help us cultivate mindfulness as well as collective deliberation at local, national, and global levels. In closing, writing has everything to do with it. Democracy is a living text that we must re-vision and re-invigorate with each generation of citizens.

The goal at this point in the journey is not constructing a monolithic discourse or grand narrative, but sustaining and extending the conversations seeded by the Writing Across Communities initiative over the past seven years beyond the boundaries of the University of New Mexico. This is the purpose of the newly established National Consortium of Writing Across Communities (NCWAC) which my colleagues and I launched in April 2011 in Atlanta during the 2011 Conference of College Composition and Communication (Kells "National Consortium"). Recognizing the tenth anniversary year of 9/11, our hope was to offer educators across the nation a generative vision for literacy education and civic engagement that transgresses the traditional boundaries of our discipline as well as the limits of institutional constraints. The NCWAC stakeholders affirm educational principles and cultural practices that promote the maintenance and wellbeing of human communities through literacy and writing. Moreover, NCWAC seeks to guide curriculum development, stimulate resource-sharing, cultivate networking, and promote research in language practices and literacy education throughout the nation, and to support local colleges and universities working to serve vulnerable communities within their spheres of influence.

The 2012 NCWAC Summer Summit in Santa Fe included three days of discussions about how we as scholars, teachers, writers, and leaders across institutional and regional sites can more effectively align the multi-faceted dimensions of our field in Rhetoric and Composition (and our multiple subfields such as Writing Program Administration, WAC, Writing Centers, ESL, Basic Writing, Second Language Writing, and Community Literacy) to better support future leaders (graduate students and new faculty) seeking to serve the vulnerable communities via sponsored literacy projects within their spheres of influence. Rather than a single book or a static product, the members of NCWAC plan to establish a dynamic online resource site to serve educators nationwide (especially junior faculty and graduate students) who are sponsoring literacy projects and working in and beyond the college classroom. The list of thirty affiliated institutions reads like a litany of hope. The hermeneutic space of the 2012 NCWAC Santa Fe Summit, marking the one-hundredth anniversary of New Mexico statehooood—the only state in the nation whose Constitution is written in both English and Spanish—offered each participant an imaginative site for considering new approaches to writing program that reaches beyond the borders of their institutions.

Writing can be both a *pharmakon*: both healing balm and an occasion for exercising agency (stirring aggravation) in a world of contingency and uncertainty. Through rhetorical listening and the act of exegesis of the text, the common thread that weaves through the stories of members of vulnerable communities, the current narratives of survivors like Marilyn Martinez and historical narratives of leaders like Vicente Ximenes, is the generative possibilities of exercising authority through diverse literacy practices. Community literacy as an advocacy movement offers an imaginative space that resists the debasement of exclusion and marginalization. In a socio-economic climate of scarcity, in a political environment conditioned by fear and shame, the capacity to read and respond to the world through the act of writing represents not only an occasion of agency but an affirmation of our humanity. Physically and mentally disabled peoples, linguistically-diverse students, transnational refugees, homeless veterans, the unemployed—the many groups we serve in our classrooms and beyond—all share a common condition of isolation and the inability to exercise agency over place. The invitation to write represents an opportunity to realize the rhetorical possibilities of turning transgressive power into transformative potential. Whatever challenge writers find themselves battling, the dignity and efficacy of self-representation through semiotics of the text are gifts we must keep in circulation.

Endnotes

1. I wish to extend my debt of appreciation to the insightful reflections on the agency of literacy offered in: Marilyn A. Martinez. Battling the Basement: The Trials and Triumphs of Marilyn A. Martinez. Santa Fe: MG Publishing, 2010: n.p.

2. The role of *nomos* and the concept of discursive democracy as a gift-giving economy are developed further in my presentation for the 2012 Watson Conference, "The Rhetorical Imagination of Writing Across Communities: *Nomos* and Literacy Education as a Gift-Giving Economy."

3. Segments of this article have been presented at the Writing Democracy Conference (March 2011), the Albuquerque Cultural Conference (September 2011), and the Watson Conference (October 2012).

4. Ellen Schrecker, *The Age of McCarthyism: A Brief History with Documents.* 2nd ed (New York: Bedford/St. Martins, 2002), 99.

5. Vicente Ximenes interview by author, October 9, 2006.

6. Vicente Ximenes letter to editor, December 20, 1951, Box 141, Folder 2, Héctor P. García (HPG) Papers. Mary and Jeff Bell Library. Texas A&M University-Corpus Christi.

7. Vicente Ximenes letter to editor, December 20, 1951, Box 141, Folder 2. HPG Papers.

8. For further discussion on *phronesis*, see: Mary Whitlock Blundell "Ethos and Dianoia Reconsidered" in Amélie Oksenberg Rorty, ed. *Essays on Aristotle's Poetics* (Princeton: Princeton University Press, 1992), 156.

9. Vicente Ximenes interview by author, March 4, 2008.

10. "Racial Issue Halts Lincoln Day Affair" *Amarillo Globe Times* n.d.; n.p. Box 146, Folder 20. HPG Papers.

11. Vicente Ximenes interview by author, March 9, 2008.

12. I remain indebted to the support and leadership of our Graduate Assistant Writing Across Communities Alliance leaders who have worked so diligently and generously over the past seven years organizing Writing Across Communities events and programs: Beverly Army Gillen, Leah Sneider, Bernadine Hernandez, Dan Cryer, Greg Evans Haley, Erin Penner Gallegos, Brian Hendrickson, and Genevieve García de Mueller.

13. I wish to acknowledge the graduate student Writing Fellows in my ENGL 640 Ideologies of Literacy Seminar who helped to envision the ENGL 102 Writing Intensive Learning Communities Pilot Project during the Spring 2012: Dan Cryer, Christine Beagle García, Genevieve García de Mueller, Brian Hendrickson, Mellisa Huffman, and Lindsey Ives.

14. A special word of acknowledgment is due to the co-founders and leaders of the ABQ Community Writing Center: Brian Hendrickson, Erin Penner Gallegos, Genevieve García de Mueller, Anna Knutson, and Deb Paczynski.

Works Cited

Aristotle. *Nicomachean Ethics*. 2nd ed. Trans. Terence Irwin. Indianapolis: Hackett, 1999.

Albrecht, Glenn. *Solastalgia: A New Concept in Human Health and Identity. Philosophy Activism Nature* (2005) 3:41-44.

Allsup, Carl. *The American GI Forum: Origins and Evolution.* Austin: Center for Mexican American Studies, 1982, 99.

Arendt, Hannah. *The Promise of Politics*. New York: Schocken Books, 2005: xx.

Beasley, Vanessa. *Who Belongs in America: Presidents, Rhetoric, and Immigration*. College Station: Texas A&M University P, 2006.

Blundell, Mary Whitlock. "Ethos and Dianoia Reconsidered" in Amélie Oksenberg Rorty, ed. *Essays on Aristotle's Poetics*. Princeton: Princeton UP 1992: 156.

Carson, Rachel. *Silent Spring*. Cambridge: Riverside P, 1962.

Hirschman, Albert O. *The Rhetoric of Reaction: Perversity, Futility, Jeopardy*. Cambridge: Harvard UP, 1991.

Guerra, Juan C. "Writing for Transcultural Citizenship: A Cultural Ecology Model." *Language Arts*. 85.4 (March 2008): 296-304.

_____. "Putting Literacy in Its Place: Nomadic Consciousness and the Practice of Transcultural Repositioning." *Rebellious Reading: The Dynamics of Chicano/a Literacy*. Ed. Carl Gutierrez-Jones. Center for Chicana/o Studies: University of California Santa Barbara, 2004: 19-37.

_____. *Close to Home: Oral and Literate Practices in a Transnational Community*. New York: Teachers College Press, 1998.

Jarrett, Susan C. *Rereading the Sophists: Classical Rhetoric Refigured.* Carbondale: Southern Illinois UP, 1991.

Kells, Michelle Hall. *Héctor P. García: Everyday Rhetoric and Mexican American Civil Rights.* Carbondale: Southern Illinois UP, 2006.

———. "Leveling the Linguistic Playing Field in the Composition Classroom." *Attending to the Margins: Writing, Researching, and Teaching on the Front Lines.* Eds. Michelle Hall Kells and Valerie Balester. Portsmouth: Heinemann-Boynton/Cook, 1999:131-49.

———. "Linguistic Contact Zones: An Examination of Ethnolinguistic Identity and Language Attitudes" *Written Communication* 19.1 (January 2002): 5-43.

———. "The Rhetorical Imagination of Writing Across Communities: *Nomos* and Literacy Education as a Gift-Giving Economy." *JAC* (Forthcoming 2014).

Kells, Michelle Hall. "National Consortium of Writing Across Communities." http://www.unm.edu/~wac/NCWAC.html

Kells, Michelle Hall. "Writing Across Communities: Deliberation and the Discursive Possibilities of WAC." *Journal of Reflections* 6.1 (Spring 2007): 87-108.

Kells, Michelle Hall and Valerie Balester. "Voices from the Wild Horse Desert." *Attending to the Margins: Writing, Researching, and Teaching on the Front Lines.* Eds. Michelle Hall Kells and Valerie Balester. Portsmouth: Heinemann-Boynton/Cook, 1999: xiii-xxiii.

Kells, Michelle Hall, Valerie Balester, and Victor Villanueva, eds. *Latino/a Discourses: Language, Identity, and Literacy Education.* Portsmouth: Heinemann-Boynton/Cook, 2004.

———. "Lessons Learned in Hispanic Serving Institutions." Eds. Cristina Kirklighter, Diana Cárdenas, and Susan Wolff Murphy. *Teaching Writing With Latino/a Students.* Albany: State University of New York P, 2007: vii-xiv.

Kells, Michelle Hall "Mapping the Cultural Ecologies of Language and Literacy" eds. Bruce Horner, Min-Zhan Lu, and Paul Kei Matsuda. *Cross-Language Relations in Composition.* Carbondale: Southern Illinois UP, 2010: 2004-11.

Kells, Michelle Hall "Writing Across Communities: The Diversity, Deliberation, and the Discursive Possibilities of WAC." *Reflections* 11.1 (2007): 87-108.

López, Ian F. Haney. *White By Law: The Legal Construction of Race.* New York: New York UP, 1996.

Martinez, Marilyn A. *Battling the Basement: The Trials and Triumphs of Marilyn A. Martinez.* Santa Fe: MG Publishing, 2010: n.p.

Pitts, Leonard. "T Shirt Ban Free Speech Issue." *Albuquerque Journal* May 20, 2010: A8.

Rose, Shirley and Chuck Paine. "On the Crossroads and at the Heart: A Conversation." *WPA: The Journal of the Council of Writing Program Administration* 35.2 (2012): 160-78.

Rousculp, Tiffany. "When the Community Writes: Re-envisioning the SLCC DiverseCity Writing Series." *Reflections* 5.1 (2006): 67-88.

Schrecker, Ellen. *The Age of McCarthyism: A Brief History with Documents.* 2nd ed (New York: Bedford/St. Martins, 2002), 99.

Woodruff, Paul. *First Democracy: The Challenge of an Ancient Idea.* New York: Oxford UP, 2005.

Appendix

ENGL 640: Ideologies of Literacy
Dr. Michelle Hall Kells

This seminar will examine the historical, cultural, economic, political, and educational dimensions of "literacy." The conceptualization, mythology, and practice of "literacy" (reading and writing) has become integral to social access in our 21st century cosmopolitan universe (full civic, economic, and cultural participation—locally, nationally, and globally). As teachers (of English Studies and Education), we need to apply a critical lens to the metaphors and models of literacy we adopt and promote.

We will examine the question of literacy as a key social value in the national imaginary. Literacy is not only a practice (and outcome of public K-16 education) but a core value of both American Constitutional culture and the Western tradition of higher learning.

Literacy is: how we reason from the data;
how we gain authority and authorship in and across diverse intellectual spheres;
how we engage (and organize) our social worlds.

We can define literacy as the processes and products related to generating, interpreting, and circulating symbolic systems of meaning (e.g. alphabetic, mathematical, digital, visual, scientific symbol systems). These are all culturally conditioned processes and products for which we need to become socialized (educated) to interpret (read) and write (produce).

The problem of the transparency of literacy is illustrated across academic, professional, and civic contexts. The value of literacy is so embedded in our social system we can't see it (even as educators). We simply take it for granted. That transparency is not a problem, so to speak, for educators and strategic planners in elite, exclusive institutions (e.g. Harvard, Stanford, etc.) that mystify access and the practices of intellectual authority. In fact, the invisibility of literacy actually serves to maintain limited access and retain authority and exclusivity to an elite group of intellectuals. However, the invisibility of literacy is a real problem for diverse, open access institutions like the University of New Mexico (and other two-year and four-year colleges across the nation) where we are seeking to distribute knowledge and authority to historically-excluded social groups. Transparency of literacy is a problem for our students who do not have the culturally-prescribed literacies of elite, privileged social groups.

The literacy skills (informational, digital, numerical, alphabetic, environmental, scientific, etc) of our professoriate and our student body affect every facet of our enterprise as an institution of higher education:

- Recruitment
- Retention
- Graduation Rates
- National Ranking & Distinction
- Placement (job and graduate school)
- Classroom success.

Literacy is not only the principal practice of what we do every day in our work and personal lives; it is a deeply held core value of American citizenship and belonging, so integral to who we are—our national identity—it is the concept around which we fashion our system of self-governance through the drafting and continuous revision (and reinterpretation) of the U.S. Constitution. Deliberative literacy (as exemplified in U.S. constitutional rhetoric) is the only core value around which we in our explosive and exponential national diversity can concur. Perhaps we could call literacy one of those "venerable" American ideals.

NOTE: This course has been designed for graduate students of Rhetoric & Writing as well as in Education. We will focus on a broad range of arguments (across genres and discourse communities in public/popular cultures). Final course projects will be adapted to the specific needs, interests, and genre-practices of the graduate students in my course with respect to their different sub-areas of Rhetorical Studies and Education.

Learning Outcomes:
Course readings, assignments, and class discussions are designed to promote the following learning outcomes:
- Apply and integrate concepts of literacy studies;
- Guide and participate in class discussions of course readings;
- Historicize the intellectual traditions of Western literacy education;
- Critically analyze notions of literacy across academic and public cultures;
- Use the writing process as recursive stages (from invention to editing) for writing tasks;
- Engage in purposeful and productive peer review;
- Connect classroom learning to teaching writing;
- Generate intellectual project (seminar paper) productive to future professional development (conference paper, MA portfolio or dissertation chapter, journal article, etc.);
- Cultivate alliances with peers and work collaboratively toward common goals.

Required Texts:
Ellen Cushman, Eugene R. Kintgen, Barry M. Kroll, and Mike Rose eds. *Literacy: A Critical Sourcebook*
Paolo Freire *Pedagogy of the Oppressed.*
James Paul Gee *Social Linguistics and Literacies: Ideology in Discourses.*
Keith Gilyard. *Composition and Cornel West: Notes Toward a Deep Democracy.*

Antonio Gramsci. *Selections from the Prison Notebooks.*
Jacqueline Jones Royster. *Traces of a Stream: Literacy and Social Change Among African American Women.*
Raymond Williams *Key Words: A Vocabulary of Culture and Society*
Victor Villanueva. *Bootstraps: From an American Academic of Color.*

A Clear Channel: Circulating Resistance in a Rural University Town

Shannon Carter

Texas A&M-Commerce

This article offers an extended treatment of two social justice efforts in a rural university town as historical examples of civic engagement with contemporary implications for Writing Democracy and similar projects. The article begins with an analysis of local activism initiated by John Carlos in 1967 while he was still a student at our university and the year before his heroic, silent protest against racism with Tommie Smith at the 1968 Olympics in Mexico City. The author then turns to a linked effort five years later by local activist MacArthur Evans, a university student from Chicago. In 1973, Evans and other university students established the Norris Community Club (NCC) in partnership with residents of Norris, the historically segregated neighborhood, to provide what they called "a clear channel of communication" between Norris and city officials. Both were successful, albeit it in very different ways. The author uses "a clear channel" as both the object of study and interpretive lens to examine these local efforts and their many implications for today.

In 1973, university students and local citizens created the Norris Community Club (NCC), a university-community partnership designed to challenge racial inequities persisting long after civil rights legislation had mandated otherwise. To accomplish the desired reform, NCC provided what they called "a clear channel of communication" between the city and residents of Norris, the town's historically segregated neighborhood (Reed, Interview). That channel mobilized the community as never before, leading to significant changes like the election of a city official who "understood the needs of the people in the Norris Community and [was] willing to do something about it" (Carter et al.)[1] and the extensive funding needed to improve neighborhood streets, sewage, and telephone services.

There is much that compels me about the Norris Community Club, a group of ordinary, local citizens—*strangers*, in fact—drawn together through "texts"[2] largely local in circulation and often ephemeral in form (see Warner). What interests me most about NCC is the ordinary, everyday quality of their work, and not their extraordinary contributions. However significant—and they *were* significant—NCC's accomplishments in terms of sustainable community changes are far less important to the current study than the ways in which NCC enabled *participation* among local publics. For nearly a century, Norris residents had felt largely excluded from such conversations, leading to significant inequities not unlike those felt across America in areas housing the greatest concentration of any city's poorest citizens. And though the transformations NCC fostered locally were always partial and mainly temporary, they were nonetheless as vital as they would be in any open and free society.

My research on NCC is situated in a growing body of scholarship that has revitalized our understanding of rhetorical agency among historically underrepresented groups, including working class and labor movements (Welch; George), Mexican-American civil rights leaders (Kells), and progressive educators (Enoch). Urban and northern markers typically signify our field's in-depth investigations of university-community relations (Coogan, Parks, Goldblatt; Cushman). Yet we still know far too little about rural literacies (Hogg; Donehower, Hogg, and Schnell), especially the activist rhetorics (Kate) enacted across rural spaces largely characterized by a rhetoric of sustainability (Owens; Donehower, Hogg, and Schnell). We know even less about university-community partnerships in communities like mine.

Figure 1. Norris Community Club, circa 1974

My primary goal in the following essay is not to analyze the specific factors contributing to NCC's successes nor its ultimate unsustainability.3 Rather I hope to articulate through this and one other local, historical example the ways in which such student-initiated efforts got started and gained local momentum. In other words, how have university students gone about creating the alternative publics necessary for desired change? What role might "mundane texts" play in these efforts—i.e., the "multiple, mundane documents, interpersonal networks, historical influences, and rhetorical moves and countermoves" that Nathaniel A. Rivers and Ryan P. Weber have argued are crucial elements of all public rhetoric? What implications might these earlier efforts have for more contemporary contexts?

Throughout, NCC's notion of a "clear channel" will serve as both the object of study and an interpretive lens through which I investigate civic engagement. On AM radio in North America, "clear-channel stations" are those most protected from interference from other stations. Theoretically then a message broadcast on a clear-channel station has the greatest likelihood of reaching its target audience with the sender's original meaning still intact. Realistically, of course, such a direct correlation between the message sent and the one received is impossible, but as long as we understand true clarity to be an impossible standard, a "clear channel" remains a useful metaphor.

I begin with NCC, especially the ways in which the circulation of everyday, mostly ephemeral "mundane texts" (Rivers and Weber) provided a local channel for democratic deliberation (Mouffe; Warner). Other local channels preceded NCC, though most were characterized by weak signal strength and overlapping radio frequencies that eventually drowned out the intended broadcast and drew listeners elsewhere. With this in mind, I turn next to a local channel initiated five years earlier by John Carlos, the sprinter from Harlem best known for his part in the Silent Protest at the 1968 Olympics. After joining ET's track team in 1966, Carlos soon found existing race relations intolerable and thus attempted to link our local community to a global "channel" circulating the rhetoric of black resistance. I describe this attempt, again drawing attention to the role played by mundane texts but this time as they strengthened overlapping radio frequencies that eventually silenced Carlos locally and drove him away altogether.

Yet perhaps even more significant than the above discussion is the renewal of local activism this rhetorical recovery has enabled. My involvement in such projects has helped bring unprecedented local attention to Dr. Carlos and his significant links to our institution, including numerous area and campus presentations in November 2011 as part of his recent book tour and, in May 2012, an honorary doctorate from this institution (see Carter, "Letter"; Hobdy). In partnership with NCC's founding members, we have also been able, once again, to turn campus and community attention toward Norris with a range of public programming and preservation efforts, including a documentary and, most recently, a multimedia exhibit funded in part by a grant from the National Endowment for the Humanities (Carter, "Remixing"). I explore how these local channels originally came into being, disappeared, and then ultimately emerged again through the very act of rhetorical recovery and rhetorical use of public programming. As I will explain in the final section, the Writing Democracy conference from which these proceedings emerged brought together NCC members for the first time in 35 years (see Carter, et al.), an event of great significance for everyone involved.

The local remains a primary factor in my analysis, though I am always mindful of what Deborah Brandt and Kate Clinton call the "Limits of the Local." As they insist, literacy practices are not "self-generating, the product of unique cultural characteristics," but rather "an outcome of historical and often violent contrasts between people of unequal power" (339). Far from a neutral canvas against which humans interact with one another, however, the local is the very space and time in which we experience our world. All history is local. All politics are local. As linguist Alistair Pennycook insists, all language use is local as "space is a central interactive part of the social" (55). Indeed, "[e]verything happens locally. However global a practice may be, it still always happens locally ... " (128, emphasis added).[4] The local spaces in which university-community partnerships form are necessarily a "central interactive part" of our social justice work.

It is thus fitting that this special issue include a study of historical examples from the local site that hosted the Writing Democracy conference from which these proceedings emerged: a mid-sized (10,000 students), PhD-granting university in a small town (9,100 population) 60 miles East of Dallas. The fluidity of the particular historical, cultural, political, and ideological forces that gave rise to the local experienced by participants in this March 2011 event are at once unique and universal. Even as participants engaged one another at a particular place (the Sam

Rayburn Student Center) and time (March 9-11, 2011), broadcasts from other local channels around the world traveled across the flat empty spaces of Northeast Texas and entered our conference rooms through conversations and smart phones, in the lived experiences of the bodies populating these spaces, in the news feeding into these rooms through iPads, laptops, and the hallway's television monitors: protests in Wisconsin follow decisions to strip the collective bargaining rights of public workers; the disaster then unfolding in Japan moves all of us to tears.

Writing democracy, then, may be understood as the vehicle through which we ensure meaningful, purposeful links across our various local contexts. A project like this requires not only *recovering* the local but also "*theorizing* the local," as David Gold has argued we must (Gold, "Beyond"). With "a clear channel" as interpretive lens, I am attempting to "theorize the local" by drawing attention to historical examples of civic engagement with theoretical and practical implications for today's efforts. Throughout I focus on the role played by the circulation of local texts in establishing viable publics necessary "to support people standing *with* others *for* something" as a "powerful alternative to ... speaking *up* or speaking *against*" (Flower 130). *This* is the clear channel NCC established locally and I hope Writing Democracy can provide, one that links local publics together through a global channel designed to, once again, "[re]introduce America to Americans," as FWP's *American Guide Series* did more than 75 years ago. America's local publics deserve a closer look.

Circulation

> *[A] public enables a reflexivity in the circulation of texts among strangers who become, by virtue of their reflexively circulating discourse, a social entity.*
>
> –Michael Warner

The history of Norris is quite similar to that of other historically segregated neighborhoods. Norris formed at the end of the 19th century as former slaves and their children began moving to the recently incorporated town of Commerce from area farms for work made available by the university, established in 1889, and the railroad industry. Not unlike other segregated communities across the Jim Crow South, Norris soon established churches, schools, restaurants, stores, and other businesses designed to provide for citizens who were denied access to these services in every other section of town. Over the next century, even as the city established and improved infrastructure and services everywhere else in town, streets in Norris would remain largely unpaved, its residents left without access to the city's sewage systems, police protection, or adequate telephone and postal service. Desegregation reached the local university in 1964 and the city's schools the following year, but neither change improved much about everyday living conditions for the town's local citizens remaining in Norris.

In 1973 a handful of university students met with residents of Norris to learn their key concerns and devise a plan for community change, leading to the formation of NCC. In a few short years, this neighborhood and, indeed, the entire town seemed altogether transformed: a historically unprecedented voter turnout elected the first African American city officials, civil service positions were filled with minority applicants long denied such opportunities, issues of key concern to Norris residents long absent from local and campus news began receiving unprecedented attention, and millions of dollars of grants and other support began pouring in to right past injustices.

NCC's ability to accomplish these goals cannot be attributed to any direct, official effort by the university. Any of the ways in which networks of reciprocity were established between the university and the community were largely ad hoc and student-led, as would be the case for most any such partnership in this era before service learning programs and similar university-driven efforts. A handful of interested faculty later learned of NCC and supported its efforts with informal training in public speaking, minor financial contributions, or similar means. The university president allowed the group to book university space in his name for their annual banquets designed "to improve relations between the Norris Community and the rest of the city" ("NCC Reception"). Such support was meaningful, albeit limited.

The texts NCC produced and circulated were "action-oriented" (Wells), driven by a tactical (temporal and spatial) logic rather than a strategic one (see Mathieu), and rhetorical in orientation. In this, NCC mirrors the "rhetorically-oriented model" Lorraine Higgins, Elenore Long, and Linda Flower advocate—one that "calls up local publics around the aims of democratic deliberation" (10). It also characterizes NCC's clear channel as one designed for the express purpose of mobilizing local publics to act on behalf of Norris.

How does a local channel created for local participation on behalf of local citizens get started? Indeed how does *any* public writing get started (see George 60)? In theorizing the local, we must pay close attention to the rhetorical ecologies (Edbauer) shaping any communicative event. The channel NCC created is, like all publics as Michael Warner defines the term, "essentially *intertextual*" (15, emphasis mine). Thus NCC's origins cannot be located in any single document, individual, or event, and it is simply not possible to trace every local or global element that made this local channel possible. We can, however, find convincing links among local activists —many direct and personal, most revealing the links among networks of texts generated to establish earlier channels and those that followed. Most notable in this respect is a series of texts generated by members of the Afro-American Society of East Texas (ASSET), especially their "Declaration of Rights" and associated materials, which they delivered to campus administrators in 1968. The action they took in this public demonstration was a concrete list of demands that included rights to African American faculty and administrators, fair and equal housing and access to campus employment, and courses in African American studies. In a few short years, all of their demands would be met, setting in motion a series of key hires and other changes that made NCC possible and productive. Just as NCC established a clear channel between Norris residents and city officials, ASSET established a channel between African American students and campus administrators.

NCC did not, of course, come out of nowhere, but most accounts date the group's unofficial start to a meeting held at a Baptist church in Norris. Soon after arriving on campus in 1973, McArthur Evans (see Figure 1, far left), a criminal justice major and campus police officer born in Selma, Alabama, and raised in Chicago, asked Douglas Stephens[5] (Figure 1, second from the left), a local citizen and fellow officer, where the city's African American citizens lived. Many of the students lived on campus, of course. But where were the local minorities who were not students? "They live off over there in 'The Hole,'" he recalls Douglas telling him. "He called it that ... He said that's where they are, 'Across the track, down in "The Hole."' From this co-worker and lifetime resident of Norris, Evans learned

> the conditions that were down in 'The Hole': sewer problems, outhouses…[sigh]. And being born in the South, I remember the outhouses. I *used* outhouses—*Hello!* [laughs]—when I was a little boy in Selma, Alabama. And so I knew about outhouses. But I couldn't believe in 1973 that people still were using outhouses and unpaved streets and communities being neglected, way off from the university down in 'The Hole'? I just couldn't see that. (emphasis in original)

He asked for a tour of Norris, then help calling together a meeting to hear the community's key concerns and help devising a plan to get them addressed. "Anyway," Mr. Evans continues, "that's where I met Mr. Reed. And through that process, the community became active, involved, and elected its first president of the NCC" (Carter et al.).

"Actually," recalls Billy Reed, "how I got started was I was a little late at a meeting I heard they were going to have down at the old church, which was an old wooden building at the time. So I decided to go down and see what the meeting was about" (Carter et al.). A veteran of the Korean War, Reed worked as a conductor for the railroad that ran through town establishing the line between Norris and the rest of the city. He was well known throughout the community, outspoken, and, unlike the majority of Norris residents, drew a salary from outside the city, making him an ideal candidate to serve as NCC's first president. With this meeting, a counterpublic came into being and, through the work of this university student-community partnership, grew and remained in circulation.

The process began by *naming* this local public. "They called it 'The Hole,'" Opal Pannell explained in an oral history interview three years ago, right before going to her file cabinet to retrieve NCC's charter and a stack of yellowed minutes and newsletters that brought this public into being originally and kept it in circulation.6 "They," in this case, referred to both the locals outside the neighborhood and the vast majority of the neighborhood's residents. "I didn't like that. That name change [from 'The Hole' to the 'Norris Community'] was our first order of business." Also one of NCC's founding members and a lifetime resident of the area who, like Mr. Reed, is a child of the Great Depression, Mrs. Pannell fought hard for Norris: "We kept telling everybody, 'We don't live in a *hole*. We *live* in the Norris Community'" (Pannell, Interview, emphasis in original; see also Carter and Conrad).

Before NCC called Norris together as a public, the absent presence of the living, breathing humans who populate this neighborhood were rendered not a public, not a community, but, in fact, a *hole*—*The* Hole, a void, a space emptied of ifs people and their long histories. "The Hole" may be similarly characterized as the static we hear on the radio dial —those spaces in between stations. We leave our radios tuned to *established* channels with a steady stream of clear programming we find relevant to our lives. We need a reason to do otherwise. Instead of relying upon established channels, students like Evans placed the AM dial on a relatively unknown channel and began to listen. Eventually he heard it, faint and distant at first but increasingly present and forceful: the people of Norris, long silenced by the far stronger overlapping frequencies of dominant publics, were speaking up and it was time for the rest of town to listen. By naming Norris, NCC helped establish a channel then, through the regular circulation of relevant texts, began giving the city a reason to tune in to Norris. By linking this local channel to global channels broadcasting black resistance elsewhere, NCC helped *compel* the city to listen and respond. "It is not our desire to scare city officials," NCC president Billy Reed explains in a 1974 editorial, "but *we demand justice at any price*" (emphasis added).

"They called it 'The Hole' because it was dark all the time there," Mr. Reed explains. "They maybe had three streetlights for the whole community." It was "'The Hole" because many residents were forced to use "outhouses rather than regular, indoor toilets ... Just a hole dug in the ground with a building sitting up over it" (Reed, Interview). To establish an organization that would represent this community, the students and citizens involved had to come up with a name. Reed, describing the first meeting of what became the Norris Community Club, recalls saying, "Well, if we are going to have an organization, we might as well have a name that coincided with the community ... [T]he Norris School was in the neighborhood where blacks attended, so I suggested that we name it the Norris *Community* ... and, of course, they agreed upon it, so that's what we did, named it that" (Carter et al.). That naming and the narrative sequencing that followed through a series of texts coordinated with great care by NCC members filled this "hole" with a collective body of "strangers united through circulation of discourse" (Warner 59). Through this process, "The Hole" became "the Norris Community." NCC essentially placed Norris on the radio dial, broadcasting this neighborhood across town. Suddenly locals were tuning in and connecting with Norris families as neighbors with a shared interest in improving the entire community, as NCC press always insisted was their goal. To establish a clear channel and remain on air, NCC had to compose and circulate a series of mundane texts not just in written form but spoken as well, including the charter establishing NCC and the bylaws that gave the organization its official shape, the phone calls exchanged with area and State officials, the agenda items NCC developed together at the local Pizza Hut during their weekly writing sessions in preparation for their appearance at the meetings of the city council, the presentations they delivered following these writing sessions, the minutes Opal Pannell took at NCC's regular meetings that later contributed to articles appearing in local press, and a host of other such texts.

Perhaps a key contributor to this circulation was NCC member Allen Hallmark, then a graduate student in journalism and NCC's only white member. A Vietnam Vet against the war, Hallmark had been deeply involved with a variety of causes associated with what he called "The Movement"—"Civil Rights, Women's Rights, Environmental Preservation ... I wanted to find out if there was some kind of movement in Commerce."

> I began exploring the town on my bicycle and when I crossed the railroad tracks into the black part of town, ... [Eventually], I found a tiny little building on a residential street that was too small to be a home. Perhaps it had a "Norris Community Club" sign on it or a notice of when the meetings were held, or else I asked around and was told about the club and when it met.
>
> I just showed up at a meeting and my entrance pretty much put a stop to all conversation for a couple of minutes. As I recall, they tried to ignore me as much as possible for the first couple of meetings, but I kept attending and gradually the ice melted and trust began to be built. (email)

Billy Reed describes Hallmark's role in NCC as "the *writer*": ... He would be with us all the time—would write about it ... Whenever we would meet," whether that be in public conversations with the city or behind closed doors, "he would be there and he would write about it" (Interview).

In charge of NCC's PR, Hallmark was a significant contributor to NCC's core programming. The articles he produced broadcast news that Norris residents helped co-create. This was news written *with* the community—not merely *about* a community or *for* a community (Deans et al.). "I thought my role was to listen to these folks who knew their community and knew ... what the community needed," Hallmark explains. "I had some skill as, you know, a budding journalist, so I thought ... my role was to take ... the message these folks came up with, take it to the local newspaper and ... get some action going." As often as possible, he told "the story of the Norris Community" on campus too. "A lot of people didn't realize what was going on," he continued, "... maybe they just shut their eyes to it, but we needed to open those eyes and get them to do the right thing" (Carter et al.).

So Hallmark wrote. When he couldn't get the local or campus newspapers to print it, he would type it up on his personal typewriter, mimeograph it at the campus, and distribute it around town himself. He knew instinctively, just as the other NCC members seemed to know, as Michael Warner argues, that "no single text can create a public ... In order for a text to be public, we must recognize it ... as a temporality of circulation" (90; 94). In order to keep that channel open, the texts had to keep circulating, and everyone involved had to participate in that circulation.

Participation

"Someone has to put down the cotton sack," Mr. Evans told my first-year students in a presentation last February, part of our Black History Month Speaker Series which he and other founding NCC members helped launch. "Someone has to drink from the white fountain" (Evans, "Black History"). His point here and in our many previous conversations and joint presentations around campus was a familiar one, though nonetheless significant. The metaphors "put down the cotton sack" and "drink from the white fountain" offer a particularly useful way to illustrate writing democracy in action, especially with respect to the crucial role played by ordinary citizens with a deep respect for the entire community and its history and a desire to listen, often *rhetorically* (Ratcliffe).

On the surface, these metaphors embody a deeply problematic logic of autonomy that guides our master narratives concerning social change—i.e., someone extraordinary (agent) does something extraordinary (action) that changes the world. Such narratives set an impossible standard for civic engagement, of course, but our human desire to celebrate and find inspiration in the extraordinary accomplishments of extraordinary people keeps such myths in circulation (see also Royster and Cochran; Hesford). Such stories can be far more attractive than more realistic ones concerning civic engagement. Few find immediately attractive an opportunity to participate in activities designed for social change yet very unlikely to produce obvious, sustainable results.

Yet these metaphors also signify autonomy's limits, as well as the historical, political and ideological forces at play in any human activity resisting the status quo. Of course, slavery didn't end because "someone put down the cotton sack." Segregation didn't end because "someone drank from the white fountain." Indeed no single individual starts a movement. Rosa Parks didn't refuse to give up her seat one day because she was "tired" (Kohl; Loab, *Soul*). This demonstration was a significant rhetorical event, but it was also one for which she and countless others had prepared for years (see also Welch). Challenges to the logic of autonomy in civic engagement do not diminish the contributions of iconic figures like Rosa Parks or any other individual involved. Instead we remember "that her initial step of getting involved was just as courageous and critical as the fabled moment when she refused to move to the back of the bus" (Loab, "The Real").

Our focus here is not on what such acts *accomplished* but rather on the ways they signify the participation of ordinary people. An agent ("someone") acting ("put down the sack," "drank from the white fountain," "refused to give up a seat") for a desired result, which is important regardless of whether or not this result comes to pass. Also crucial to these actions as rhetorical events symbolizing common goals (equality) and/or policy change (abolition of slavery, desegregation) are the rhetorical ecologies that give them meaning—not as an individual actor who is too tired or thirsty to adhere to behaviors scripted by society but as a rhetor involved in a rhetorical event enabled by a counterpublic and shaped by a particular series of historical, political, ideological, temporal, and spatial concerns (see Warner; Crowley; Ratcliffe). Rhetorical events like these rely upon a vast array of far more mundane texts, aural and written, as Rivers and Weber reveal in their "ecological read" of the Montgomery bus boycott. Mundane texts were similarly complicit in bringing local activist efforts like NCC into being.

Urging us to separate ideology from activism, William Exum argues, "ideological beliefs are a necessary basis for action, but" challenging the status quo "does not necessarily produce activism" (14). Indeed, Evans insists upon action—as a young college student in the early 1970s and today, as a retired pastor meeting again with local citizens and college students to learn what the community needs. He urges those who can, as he puts it, to "get busy" in responding to those needs. Thus perhaps the formula for activism suggested by NCC's history may be best described thus: An agent ("someone") acting ("put down the sack," "drank from the white fountain," "refused to give up a seat") only after (1) extensive research and meetings with others likewise passionate about changing the systems that forced that sack into their hands (slavery, then sharecropping systems), their bodies to the back of the bus and their thirsts quenched from the usually warm, frequently filthy "colored fountain" and (2) further study and additional work both within and beyond existing channels to determine the role to be played by particular demonstration (the sack/the fountain/the seat) and its potential contribution to the movement's overall goals. Such a narrative lacks the punch of the actor-action-results formula, but it certainly leaves significant room for wide scale participation. In this way, an individual action —putting down the sack/drinking from the white fountain/refusing to give up one's seat—can help establish a channel for communication across and about difference, not to reify racism's existence but to remedy its effects.

Also crucial to our understanding of civic engagement, particularly on behalf of local, little known causes, is close attention to the location in which these actions take place and the rhetorical function of identification (Burke) against that local landscape and its particular history. In other words, someone (agent) acts (puts down the sack, drinks from the white fountain) in some identifiable place and at some identifiable time. Local channels are deeply reliant upon such factors. In the current analysis, both agents (NCC and John Carlos) act in Commerce, Texas, right before and soon after 1970, the point at which the Great Migration that dominated the 20th century began to return the nation's African American citizens to the southern states (Wilkerson; "The New"; Frey).7

Put down the sack. Texas, especially rural Texas, is itself a disorienting mashup of competing narratives. Published in 1940, the Texas volume of the Works Progress Administrator's *American Guide Series* captures the unique dualities of this large State thus: "More Southern than Western is the State's approach to most political and social questions; more Western than Southern are the manners of most of its people" (Writers' Program 5). East Texas was peculiarly southern with the State's greatest concentration of cotton and related crops and, therefore, slaves. Texas's harsh terrain and extreme temperatures, however, coupled with its unique history—as part of Spain until 1821 and then Mexico until 1836—meant it was also later to begin agricultural industry than much of the rest of the South. It was ranching, not farming, that captured the imagination and foregrounded the State's identification as more Western than Southern. The significant population of Mexican-Americans drew Texas still farther West than South.

Perhaps it is this very duality (South/West) that dislodges Texas from our larger understanding of the civil rights movement. Perhaps it is its position as part of the "New South." Whatever the reason, as historian Neil Foley insists,

> ... [T]he fact remains that most Anglo Texans were descended from transplanted Southerners who had fought hard to maintain the "color line" in Texans and to extend its barriers to Mexicans. Many Anglo Texas thus often wore two hats: the ten-gallon variety as well as the white hood of the Invisible Empire. (2)

The white community of Commerce no doubt resisted identification with its slave-holding past and were likewise reluctant to accept arguments challenging the equity of the sharecropping systems that followed. Texas wealth—largely absent from this region of the state—was built not on farming but on oil, and those who did raise crops were likely to do so on small farms not infrequently owned by someone else. Poverty dominated Northeast Texas when William L. Mayo, a pioneering educator from the mountains of Kentucky, arrived in 1889 to establish the white teacher's college that Evans and Carlos would later attend. The institution Mayo built was designed to serve the area's white farmers and their children, "regardless of their ability to pay" (see Gold), and the vast majority of area residents couldn't afford to pay college tuition. Thus, to "put down the cotton sack" in this region meant challenging not only white owners but perhaps threatening the poor white locals who may have owned little more than the region's recently freed slaves (see Philips; Foley; Bell). For the dominant publics living in and around Commerce during Reconstruction and the first few decades of Jim Crow, a clear channel for communication about slavery/sharecropping and its injustice would require far more than an individual act of resistance ("put down the cotton sack"), regardless of how representative it might be of resistance elsewhere.

Drink from the White Fountain. Segregation was, of course, a deeply divisive issue in Commerce. However, the events that most characterize local struggles here and, indeed, throughout much of the rest of the southern states, were fought not in the streets among local publics but in mundane documents ranging from interoffice memoranda among campus administrators, letters exchanged between campus leaders and area, state, and federal officials, legal documents, and petitions (Shabazz; Sokel; Dittmer).

A particularly useful example of this can be found in the circulation of documents surrounding two local segregationists and bitter enemies: US Senator Sam Rayburn, this university's most famous alumnus, and James G. Gee, ETSU president from 1947-1966. From 1913 until 1961, Sam Rayburn represented this rural district dominated by voters loyal to Jim Crow and remained himself equally loyal to his constituents and, especially, ETSU, the institution that had given this poor farmer without a high school diploma a chance at a college education. Despite his stance on the issue (which some argue had softened considerably after decades in Washington DC) and the likely threat to his voting base it posed, he was an even more loyal Democrat and, as Speaker of the House, helped sign into law the most significant civil rights legislation since Reconstruction: the Civil Rights Act of 1954. His public connections to Lyndon B. Johnson, combined with this piece of legislation, made him a bitter enemy to a number of powerful local leaders.

His harshest local critic by far was President Gee. However, like Rayburn, Gee would find himself overseeing public transformations that effectively ended de jure segregation. Though a loyal segregationist, he did not challenge what he called the "inevitability of racial integration" (Gee). Instead he formed "a secret committee" whom he charged with studying desegregation elsewhere and offering recommendations. The primary and stated goal for our campus was what Gee and the committee called "a dignified integration," arguing demonstrations against desegregation would threaten the local community's sustainability far more then any new admission policy ever could (Carter and Conrad; Wilkinson; Shabazz). In June 1964, Gee followed the committee's recommendations to the letter when he announced the lifting of "racial barriers" to admissions. By most available accounts, desegregation at ETSU occurred largely without incident, at least in terms of violent demonstrations. In this sense, perhaps it was, indeed, a "dignified integration," a characterization that remains a significant point of pride for local citizens.

By the time African American students like Carlos and Evans enrolled, local whites largely accepted racial integration's inevitability. Increasingly, however, the material changes that accompany that process —especially in this era of student revolt and black power/women's rights rhetoric—began to be characterized by many locals as "the racial problem." "In regard to the increasingly troublesome 'racial problem' in Commerce," says a local sophomore in a 1970 letter appearing in the campus paper, "… things may be getting worse" (Helmsly). For him and many other whites, evidence of this was the increasingly common presence of "incidents" like the one he describes in his letter. Not only had an African American box office worker recently challenged a white patron who had treated her unfairly, but the local press had printed letters from others praising black resistance. He appears as outraged as he was eloquent:

> It is really sad to me that these people are still fighting a battle that was over years ago. I hope that one day they will get enough White money from the White taxpayers to pay for the education they will receive from White institutions with White professors so they can learn just exactly what it is they are fighting against. (Helmsley)

The fight "over long ago" included abolition of both slavery and segregation, of course. The fight that remains, according to critical race studies, is the systemic racism that persists across an America that allowed the sale of humans and laws built on a logic of white supremacy. In our color-blind society, race had been rendered invisible while racism's effects remain firmly entrenched in everyday life. While racism as a national problem, even at the height of the civil rights movement, may appear abstract, distant, and symbolic, the local, the everyday, is rarely abstract. When that local is sparsely populated (rural), when resources are scarce, as is the case here, major changes at local levels are hard to enact. In fact, "… racial segregation is more than a series of quaint customs that can be remedied effectively without altering the status of whites" (Bell 19b). Thus, perhaps, we can understand the town's slow uptake on social justice issues like these, as I will explain. In similar ways, as Catherine Prendergrast has argued, race has become what she calls "an absent presence" in our discipline—the ever present element we learn to look past or look around, forgetting the important ways race remains in our classrooms and our scholarship just as it remains a defining element in the rest of our everyday lives.

For NCC, the remedy for racism's current challenges was inherently *rhetorical*—establishing a clear channel of communication that essentially rhetoricized race in many of the same ways Nancy Welch has urged us to "rhetoricize class" (11). To rhetoricize race is to approach it not as a cultural identity but instead the available means for persuasion and decision making power within and against the limits embedded in the systemic racism that shapes everyday life—especially in the Jim Crow South in the decades immediately following desegregation.8 For John Carlos, the remedy was largely *ideological*, drawing together a counterpublic based on a shared identity which, in Nancy Fraser and Michael Warner's articulation of the term, act in direct opposition to cultural norms. The counterpublic Dr. Carlos hoped to establish at ET five years before had many similarities with the one NCC brought into being in the early 1970s. Both attempted to disrupt injustices by transforming public discourse surrounding everyday racism. Yet while Carlos worked to link this discourse to global discourse surrounding a shared identity, NCC was fundamentally concerned with rhetorical agency and issues of local concern. NCC's channel was, after all, a local station in ways Carlos's channel simply *could* not, perhaps *would* not be.

Resistance

> *We declare our right on this earth to be a man, to be a human being, to be respected as a human being, to be given the rights of a human being in this society, on this earth, in this day, which we intend to bring into existence by any means necessary.*
>
> –Malcolm X

In 1968, at the Mexico City Olympics, sprinters John Carlos and Tommie Smith rhetoricized race, calling global attention to the persistence of racism by taking full advantage of the means of persuasion available to them as black athletes representing the nation to the world (see Figure 2). That single iconic image of two African Americans, black-gloved fists raised and heads bowed as the national anthem played and millions booed, remains indelibly etched in our collective memory. Until recently, however, the message they intended, like the meaning behind much of the rhetoric of black power (see Stewart, Burgess, Scott and Brockriede), was rewritten and then altogether silenced by the racist politics the movement opposed.9

ET recruited John Carlos from Harlem in 1966, just two years before this global demonstration of what Edward P.J. Corbett would call "The Rhetoric of the Closed Fist."10 In Harlem, Dr. Carlos had walked with Malcolm X—literally, catching as many of Malcolm X's frequent presentations at the mosque on 116th street as he could, then following him around the neighborhood "like a scampering puppy dog" (Carlos and Zirin 26), peppering him with questions along the way. As part of the counterpublic called up in the discourse surrounding collective resistance "by any means necessary" (Malcolm X), Carlos was highly attuned to racism's complexity and ubiquity.

Figure 2. Carlos, 1968 Olympics (far right)

Figure 3. Carlos, ETSU Track Team (1966-67)

He knew racism's key challenges were just as present in the North as they were everywhere else. Yet he had never before experienced the covert forms of racism segregation presented —not personally, at least. Along with his young wife and their two-year old daughter, "We agreed to make a home for ourselves in Commerce," Dr. Carlos recalls decades later. "But every last shred of dignity that we took with us to Texas was challenged" (Carlos and Zirin 64).

His direct link to an action designed to bring about necessary change can be traced to a rather unlikely place: his mailbox at the Commerce Post Office. There, he picked up the latest issue of *Track and Field* and found in it a renewed opportunity for active update in a counterpublic designed to challenge the systemic injustices he was experiencing firsthand. In that issue, he read about the Olympic Project for Human Rights (OPHR) that was just beginning to take hold in the fall of 1967 at San Jose State. "I was reading that at the same time I was … actually living these same issues at East Texas State University," Carlos explains in a recent interview (Kojo). NCC offered African American citizens a local channel through which they could communicate issues of local concern; OPHR, on the other hand, offered African Americans another *global* channel through which they could communicate issues of *global* concern. Through the global channel OPHR provided, Carlos could help challenge injustice world-wide, joining other African Americans in a boycott that, if successful, could largely cripple America's chances of success in the 1968 Olympics. "Why should we run in Mexico," OPHR insisted, "only to crawl at home?"

In constituting the counterpublic thus named ("OPHR"), black athletes around the nation began to come together as agents of social change prepared to act (boycott), demonstrating (a) racism exists, (b) America needs African American citizens to achieve greatness, and therefore, (c) America must treat her African American citizens equitably. The local channel NCC provided, by comparison, drew local citizens together as agents of social change prepared to act (vote, share unflattering news about city beyond the local), demonstrating (a) inequalities exist in Norris, (b) Norris is part of the local community and the concerns of Norris affect the entire town, and therefore (c) Commerce must address persistent inequities. Both channels grew larger audiences as the frequency and number of "texts" both spoken and written about Norris increased in circulation. Listeners alone don't result in community transformation, however; access to a channel for communication does not necessarily give activists control over the messages received by the dominant power structure.

Across the nation, black athletes likely to be en route to the Olympics found themselves surrounded by reporters asking them about their position on the boycott. Within weeks of reading that *Track and Field* article in the Commerce Post Office, a series of local and campus interviews with Carlos "set this little campus on its ear" (Carlos and Zirin 72). "The social climate here for the Negro is discriminating and terrible," Carlos told a campus reporter in 1967 (Anderson, "Carlos"). In a *Dallas News* article appearing a few days earlier, Carlos describes his key concerns this way: "You go out of state to a track meet and you are representing not only your school but the entire state. Yet you come back and find restaurants that say they don't serve Negroes … [Y]ou go into a place to shoot a game of pool and they tell you Negroes aren't allowed" (Stowers). "If conditions don't change," Carlos is quoted as saying to a student reporter, "*something is going to happen at ET*" (Anderson, "Carlos," emphasis mine).

The other African American athletes at ET during the time did not publicly challenge the validity of Carlos's statements to the press concerning discrimination, and many may have even supported his proposed, albeit vague, response ("something is going to happen at ET"). A number of white students were particularly vocal in their support of Carlos and his statements. No one denied the ongoing challenges of desegregation. Yet any collective resistance that began to mobilize locally in response to OPHR and the challenges it represented was quickly silenced in a surprisingly effective preemptive strike by campus administration.

Immediately after the campus paper published its interview with Carlos, the Athletic Director called all the black athletes together to discuss "all this boycott nonsense" (Carlos and Zirin). Following a two-hour meeting, the athletes involved issued a jointly authored "resolution" to the press: "besides the normal prejudices that are encountered in everyday life," they explained, "there is no dissension or static between the two groups" (qtd. in Anderson 1). Carlos insisted that static was necessary, as those "normal prejudices ... encountered in everyday life" must not be allowed to continue. He was willing to sacrifice everything he had worked for his entire life to stand out against the persistence of racism in everyday life, and he would do exactly that the very next year atop the Olympic podium in Mexico City.

The resolution —perhaps coerced by campus administration, perhaps not — nonetheless silenced any potential of a local channel established through a shared identity with the now globally recognized OPHR. "We didn't appoint [Carlos] as a spokesperson," the resolution insisted. "[I]n fact, it is the general opinion among negro [sic] athletes that we are not behind Carlos" (qtd. in Anderson 8). The local channel that had begun broadcasting global programming about black resistance went immediately silent. Carlos gathered up his family and left, returning to campus decades later as part of a book tour that includes a chapter about his time here called "Trouble in Texas," a community now welcoming him with open arms.

A Clear Channel

> *Public discourse postulates a circulatory field of estrangement which it must then struggle to capture as an addressable entity. [...] [I]n order for this to happen, all discourse ... must characterize the world in which it attempts to circulate, and it must attempt to realize that world through address.*
>
> –Michael Warner

In Harlem, through the discourse surrounding Malcolm X and other vocal elements of this counterpublic, Carlos found direct access to a channel through which he and other local African Americans might communicate their ongoing frustrations and concerns with the oppressive social and political structures. "His power," Dr. Carlos explains of Malcolm X's appeal across Harlem "and the response of the audience, grew out of the fact that he was articulating ideas we were all thinking about all the time but didn't really have a language or vocabulary to express. For me, it was like he grabbed onto my frustrations and turned them into logic" (Carlos and Zirin 29). Yet it would not be enough to turn "frustrations into logic" if no one was listening. Without a clear channel through which to broadcast these perspectives, without listeners, the reach is limited. At that moment, however, the movement's strength held that channel open, circulating its discourse around the nation through newsstands, television screens, public speeches, and personal conversations.[11]

In 1965, the year before Carlos left Harlem for our university, his role model was assassinated. The channel established and maintained by the rhetoric of black power remained on air nonetheless, gaining new listeners all the time. While in Commerce, Dr. Carlos remained tuned in, of course, and students and citizens across Commerce were indeed listening. To some extent, they were even beginning to mobilize around such issues. Yet the local reception for this channel was weak and loyal listeners too few in number. Thus we see the limits of such broadcasts in this local instantiation of the global channel for collective resistance represented by leaders of the black power movement and OPHR in particular. Perhaps the urban, northern, and "outsider" identity markers Carlos brought with him to an area that largely identifies as rural and southern challenged his efforts to link local concerns with this globally recognized channel. Perhaps Carlos's very status as an outsider may have threatened local sustainability. Regardless of the reasons, local reception for his form of protest was largely unavailable.

The channel NCC provided, on the other hand, relied upon local issues of shared concern. It is also not insignificant that Carlos had previously attempted to link Commerce to other channels nor that in the five years since multiple local and campus movements combined with national and international events had begun to produce significant local transformations. Indeed numerous local and global factors impacted the local reception of both the channel Carlos attempted to establish and the one NCC was able to provide. The circulation of largely mundane texts played a significant role in local broadcasts across these channels, limiting and expanding their reach.

The clear channel of communication NCC provided depended upon the frequent circulation of Norris Community news, especially that generated with Norris residents like the items Allen Hallmark wrote to shine "a spotlight ... on Norris" (Carter et al.). Equally important, however, were the letters exchanged between local residents and elected officials at both local and state levels, documents NCC members created and circulated to establish a local chapter of the NAACP, grant materials created to bring to Norris the millions of dollars it required but the city found itself unable to provide, tickets for the annual banquet designed to "improve relations between the Norris Community and the rest of the city" ("NCC Reception") and raise funding for Norris improvement projects, as well as the records kept to ensure finances remained in order. NCC conducted surveys across Norris, kept strict records of their regular meetings, and maintained a newsletter. Even the sign on the door of NCC's meeting space helped circulate Norris, bringing in new members like Hallmark. All of these factors and more contributed to the ongoing maintenance of the clear channel NCC provided.

In similar ways, a wide array of mundane texts surrounded Carlos's local efforts, just as they do civic engagement anywhere. The discourse that effectively shut down Carlos's campus attempts were likewise shaped by a variety of mundane texts and exchanges, including the various letters, phone conversations, and other documents that called together the black athletes for the two-hour meeting that resulted in the resolution that "we didn't appoint [Carlos] as our spokesman," as well as the documents that led to this statement and its subsequent publication in campus news. Communication channels like these won't open by sheer will, nor will any channel remain open after the discourse that brought it into being in the first place stops circulating.

Student populations are temporary populations and racism is not a "curable aberration" but institutionalized, systemic, persistent (Bell; Williams, Delgado). Civil rights secured by NCC thus began to lose ground as the student leadership graduated, representation among city leaders shifted to become dominated by those far less sympathetic to Norris's remaining concerns, and the era of student activism gave way to the 1980s. By the time I began my current study of civic engagement in this local context, the forward march evident in that feverous period of reform seemed stalled, indeed rolling ever backward. The naming NCC provided gave way to "The Hole" and race was rendered, once again, "invisible," even as racism seemed increasingly present—though certainly no more present in this local context than elsewhere across the nation (see especially Alexander's *The New Jim Crow* and Conley's *Being Black*). Yet in the very act of naming NCC again in my research, local public programming, and digital storytelling, we have begun circulating discourse about NCC that again calls it into being.

A New Channel

Jacqueline Jones Royster reminds researchers "whatever the knowledge accrued … it must be both presented and represented with this community." Indeed, the community is not the object of our study but in fact "co-knowledge creators" (Royster). In the years since I first learned of NCC's existence, I have been regularly moved by the generosity of these individuals and their desire to help recover NCC's story and renew its key work. They've joined me on countless panel presentations throughout the area, contributed to various multimedia projects, emailed, called, or mailed artifacts and other details they thought might be of interest to me or otherwise useful in reconstructing NCC's history and sharing it with others. Each conversation I have with these individuals leads to other individuals no less enthusiastic about sharing their memories and no less generous with their time. Each conversation leads to new archival materials for our library collections, which these individuals eagerly donate, and new research and outreach opportunities for my students, which they eagerly embrace.

Throughout, it remains absolutely clear such work is necessarily composed *with* the community not *about* the community (Royster; Deans). I am an outsider to the civic engagement efforts I describe in this article and my other work. I am not from Commerce, though I have spent much of my life in Texas. I am white, raised in middle class neighborhoods of Southern California and then South Texas. Before moving to Commerce in 2001, I had never lived in a rural area, and for most of the project under discussion, I have lived not in Commerce but in a large Dallas suburb about an hour's drive away, and I am part of a generation widely regarded as apolitical, apathetic, and uninvolved (Generation X). I bring to these efforts not a controlling interest but rather my disciplinary expertise, the existing university resources I am able to leverage on behalf of such locally driven projects, and the ongoing support of colleagues across campus.[12]

I bring to this community partnership the support of internal research grants, external grants from NEH and Humanities Texas, and significant contributions from our university president (Dan Jones), provost (Larry Lemanski), and dean (Salvatore Attardo), which helped fund the Writing Democracy conference and, in recent years, the Converging Literacies Center (CLiC), a research initiative designed to "promote a better understanding of how texts and related literacy practices may develop, sustain, or even erode civic engagement across local publics, especially among historically underrepresented groups" (Carter, "Writing"). With this support and CLiC's mission to "develop educational and outreach initiatives designed to address relevant civic issues," I can bring to the community graduate student support that helps coordinate local presentations, research and writing toward important preservation projects, and ongoing attempts to capture these local stories through digital media. I bring contributions from my department and others toward cookies and coffee for our various campus presentations and the increasingly significant audiences these activities draw from both the campus and the community.

I regularly introduce undergraduate and graduate students to the many action research options available in local contexts like ours, which frequently leads to research and outreach that far surpasses my expectations or imagination. My students launched a voter registration drive in Norris (2012), began working with an area African American museum to secure funding for the restoration of an adjacent Rosenwald School (ongoing), and collaborated with long-time Norris resident and church historian Harry Turner to apply to have installed a Texas Historical Marker at the church hosting the original NCC meetings (installed 2011). In early 2010, after giving my graduate students a tour of Norris, Turner invited several of the international students back to speak to church members about their experiences growing up in Saudi Arabia, Nigeria, Thailand, Italy, and elsewhere. Each time, the presentations drew more than forty local citizens, the vast majority of whom have never spent any time outside Texas. My first-year students have conducted research on the various aspects of Norris history; my graduate students have presented research on Norris at regional and national conferences. Norris residents regularly attend my student's campus presentations of their work, and these individuals and countless others have presented alongside me on campus and in the community. Indeed, it seems altogether impossible that we can exhaust this local context and its history of activism, and every local context is likely to be similarly rich with opportunities. The "co-knowledge creators" throughout our local communities are important for dozens of reasons, not the least of which being, as Eli Goldblatt reminds us, *"because we live here."*

Endnotes

1. Ivory Moore, the first African American campus administrator and member of the city council, would go on to serve another 18 years on the city council, eventually becoming the first African American mayor of Commerce, Texas. Mr. Moore wrote his first successful grant while still a teenager in rural Oklahoma for the Works Progress Administration. He would go on to write millions of dollars in grants to serve Norris and campus minorities. Moore and other important local activists I cannot address for lack of space play a substantial role in my current book project on how local people excluded from public spaces garnered rhetorical agency in the decade after desegregation reached this area. In 2012, we were fortunate enough to begin the process of establishing an Ivory and Lennie Moore Collection in our university archives. The Moores tell us they are honored and continue to thank me for the opportunity. I am humbled by their humility. The honor, of course, is ours.

2. Throughout, my use of the term "texts" refers to both oral and written "texts," echoing Michael Warner's use of "texts" in his "text-based publics."

3. Unsustainable, at least in terms of the "strategic logics" employed by the university side of the partnership (see especially Jessica Restaino and Laurie Cella's forthcoming collection Unsustainable: Owning Our Best, Short-Lived Efforts at Community Writing Work)

4. I recognize that new media's participatory nature significantly expands our reach beyond "the local," at least in the abstract. However I also realize that, whatever mechanism I use to interact with the world, my physical body must always be located locally and thus must experience the world locally.

5. Not his real name, though the image in Figure 1 is his own.

6. Before this point, the vast majority of local citizens had either forgotten about or had never heard of NCC. Please see Carter and Conrad "In Possession" for additional details. Digital copies of these items and others from NCC's early history are now available in our university archives, generously donated from the personal files of Billy Reed and Opal Pannell.

7. According to this study, "college-educated individuals lead the new migration into the South. The 'brain gain' states of Georgia, Texas, and Maryland attracted the most black college graduates from 1995 to 2000, while New York suffered the largest net loss" (Frey 4).

8. In this use of race, I borrow directly from Nancy Welch's articulation of class. To disrupt injustices, Welch suggests, we "rhetoricize social class," and, in doing so, "shift our definition of class from a focus on cultural identity to a focus on one's available means for executing decision-making power within and against privatization's strict limits on public rights and voice" (Living Room).

9. Time's coverage dripped with the same dismissive rhetoric that characterized much of the press surrounding the event: "'Faster, Higher, Stronger' is the motto of the Olympic Games. 'Angrier, nastier, uglier' better describes the scene in Mexico city last week" (62). "It was not a gesture of hate," explains Tommie Smith in a 1991 interview for Sports Illustrated. "It was a gesture of frustration" (Moore 7).

10. Given such characterizations and the historical and spatial context surrounding these efforts, it may be tempting to distinguish Carlos's efforts as

representative of Edward P.J. Corbett's "Closed Fist" and NCC's rhetoric as "Open Hand" (Carlos). That would be a mistake.

11. Though Corbett found rhetoric's Closed Fist problematic, many have pointed to its necessity. Indeed, in such circumstances the "Open Hand" may do little more than reify norms, silencing difference and perpetuating inequities (see Brown; Murdock). As Nancy Welch argues in this issue, "civility functions to hold in check agitation against a social order that is undemocratic in access to decision-making voice and unequal in distribution of wealth" (page). NCC's rhetoric cannot be exclusively characterized as "open hand" any more than Carlos's rhetoric was exclusively "closed fist." In their public rhetoric, NCC made it clear they would remain civil in their approach only as long as doing so proved fruitful. When those options were closed to them, however, they were prepared to "close that hand" (ibid, 291). The entire nation was tuning in to hear Malcolm X, Stokely Carmichael, Angela Davis, and others likewise circulating discourse that members of this counterpublic recognize and participate in themselves.

12. Especially important in this respect are library director Greg Mitchell, archivist Andrea Weddle, and athletic director Carlton Cooper. I am grateful for our ongoing collaborations and their many contributions.

Works Cited

Anderson, Tom. "Carlos Hedges On Joining Up with Boycotters." *East Texan* 6 Dec. 1967: 1; 8.

———. "Negro Athlete Refutes Statements." *East Texan* Dec. 1967: 1; 8.

———. *Faces at the Bottom of the Well: The Permanence of Racism*. 1992: Basic Books, 1992.

Brandt, Deborah and Kate Clinton. "Limits of the Local: Expanding Perspectives on Literacy as Social Practice." *Journal of Literacy Research* 34 (2002): 337-356.

Burgess, Parke G. "The Rhetoric of Black Power: A Moral Demand?" Quarterly Journal of Speech 1968: 122-133.

Carter, Shannon. "A Clear Channel." Remixing Rural Texas: Local Texts, Global Contexts. Converging Literacies Center (CLiC). Video. Aug. 2012. Web. 2 Aug. 2012.

———. "Letter of Nomination." Personal Blog. 1 Oct. 2011. Web.

———. "Remixing Rural Texas: Local Texts, Global Contexts." National Endowment for the Humanities Office of Digital Humanities. July 2011. Web.

———. "Writing Democracy in the Engaged University: A CLiC White Paper." May 2011. Retrieved 15 June 2011. Web.

Carter, Shannon and James H. Conrad. "In Possession of Community: Toward a More Sustainable Local." *College Composition and Communication* 64.1 (September 2012): 82-106, Forthcoming. Print.

Carter, Shannon, James H. Conrad, Larry Matthis, MacArthur Evans, Allen Hallmark, Harry Turner, Opal Pannel, and Billy Reed. "Writing for (a) Change." *Writing Democracy*. March 2011, Texas A&M-Commerce. Web.

Carlos, John and Dave Zirin. *The John Carlos Story*. Chicago: Haymarket Books, 2011.

———. Interview by Kojo Nnamdi. *The Kojo Nnamdi Show.* 4 Oct. 2011. Web. 14 Nov. 2011.

Coogan, David. "Community Literacy as Civic Dialogue." *Community Literacy Journal* 1.1 (Fall 2006): 95-108. Web.

Corbett, Edward P.J. "The Rhetoric of the Open Hand and the Rhetoric of the Closed Fist." *College Composition and Communication* 20.5 (1969): 288-296.

Cushman, Ellen. *The Struggle and the Tools: Oral and Literate Strategies in an Inner City Community.* New York: SUNY P, 1998. Print.

Deans, Thomas, Barbara Roswell, and Adrian J. Wurr. "Teaching and Writing Across Communities: Developing Partnerships, Publics, and Programs." Thomas Deans, Barbara Roswell, and Adrian J. Wurr, eds. *Writing and Community Engagement: A Critical Sourcebook.* New York: Bedford/St. Martins, 2010. 1-12. Print.

Donehower, Kim, Charlotte Hogg, and Eileen E. Schell. *Rural Literacies.* Southern Illinois UP, 2007. Print.

Edbauer, Jennifer. "Unframing Models of Public Distribution: From Rhetorical Situation to Rhetorical Ecologies." *Rhetoric Society Quarterly* 35.4 (2008): 5-24. Print.

Enoch, Jessica. *Refiguring Rhetorical Education: Women Teaching African American, Native American, and Chicano/a Students, 1865-1911.* Southern Illinois UP, 2008.

Exum, William. *Paradoxes of Protest: Black Student Activism in a White University.* Temple UP, 1985. Print.

Flower, Linda. *Community Literacy and the Rhetoric of Public Engagement.* Southern Illinois UP, 2008. Print.

Foley, Neil. *White Scourge: Mexicans, Blacks, and Poor Whites in Texas Cotton Culture.* Berkeley: University of California Press, 1997.

Frey, William H. "The New Great Migration: Black American's Return to the South, 1965-2000." The Brookings Institution, 2004.

Gee, James G. University President Papers, collection 2008.28, James G. Gee Library Special Collections, Texas A & M University-Commerce.

George, Diana. "The Word on the Street: Public Discourse in a Culture of Disconnect." *Reflections* 2.2 (2002): 5-18.

Gold, David. "Beyond Recovery: Contemporary Challenges in Rhetoric and Composition Historiography." Writing Democracy: A Rhetoric of (T)here, 2011. Keynote. Paper.

———. *Rhetoric at the Margins: Revising the History of Writing Instruction in American   Colleges, 1873-1947.* Carbondale: University of Southern Illinois, 2008.

Goldblatt, Eli. *Because We Live Here: Sponsoring Literacy Beyond the College Curriculum.* Cresskill: Hampton P, 2007. Print.

Hallmark, Allen. Personal Email to Author. 10 June 2010.

Hemsley, Edward. "Letter to the Editor." *The East Texan.* November 1970. Print.

Hesford, Wendy S. "Human Rights Rhetoric of Recognition." *Rhetoric Society Quarterly* 41.3 (2011): 282-289. Print.

Higgins, Lorraine, Elenore Long, and Linda Flower. "Community Literacy: A Rhetorical Model for Personal and Public Inquiry." *Community Literacy Journal* 1.1 (Spring 2006): 9-43. Print.

Hobdy, Will. "John Carlos Returns 'Home." *The Kuumba Heritage*. 22 Nov. 2011: 4. Web.

Hogg, Charlotte. *From the Garden Club: Rural Women Writing Community*. University of Nebraska P, 2006. Print.

Kates, Susan. *Activist Rhetorics and American Higher Education, 1885-1937*. Southern Illinois UP, 2001. Print.

Kells, Michelle Hall. *Hector P. Garcia: Everyday Rhetoric and Mexican American Civil Rights*. Southern Illinois UP, 2006.

Kohl, Herbert. *She Who Would Not Be Moved: How We Tell the Story of Rosa Parks and the Montgomery Bus Boycott*. New Press, 2007.

Loab, Paul Rogat. "The Real Rosa Parks." *Huffington Post*. 31 Oct. 2005. Web. 14 May 2012.

———. *Soul of a Citizen. Living with Conviction in a Cynical Time*. St. Martin's Griffin, 1999. Print.

Malcolm X. *By Any Means Necessary (Malcolm X. Speeches and Writings)*. New York: Pathfinder Press, 1992. Print.

Marback, Richard. "Corbett's Hand: A Rhetorical Figure for Composition Studies." *College Composition and Communication* 47.2 (1996): 180-198.

Mathieu, Paula. *Tactics of Hope: The Public Turn in English Composition*. Portsmouth: Boynton/Cook, 2005. Print.

Mouffe, Chantel. *The Democratic Paradox*. Verso, 2000.

"NCC Reception Being Planned." *Commerce Journal* 13 June 1975.

"Norris Club Co-Founder Leaves Town." *Commerce Journal* 5 June 1975.

Pannel, Opal. Interview with Shannon Carter and James H. Conrad. 2009. Archives. James G. Gee Library, Texas A&M-Commerce.

Pennycook, Alastair. *Language as a Local Practice*. New York: Routledge, 2010.

Phillips, Michael. *White Metropolis: Race, Ethnicity, and Religion in Dallas, 1941-2001*. Austin: University of Texas Press, 2006. .

Prendergast, Catherine. "Race, the Absent Presence in Composition Studies." *College Composition and Communication* 50.1 (1998): 36-53. Print.

Ratcliffe, Krista. *Rhetorical Listening: Identification, Gender, Whiteness*. Southern Illinois UP, 2005. Print.

Reed, Billy. Interview with Shannon Carter and James H. Conrad. 2009 and 2010 Archives. James G. Gee Library, Texas A&M-Commerce.

———. "Letter to the Editor." *The Commerce Journal* April 1974. Print.

Rivers, Nathaniel A. and Ryan P. Weber. "Ecological, Pedagogical, Public Rhetoric." *College Composition and Communication* 63.2 (December 2011): 187-218.

Royster, Jacqueline Jones. *Traces of a Stream: Literacy and Social Change among African American Women*. Pittsburgh: U of Pittsburgh P, 2000.

Royster, Jacqueline and Molly Cochran. "Human Rights and Civil Rights: The Advocacy and Activism of African-American Women Writers." *Rhetoric Society Quarterly* 41.3 (2011): 213-230. Print.

Staff. "The First Bridge." *The Commerce Journal* 13 Sept. 1973.

Stewart, Charles J. "The Evolution of a Revolution: Stokely Carmichael and the
    Rhetoric of Black Power." *Quarterly Journal of Speech* (1997): 429-446.
Stowers, Carlton. "Carlos Hits Prejudice: East Texas Sprinter May Join Boycott."
    Dallas News 3 Dec. 1967.
Warner, Michael. *Publics and Counterpublics*. New York: Zone Books, 2005. Print.
Welch, Nancy. *Teaching Writing in a Privatized World*. Boynton/Cook, 2008. Print.
Wells, JD. "NAACP Speaker Talks to NCC." *The Commerce Journal* 8 Nov. 1973.
Wells, Susan. "Rogue Cops and Health Care: What Do We Want from Public
    Writing." *College Composition and Communication* 47.3 (1996): 325–41. Print.
Wilkerson. *The Warmth of Other Sons: The Epic Story of America's Great Migration.*
    Vintage, 2011.
Wilkison, Debra. "Eyewitness to Social Change: The Desegregation of East Texas State
    College." M.A. thesis, East Texas State University, 1990. Print.
Writers' Program at the Works Progress Administration in the State of Texas. *Texas: A
    Guide to the Lone Star State*. Austin: Bureau of Research in the Social Sciences at
    University of Texas, 1940.

Acknowledgments

I am grateful to the Texas A&M-Commerce, especially Office of the Provost, College of Arts and Humanities, and Department of Literature and Languages, for their support throughout this project. Most significant in this respect is the funding provided for this ongoing research and archival development, including Faculty Development Leave Fall 2010 for my current book project, support for the Writing Democracy conference on which this volume is based, and additional funding for related digital humanities projects. Of particular note is the remix "A Clear Channel," which serves as a companion piece for the current article. "A Clear Channel" is also part of *Remixing Rural Texas: Local Texts, Global Contexts*, which has been funded by a grant from the National Endowment for the Humanities Office of Digital Humanities and additional support from the Office of the Provost.

Shannon Carter, an Associate Professor of English at Texas A&M-Commerce, is the author of *The Way Literacy Lives* (SUNY Albany, 1998), as well as essays in *College English, College Composition and Communication, Community Literacy Journal*, and *Kairos*. She is currently working on her second book, a rhetorical historiography of race and civic engagement in this rural university community during the last half of the twentieth century. Her interests include digital media, especially video, and her recent work takes up these themes in a series of short video documentaries remixed almost entirely from existing local history collections. She currently serves as PI on Remixing Rural Texas, which received an NEH Office of Digital Humanities Start Up Grant.

Next Steps for Writing Democracy

The Political Turn: Writing "Democracy" for the 21st Century

This workshop extends a conversation about the 1930s Federal Writers' Project begun in 2011 and continued at CCCC 2012 to focus specifically on defining what we mean by the term "democracy."

Over the past fifty years, we have seen a "linguistic turn," a "social turn," and a "public turn." In this moment of mounting, worldwide economic, environmental, and cultural uncertainty, we submit that it is time for a "political turn." Despite some indications of a slow recovery from the crash in 2008, the U.S. continues to face mounting household and student debt, foreclosures, and long-term unemployment. The richest 1% own a third of the nation's net worth; income of the 24 million least wealthy Americans decreased by 10% in 2010; and one in every 7 Americans lives below the poverty line (*Guardian* 11/16/11). It is this gross economic inequality that gave rise to the Occupy Wall Street movement in September 2011 and its powerful slogan, "We are the 99%." In the environmental arena, we have born witness to the effects of climate change and the persistence of unscientific political discourse about it; the threat of nuclear disasters like the explosion at the Fukushima Daiichi Nuclear Plant in March 2011; and the impact of market-driven energy policies and procedures like hydro-fracking. And on the cultural front, we live in a period most acutely marked perhaps by the fact that incarcerated people in the U.S. represent 25% of the world's prisoners and of those 70% are nonwhite. According to Michelle Alexander, author of *The New Jim Crow: Mass Incarceration in the Age of Colorblindness*, "more African Americans [are] under correctional control today—in prison or jail, on probation or parole—than were enslaved in 1850, a decade before the Civil War began."

At CCCC 2012, we held a workshop on the relevance of the 1930s Federal Writers' Project to contemporary college writing programs, service-learning programs, and scholars across the country engaged in university-community partnerships. We continued earlier explorations begun at the 2011 Writing Democracy conference at Texas A&M-Commerce to explore how together these programs might create a roadmap for rediscovering 21st century America with FWP 2.0, using some of the same tools of ethnography, state or local guides, oral history, and folklore used by the federal writers during the Great Depression. Among the contributions at the CCCC 2012 workshop were Jeff Grabill's commentary on the relevance of John Dewey's *The Public and Its Problems* to thinking through the rhetorical appeal that gives rise to a public and Steven Parks' discussion of the publicly funded Federation of Worker Writers and Community Publishers, a nonprofit organization begun in 1976 in England whose aim is "to increase access to writing and publishing, especially for those who may sometimes find it difficult to be heard in our society." Historian Jerrold Hirsch, author of *Portrait of America: A Cultural History of the Federal Writers' Project*, provided a historical context for the discussion. Kathi Blake Yancey described the Center for Everyday Writing at The Florida State University and Laurie Grobman discussed her student research projects in Latino, African American, and Jewish communities, all leading to the publication of books.

The proposed 2013 workshop emerges directly from conversations in St. Louis about the FWP as a historical and cultural model. For as productive as those conversations were, they also sparked new areas of concern. It became clear that deeper conversations of what we mean by the term "democracy" and how such a project could go beyond merely linking community-based writing and other university-community partnerships needed to occur. We needed to identify comparable subjects for a reprise in 2012 of the federal writers' invitation to people whose voices had not been heard in the 1930s—Native Americans, the last generation of ex-slaves, immigrants, and workers—to tell their stories. For this workshop, then, we intend to build an agenda that might begin to serve as today's equivalent of the FWP's commitment to democracy, pluralism, and inclusiveness.

The primary goal of the proposed CCCC Workshop, then, is to deepen the conversation about democracy that began in earnest at the 2012 gathering, and thus enact a political turn we believe is necessitated by the current conjuncture as well as our particular project of "writing democracy" and reviving the FWP. Our plan is as follows: During the academic year 2012/2013, we are going to sponsor a disciplinary wide conversation on the meaning of democracy by creating an on-line "This We Believe" website, where teachers and students can submit two minute essays on the connection between writing, writing classrooms, and democracy. These essays will serve as the launching point for our workshop as well as framing devices throughout the day. The day will include three panels featuring Olympic athlete John Carlos, renowned for having raised his fist in a black power salute in the 1968 Olympics in Mexico City, Nancy Welch, Kurt Spellmeyer, and Carmen Kynard. Each panel will help us 1) place the focus on "democracy" into a historical context; and 2) theorize the meaning of democracy in 2013. Additionally, the workshop will use the community organizing methods of Marshall Ganz to enable participants to develop a year-long agenda for FWP 2.0, based upon the earlier panel presentation, along with a series of benchmark goals, to be achieved by C's 2014.

9:00	Introductions: SC/DM/SP	
9:15	**Democracy and the Open Hand/Closed Fist** Carlos, Carter, Welch (60 Minutes)	
10:15	**"This We Believe"** (45 Minutes)	
11:00	Break (15 Minutes)	
11:15	**Theories of Democratic Writing**	

	Spellmeyer/Mutnick (60 Minutes)
12:15	Lunch
1:00	**Democratic Struggle: Writing On Line, Off Campus, and In the Streets** Kynard, Kuebrich, Parks (60 Minutes)
2:00	**Organizing for Change:** Afternoon Workshop
4:30	**Federal Writers Project 2.0 Campaign Plan** (30 Minutes)
5:00	Conclusion

Participants

    Co-Chairs:
        Deborah Mutnick
        Shannon Carter
        Steve Parks

    Presenters/Facilitators:
        John Carlos
        Carmen Kynard
        Nancy Welch
        Kurt Spellmeyer
        Laurie Grobman
        Brian Bailie
        Ben Kuebrich
        Eli Goldblatt

Writing Democracy 2012-2013

This We Believe
A Project of FWP 2.0

Seventy-five years ago during the Great Depression, a division of the Works Progress Administration called the Federal Writers' Project (FWP) employed writers and researchers to create "a new roadmap for the cultural rediscovery of America" via local guidebooks, oral histories, and folklore. Today, college writing programs, service-learning programs, and scholars across the disciplines are engaging in university-community partnerships that might together create a similar roadmap for rediscovering 21st century America.

After the 2008 crash, numerous commentators suggested the idea of a new FWP. Although it became clear by late 2009 that Obama's stimulus package would not fund such a project, the idea inspired a conference, Writing Democracy: A Rhetoric of (T)here, in March 2011 at Texas A&M-Commerce. Over 150 scholars, students, and community members convened to examine concepts of place, local publics, and popular movements in an attempt to understand and promote democracy through research, writing, and action. Since that time, those involved have continued to talk and develop strategies for linking writing to democracy.

"This We Believe" is an attempt to expand and archive those conversations. Over the next year, FWP 2.0—our name for a fledgling 21_{st} century Federal Writers' Project—will be reaching out to students, teachers, and everyday citizens asking them to record a short, two-minute response to any of several questions. Their answers will be made available on this site, where others can respond and expand upon the conversation. Ultimately, we hope to take representative conversations and produce a book for use in classrooms across the country –bringing the peoples' concerns and hopes for democracy directly to students. We also hope to host another Writing Democracy Conference in 2013.

We invite you to take a moment and record a response to one of the following questions. Simply visit the "This We Believe" page at writingdemocracy.org, the select one of the following questions. You will be taken to a page that will allow you either to record or to upload your response.

1. To paraphrase Raymond Carver, "what do we talk about when we talk about democracy"?
2. What does U.S. democracy in 2012 look like to you? How do its realities compare to your dream of democracy in our nation and in our world?
3. How does writing, as cultural work, serve the project of democracy as you've described and dreamed it above? What possibilities does writing hold for helping us to reimagine and reinvigorate U.S. democracy locally and nationally?

4. In this time of growing interconnectedness and economic globalization, what opportunities and challenges face democracy beyond national borders?

We look forward to you joining the conversation.

This We Believe Project Directors
    Shannon Carter
    Timothy Dougherty
    Deborah Mutnick
    Steve Parks
    Rachael Shapiro

Book and New Media Reviews

From the Review Desk
Jim Bowman

St. John Fisher College

As my upper division rhetoric students settled into a service-learning project designed to help develop the communicative capabilities of an organization that provided uninsured and underinsured city residents of Rochester with affordable healthcare, the platitudes flowed easily. They justified the utility of their efforts on safe, ethical grounds. We were "helping those in need" and "supporting a worthy organization." I worried, though, that our "safe" capacity-building work might be conspiring against a more honest look at what drives the differences in perspectives between comparatively privileged college students and the volunteers, staff, and constituents at the healthcare organization we worked with. After screening and discussing Michael Moore's polemic documentary *Sicko*, this benign "cover story" began to take on water. The asymmetric experiences that led to different takes on "healthcare literacy" became part of our own complicated class story. I will probably never know whether these more open discussions of perspectival difference had any impact on the students' work, but I was certainly more confident that our efforts thereafter were done with a great deal more self-awareness of how and why people approach the literacies of healthcare so differently.

In the midst of ambitious community-based projects, educators can sometimes neglect to attend effectively to the different perspectives on literacy held by those in higher education and those in community organizations. The texts and reviews of this edition display this tension productively and explore literacy from many of the diverse positions that inform meaningful collaborations between communities and institutions of higher education. Ben Kuebrich's keywords essay on "community publishing" provides us with valuable insights into the growth and challenges of writing projects that are ideally driven by the needs of community organizations that represent dynamic, evolving constituencies. He notes, for example, the difficulty in measuring the impact of community-based projects and publishing efforts. Those in higher education can better position themselves to gauge the impact of our efforts when they listen to community partners. As he points out, the news of a project's impact will not break in our journals but rather in the daily interactions we share with the communities we serve and for whom literacies matter most. *Literacy in Times of Crisis*, edited by Laurie MacGillivray and reviewed by Patricia Burnes, begins from the given assumption that literacy is embedded in social practices. Attention to how moments of crisis demand, produce, disable, or otherwise affect literate activity affords scholars, teachers and community activists insight into the inescapable power of literacy. For language educators of all sorts who are determined to see their efforts empower others, the collection as a whole provides a message both sobering and inspiring. Linda Flower's *Community Literacy and the Rhetoric of Public Engagement*, reviewed by Christine Martorana, demonstrates how community-oriented academics are at their best when they operate self-reflectively to deploy their own literacy skills and institutional power to support the complicated work of community activism. And finally, *Writing Home*, the literacy narrative of Eli Goldblatt reviewed by Rebecca Lorimer, provides inspirational nourishment for practitioners of community literacy, whose work can always profit from a critical, descriptive look inward and backward, to the sources of their own personal paths to literacy.

Keywords: Community Publishing

Benjamin D. Kuebrich

Syracuse University

"Community publishing" sounds like a relatively quaint thing. In fact, the quaintness is built into the term "community." As Raymond Williams noted in his *Keywords*, "community" has always been a "warmly persuasive word" that "seems never to be used unfavorably" (76). Joseph Harris, who builds on and applies William's definition to composition classrooms, gives two warnings about the use of this "vague and suggestive" term (99-101). First, community can be any group, any discourse community, and thus floats as a relatively empty signifier. The second use of "community" distinguishes one group as insiders who have shared purpose, language, and experiences in contrast to others. While more descriptive, Harris notes how this concept of community often glosses over the internal tensions and differences we know to exist in all communities. In *Tactics of Hope*, Paula Mathieu looks for a term to describe her work outside the university, also expressing dissatisfaction with "community." She settles for "street" because "its problems seem generative"(xiii). Most scholars and most of our students live in what they call communities, not in the streets; the street denotes a place outside the university that isn't always warm and favorable.

Despite its shortcomings, community publishing is our keyword, and I hope my opening digression restores some of the concept's ineffable complexities while acknowledging it as a contested phrase. As Miller, Wheeler, and White adeptly note in their keyword on reciprocity, we as a discipline have "resigned ourselves to the term 'community' to refer to para-university communities," not yet able to find a term that accurately represents the partnerships, tensions, connections, and differences of groups that we work with (176). Even while we develop the vocabulary to more accurately describe the practice, community publishing is thriving.

The release of the collection *Circulating Communities: The Tactics and Strategies of Community Publishing* earlier this year, edited by Paula Mathieu, Steve Parks, and Tiffany Rousculp, marks the high point in a stream of scholarship on community publishing. Its eleven essays, each describing different community publishing projects, demonstrate the creativity of community publishers. *Circulating Communities* builds on the momentum of other recent and influential texts, including Parks' *Gravyland* (2010), *The Republic of Letters* (2009), Linda Flower's *Community Literacy and the Rhetoric of Public Engagement* (2008), Eli Goldblatt's *Because We Live Here* (2007), and Mathieu's *Tactics of Hope* (2005). The inclusion of community publishing scholarship and community-based writing in a number of recent collections provides yet more evidence of the field's growing interest in community publishing, such as *Writing and Community Engagement: A Critical Sourcebook*, which includes ten pieces written "from the community."

While there is much diversity in community publishing, its shared characteristics normally consist of the following:

1. The writers are among groups that traditionally do not have access to publication, either because of material constraints or because of the social construction of standards for cultural and political expression. The introduction to *Circulating Communities* describes how community publications move "underrepresented voices" to print, including "people of color, women, working-class radicals, gay and lesbian groups, and homeless advocates, among others" (1-6).

2. Writing is done *by* the community, as Mathieu et al describe; this is in contrast to other forms of community literacy that write about, with, or for the community (15). Nick Pollard and Pat Smart describe writing from the Federation of Worker Writers and Community Publishers in the UK as "emphatically culture from the bottom up" and that the goal is "making workers' voices heard and making them count—on our own terms" (21, 31). Descriptions of community publishing often emphasize the agency of community residents. When university collaborators are involved, the goal is to provide resources from the university and/or facilitate some of the publishing process, not to define the purpose, content, audience, or tone of publications. Communities should have full and final editorial control.

3. The writing is normally confined to a geographic locality. Pollard and Smart describe how the term "community publisher" reflects the localness of topics, authors, and distribution (21-25). The publications may take on topics of national and international significance, but often view them with an eye toward local implications. While online self-publishing is an easy way to go public with writing, community publishing remains largely print-based or born in print and then digitized as a secondary means of publishing. Community publishers are often in "resource poor" communities where the digital divide prevails and the power of being in print can build community and cultural value (Mathieu et al 2).

4. Community publications write for social change and for the promotion of diverse language use and culture. Mathieu et al describe how community publications often "confront power dynamics and political systems" (3). They also describe a variety of community publishing projects that "blur the lines between political and literary writing" and "change the terms of who can and should be considered a writer" (3-6). These publications advocate for underrepresented viewpoints and their publication demonstrates that everyone is an intellectual/philosopher/writer. Thus, social change happens on multiple levels through community publishing.

5. Community is made or enriched in the process of publication. Describing a local campaign built in response to an incident of homophobic vandalism, A. V. Luce asks scholars to focus not only on the product and outward effect of community publication but also the effect of community formation through the process of writing and publishing (202). Community publishing, then, represents not static, ready-made groups of people with a message to promote, but instead, as scholars like Michael Warner remind us, communities and publics that are made through texts, not prior to them.

Many recent and historical community publications have followed the above criteria. In writing a history of the Federation of Worker Writers and Community Publishers, Pollard and Smart note that while the FWWCP began in 1976, "working-class writing and community publishing has probably existed in some form or other since the invention of the printing press" (22). The first section of *Republic of Letters*—a book-length treatment of the history, theories, and writing from the FWWCC—notes the rise in political agency during the 1960s when working-class groups determined that formal political structures did not represent them, so they "began to represent themselves" (11). Other texts in composition also mark the rise in political, community-based writing during this period, including Jacqueline Rhodes' *Radical Feminism, Writing, and Critical Agency: From Manifesto to Modem*, which tracks feminist political and community-based writing from the late 1960s to the present. These historical examples provide us with an ideal form of community publishing, where groups who traditionally lack resources and access self organize to publish on their own, developing communities and movements that work for social justice.

A number of important texts in composition link this period of political agency and self-sponsored community publishing with contemporary practices. For starters, the NCTE's Students Right to Their Own Language Resolution provoked progressive composition scholars to act in line with a more capacious understanding of the social and cultural power of language variation, expanding the field's definition of effective writing. Adding more ethnographic data to language acquisition and literacy standards, Shirley Brice Heath's *Ways With Words* assesses the divide between home and school language in two nearby, racially segregated communities. Finally, Anne Gere's "Kitchen Tables and Rented Rooms: The Extracurricular of Composition" analyzes community publishing from composition's disciplinary perspective, describing self-sponsored writing groups that are "constructed by desire," some of which published and held community readings for activist ends (80). In Gere's early piece of scholarship on community publishing, she argues that self-sponsored, community writing has something to teach composition, but she makes no argument for scholars in composition to engage in or facilitate the practice.

So what happens when universities engage in community publishing work? If our concept of community is defined as para-university, and as those without access to publication, what role do universities have in sponsoring and supporting community publishing? The tensions and traditional divisions of community partnership are a necessary starting point for much of the scholarship in community publishing and community literacy. This is true especially of *Unsustainable: Reframing Short-Lived Community Writing Work*, a forthcoming collection co-edited by Laurie JC Cella and Jessica Restaino. The collection works to refigure how we think of value in community partnership and to reconsider the community/university binary that constrains our work, but this starts with an acknowledgement that most of the essays in the collection "identify a structural, deal-breaking incongruity, one that renders university/community collaboration incompatible" (359).

In a dialogue on community publishing, Nick Pollard and Steve Parks identify some of these specific discontinuities. In contrast to the self-sponsored community publishing done by the FWWCP, Parks wonders if "that purity can be replicated within a university/community partnership" (58). Pollard argues that the lack of grass-roots involvement, the professional standards of university-sponsored publications, and the use of outside grants could demotivate writers and constrain possibilities for truly representative publications (60-64). He fears that university funded, collaborative publications will ultimately be "written for, not with the community" (64).

Similarly, Mathieu's critique of traditional service learning practices in *Tactics of Hope* argues that "the more we try to institutionalize the relationships between universities and neighboring streets and communities, the farther we stray from a rhetorically responsive engagement that seeks timely partnerships" (xiv). Instead, Mathieu seeks tactical, rhetorical orientations toward community work to replace strategic orientations based on university goals and timelines. Since community publishing locates its agency and rhetorical production in the community, these initiatives seem primed for the rhetorically responsive, tactical orientations that Mathieu suggests. Still, the distinction between tactical and strategic orientations presents a challenge for community publishing in composition and rhetoric since university partnership necessarily dilutes the process by adding external values and expectations. With student learning objectives and the necessity to publish or perish, university partners have an especially fine line to walk between the requirements of the academic world and the commitment to community-defined publication goals and editorial processes.

Within this context, even well-planned and well-meaning partnerships can end up burning community members. The community engagement "horror story," in fact, has become something of its own genre. Near the end of Mathieu's *Tactics of Hope*, she summarizes a story from a woman named "Jane" who is a formerly homeless veteran and outreach worker for a community group (122). Jane partnered with a large non-profit and two local universities to create a book about the experiences of the local homeless population, planning to use proceeds from the book to fund small grants for life and work items needed by the homeless community. What began as an ambitious and creative partnership ended with a university professor taking over the project, publishing a book with himself as the editor, exploiting the community for their stories, and taking total control of editorial decisions. Money from the book went back to the large non-profit, not to the local homeless community. Pollard warned that community-university partnerships would end in books being written for instead of by the community, but this example of partnership-gone-wrong is clearly neither. It is a story about how the extremes of a university-centered approach can damage local communities, leaving them to feel powerless against the resources and standing of the ivory tower. Luckily, there is now plenty of scholarship available to learn from the successes and failures of projects in community publishing, and many community publishers have created seemingly sustainable partnerships. See Mathieu's *Tactics of Hope* for ten suggestions from Jane on working with community partners (124-125).

From non-profits, universities, and community's self organizing, homeless populations and advocates are publishing street papers, scholars and citizens are facilitating writing groups and publishing work from local prisons, and residents are re-presenting their history and culture. The diversity and unique purpose of each publication cannot be addressed here, but curious readers can research successful projects in their area: the *Journal of Ordinary Thought* and *Streetwise* in Chicago, *Real Change* in Seattle, Write Around Portland, the *Homeward Street Journal* in Sacramento, the Salt Lake City Community Writing Center and their yearly *sine era* collection, the Colorado Community Literacy Center and their regular publication of women's prison writing in *Speak Out!*, *New City Community Press* and the Open Borders Project in Philadelphia, the *Gifford Street Community Press* in Syracuse, Write On! in Durham, the Arkansas Delta Oral History Project, the Neighborhood Story Project in New Orleans, the Federation of Worker Writers and Community Publishers in the UK, and 826 National in most major US cities. There are surely many more examples that I am forgetting or do not know of. If you are looking for practical advice on starting a writing group in your community, see the "tip sheet" at the end of Parks' and Pollard's "The Extra-Curricular of Composition: A Dialogue on Community Publishing."

Despite a surge of community publishing and scholarship in the area, there is still work to be done assessing the effects of community publishing on local populations, altering the definitions of academic success to value the long haul of community-based work, and experimenting with digital spaces of community publication.

After descriptions of their community engagement work in "Community Literacy," Peck, Higgins, and Flower write, "the question we must continue to ask is, does it make a difference?" The lists of scholarship and community practices above tells us that, despite some pitfalls, community publishing is working toward social change in communities, redefining our culture's idea of the writer, and adding complexity and nuance to debates concerning underprivileged populations. There are plenty of reasons to believe we are doing good work, but more thorough assessment is needed. As Deans, Roswell, and Wurr note in the introduction to *Writing and Community Engagement*, "most of the published studies on community writing take the form of critical reflections on practice," while few studies use empirical research or other data-supported methods to assess the long and short term effects on local communities (8-10). We need to know how the ideas in these publications circulate, how community writers are affected by the process of publication, and whether texts aimed at social justice can actually transform social conflicts--a wide ranging list of outcomes that won't be easy to determine.

In addressing the discontinuity between university and community goals, calls for revising the criteria by which we distinguish academic success—for faculty, graduate students, and undergraduates—have been getting louder. In the final pages of Goldblatt's *Because We Live Here*, he laments the "brutal politics of tenure and employment in contemporary higher education," asking for scholars in the field to slowly build in value for community engagement work. Similarly, in the conclusion to *Unsustainable*, co-editor Jessica Restaino asks, "How might scholarship be more broadly defined to encompass a collaboratively-written community publication? [...] What opportunities do we have to think about our teaching along alternate timelines, beyond the singular semester?" (370-71). Scholars should not have to wait until they have tenure to build in a few hours each week for community-engaged work, and students in community engaged courses need creative assessment criteria that respond to the unique purposes of each project.

Finally, questions remain about the future of publishing technologies and community publishing. In A.V. Luce's description of the "Faces of Pride" campaign, a blog helps to facilitate a community publishing project. In response to a local art gallery selling a poster saying, "Generation 'Q': Young - Proud - Queer," a vandal scrawled "There is no such thing as a proud queer!" on the storefront window in permanent marker (202). As news of the incident quickly spread, the Associate Director of the campus LGBTQ resource center made a blog to display images of local advocates holding signs like "proud queer" and "proud ally." These photographs were soon printed and displayed behind the vandalized window, creating a powerful juxtaposition between hatred and pride. Online publishing obviously facilitated the publication of these images and voices, which were published locally while also reaching a broader audience online. Examples like the Open Borders Project (see Lyons) further demonstrate the possibilities of community building and empowerment through digital storytelling. While current socio-economic conditions make digital publishing impossible in some communities, the landscape is rapidly shifting and community publishers are creatively thinking about how technology can facilitate community building and community action.

Extrapolating from Pollard and Smart's description of the FWWCP, community publishing can perhaps be described as *the means of making writing and publishing available to all, and making it count on the community's own terms* (31-33). Of course, each part of this description presents a challenge: How do university partners best create conditions under which community residents write on their own terms? What counts as "making it count"? That is, how do community publishers know when they've made a positive difference? What constitutes writing and publishing in our shifting digital landscape? The great thing about community publishing is that answers to these questions rarely come from journal articles; they come instead through collective action, experiment, and commitment to making a more just and inclusive society.

Works Cited

Cella, Laurie J.C., and Jessica Restaino, eds. *Unsustainable: Reframing Short-Lived Community Writing Work*. (Forthcoming)

Deans, Thomas, Barbara Roswell and Adrian J. Wurr, eds. *Writing and Community Engagement: A Critical Sourcebook*. Urbana: National Council of Teachers of English Press, 2000. Print.

Flower, Linda. *Community Literacy and the Rhetoric of Public Engagement*. Carbondale: Southern Illinois University Press, 2008. Print.

Gere, Anne R. "Kitchen Tables and Rented Rooms: The Extracurriculum of Composition." *College Composition and Communication*. 45.1 (1994): 75-92. Print.

Goldblatt, Eli. *Because We Live Here: Sponsoring Literacy Beyond the College Curriculum*. Creskill, N.J.: Hampton Press. 2007. Print.

Harris, Joseph. *A Teaching Subject: Composition Since 1966*. Upper Saddle River, NJ: Prentice Hall, 1997.

Heath, Shirley Brice. *Ways With Words*. Cambridge: University of Cambridge Press, 1983. Print.

Luce, A.V. "'A Bunch of Us Beg to Differ!': Queer Community Publishing and Rhetorics of Pride." *Circulating Communities: The Tactics and Strategies of Community Publishing*. Eds. Paula Mathieu, Steve Parks, and Tiffany Rousculp. UK: Lexington Books, 2012. 201-216. Print.

Lyons, Mark. "Listen to My Story: The Transformative Possibilities of Storytelling in Immigrant Communities." *Circulating Communities: The Tactics and Strategies of Community Publishing*. Eds. Paula Mathieu, Steve Parks, and Tiffany Rousculp eds. UK: Lexington Books, 2012. 71-82 Print.

Mathieu, Paula. *Tactics of Hope: The Public Turn in English Composition*. Portsmouth, NH: Boynton/Cook, 2005. Print.

Mathieu, Paula, Steve Parks, and Tiffany Rousculp. *Circulating Communities: The Tactics and Strategies of Community Publishing*. UK: Lexington Books, 2012. Print

Miller, Elizabeth, Anne Wheeler, and Stephanie White. "Keywords: Reciprocity." *Community Literacy Journal* 5.2 (2010-2011): 171-178. Print.

Morley, David and Ken Worpole eds. The Republic *of Letters: Working Class Writing and Local Publishing*. Syracuse UP, 2009. Print.

Parks, Steve and Nick Pollard. "The Extra-Curricular of Composition: A Dialogue on Community-Publishing." *Community Literacy Journal* 2 (2009): 53-78. Print.

Parks, Steve. *Gravyland: Writing Beyond the Curriculum in the City of Brotherly Love*. 2010. Syracuse: Syracuse University Press, 2010. Print.

Peck, Wayne Campbell, Linda Flower, and Lorraine Higgins. "Community Literacy." *Composition and Communication* 46.2 (May 1995): 199-222.

Pollard, Nick and Pat Smart. "Making Writing Accessible to All: The Federation of Worker Writers and Community Publishers and TheFED." *Circulating Communities: The Tactics and Strategies of Community Publishing*. Eds. Paula Mathieu, Steve Parks, and Tiffany Rousculp eds. UK: Lexington Books, 2012. 21-34. Print.

Rhodes, Jacqueline. *Radical Feminism, Writing, and Critical Agency: From Manifesto to Modem*. Albany: SUNY Press, 2005. Print.

Warner, Michael. *Publics and Counterpublics*. New York: Zone Books, 2002. Print.

Williams, Raymond. *Keywords: A Vocabulary of Culture and Society*. New York: Oxford UP, 1985.

Literacy in Times of Crisis: Practices and Perspectives.
Laurie MacGillivray, Ed.
New York and London: Routledge, 2010. 216 pp.
ISBN 978-0415871648. $44.95.

Reviewed by Patricia Burnes
University of Maine

Literacy in Times of Crisis: Practices and Perspectives is an ambitious book. Each chapter in the major, middle section is a report from a research project into what happens to and through literacy in times of crisis. The range of crises being studied is impressive: natural disasters, homelessness, teenagers facing motherhood, immigrants caught between cultural assumptions about marriage, children enduring custody battles, and others. Despite the wide divergence in situations explored, all contributors share a belief in literacy as social action through which people shape and reshape their identities and create the structures through which life becomes comprehensible. This view of literacy is hardly new. But by asking what happens when crises or unexpected events "overwhelm the systems that make things work" (1), editor Laurie MacGillivray and her contributors challenge and expand previous understandings of the relationships between individual literacy and cultural identity. They also address the relationships between individual identities and the social structures that make purposeful action possible. Framing their accounts are statements by three teachers, who first anticipate and then reflect on the major chapters in terms of their teaching and, in one case, larger community concerns. These final reflections help readers make useful connections among at least some of the great range of perspectives presented earlier; they also point beyond the book by providing a glimpse of the research and theorizing still needed if dedicated professionals are to learn how to serve their communities through the practices of literacy in times of crisis.

Some of the book's chapters testify very particularly to the role of literacy in individual circumstances; others work to help readers better understand literacy as a force central to the life of a community. April Whatley Bedford's overture chapter does both. She describes having been evacuated from New Orleans in anticipation of Hurricane Katrina, something which left her separated from everyone she knew and desperate for information. Although she had never used blogs and had only a vague idea of what they were, she went on-line, found several, and became an avid reader and contributor, relaying what she knew of the storm and learning from others. Significantly, she writes that immediately after being evacuated she had bought a journal, thinking that she would record her thoughts and feelings—as had been her habit for much of her life. This time, though, she found she had no desire to write anything that did not contain information about the storm. She retired the journal and turned to the blogs and emails that filled her days, entering and helping to sustain a virtual community by writing messages that friends later told her were among the most powerful texts she had ever composed.

Similar connections among literacy, identity, and community are obvious in Kara L. Lycke's chapter reporting research she had completed at a center for teenage mothers. Concentrating on two of the many cases she had studied and relying on vivid quotations to help us imagine those two young women, Lycke presents the substantial changes in lifestyle and long-range goals occasioned by motherhood and the literacy practices that enabled and expanded those changes. For a young woman from a highly supportive family, motherhood meant more serious reading and renewed concentration on school work with an ever tighter focus on the career that had always been her goal. For a young woman with a weaker family structure, motherhood meant putting aside reading practices she had once enjoyed (romance novels, mystery stories, love poetry) and turning instead to the online and print resources she was coming to know through a school program for unwed mothers. Lacking what Deborah Brandt calls "sponsors of literacy" in her immediate environment, the young woman found ways to create her own contexts for responsible motherhood. Like many of the book's chapters, Lycke's is valuable both for expanding research on its particular topic—the potential maturity of teenage, single mothers—and for expanding our understanding of the cultural power of literacy.

A similar if more complex account of shifts in reading practices in times of crisis comes in Gisele Ragusa's chapter on literacy strategies employed by families confronted with diagnoses of childhood disability. She reports on her study of seven families, each of whom had to cope with a disability diagnosis. In all the families, reading for pleasure declined significantly once the diagnosis had been made while reading for information, both on one's own and through computer-based networking, increased. The latter activity, Ragusa came to believe, served as a significant substitute for extended family support. In her closing advice to caregivers, she argues that disability-related information, whether electronic or print, needs to be current, accessible, and positive. Also testifying to literacy as creation of community is the research presented by editor Laurie MacGillivray, who reports on the Bible-reading practices of children and their mothers in homeless shelters. The quotations provided by MacGillivray provide emphatic evidence for her claim that young people come to know themselves in connection with the reading of Scripture. McGillivray shows how such reading can provide security and a reliable sense of one's place in the world, all the while also helping to form and to support strong habits of reading.

Not all the chapters show literacy as a way to transcend crisis; literacy practices are also presented as ways to understand and cope with difficult circumstances. In her second contribution, chapter 5, Ragusa reports her study of what happened when children from various ages kept dialogue journals with their mothers to cope with the trauma of divorce. Both the substantial quotations Ragusa provides as well as her description of changes over the six-month duration of the project provide compelling support for her claim that keeping the journals offered the means to both enriched literacy and emotional maturity in difficult times. Further evidence of the therapeutic possibilities of literacy in times of crisis comes in chapter seven as researcher Mary K. Thompson reports on the desperate case of a teenage victim of numerous crises, one participant in a study she was doing of the writing of Asian-American teenagers. The chapter reveals the teenager's success in using fanfiction and extremely personal poetry (shared only with the researcher) as ways to create new social worlds for herself and to achieve some degree of emotional balance in her traumatic life.

In contrast to the narrow foci of these first six chapters, MacGillivray closes the major part of the book with three chapters presenting society-wide literacy practices that throw into crisis the lives of those affected by them. Loukia K. Sarroub begins by reporting her research on the contradictory relationships between marriage and literacy in the immigrant communities she had studied. Although necessary for the rights of citizenship, she reports that the achievement of print literacy for her subjects could be an impediment for marriage in terms of their home cultures. For each, print literacy was a situated social practice, but situated in only one of the two cultures through which they achieved identity. Caught between two cultures, the women struggled to find ways to use the new rules to their own advantage rather than being defined by them.

A similar story of official pronouncements disserving individual needs comes in Rebecca Rogers and Kathryn Pole's account of a struggle between city and state leadership to take over the St. Louis Public School system in 2007. Through meticulous critical discourse analysis, the co-authors show how those parties interested in a state takeover were able to turn what had been a longstanding series of problems with public education into what the public was led to perceive as a crisis. State takeover advocates used decontextualized pronouncements that finally claimed more attention than the statements coming from those immediately affected by the proposed action. Rather than providing a way to cope with crisis (as the literate practices detailed in the earlier chapters did), the literacy at work here created a crisis that those parties with the most money and the most to gain could use to their advantage. In the last of the major chapters, Susan Florio-Ruane provides an overview of ways in which government officials have used crisis narratives to change teachers' practices and at the way teachers have both accepted and resisted those attempts. Drawing her examples from a plea for a return to first principles from the Educational Policies Commission in 1937—from the Sputnik-related creation of the National Defense Education Act and of the various programs enacted through the National Science Foundation, and from what she terms the failed crisis narrative of No Child Left Behind Act—Florio-Ruane demonstrates that the language of crisis can be used to prompt unthinking obedience to harmful practices and that educators must exercise their best professional judgment to resist such attempts. She concludes with a plea that educators follow only those mandates that accord with their professional knowledge, experience, and judgment.

The book ends with reflections by three teachers, each of whom writes about how her work already reflects some of the book's concerns and what larger adjustments she might make. Tracy Sweeney, an early career teacher, writes of the repeated importance the chapters give to new, ever-changing literacy practices and of her determination to introduce those to her students as well as to find ways to make her classroom more responsive to their out-of-school needs. Jane Ching Fung, a veteran teacher, sounds similar themes, stressing the importance of getting to know the students she teaches and of finding ways to balance community-based literacy activities with the more typical test-preparation work that can consume so much of a teacher's time. The final commentator, Elizabeth Moje, a teacher-educator and researcher, stresses the importance of writing for expressive and problem-solving purposes, emphasized in many of the chapters, but goes on to note the challenges and conflicts that teachers will face in attempting to enact many of the practices presented in the book. Those under pressure to teach large numbers of students and to meet district-wide guidelines and deadlines, she points out, may not be able to devote the kind of time to individual students that some of the chapters suggest, nor can they always do that without being tempted to pathologize the students and unwittingly withhold the level of rigorous attention they are giving the students' classmates. She goes on to raise the crucially important question of power, pointing out that none of the literacy practices described in the preceding chapters will bestow by themselves the kind of agency that people in desperate situations need. Such agency, Moje points out, is finally the business of all adults in a society to promote.

Moje's statement provides an ideal way to help readers make the implications of this book their own and find ways to act on them. Once literacy is recognized as embedded in social practice—and all the chapters in this book present literacy that way—then the crucial question of agency becomes the business of teachers and community workers alike. Teachers can indeed, as Sweeney points out, give students practice in many kinds of literacy and perhaps help them reflect on when and how particular practices are useful; and teachers can also, as Fung insists, be mindful of students' lives within and outside of schools and work to help students make connections. But Moje is surely right to say that the central question of how victims are restored to agency requires more than the learning of particular literate practices. Other recent accounts of connections between literacy in school and the larger society raise similar questions. In her exhaustive *Literacy in American Lives*, Deborah Brandt shows connections between individual literate practice and the needs of the larger society as crucial to personal success and failure and ends by asking how schools can possibly decide between serving the larger needs of the society that supports them or the individual needs of students. James Gee forwards a similar question in his chapter "New People in New Worlds," in Cope and Kalantzis's *Multiliteracies: Literacy Learning and the Design of Social Futures* by pointing out that "All language is meaningful only in and through the contexts in which it is used" (63) and then explaining the great need schools have to immerse students in the languages they will use to create their lives.

Although MacGillivray and her contributors do not raise directly the question of community/school relations, many of their chapters point indirectly to those connections. Some of the most successful of the cases show victims able to align themselves with the language of a surrounding community and to come thereby to renewed agency. And at least one of the chapter's—Sarroub's, on the conflicts endured by immigrant women newly literate in the language of their second country—points to the opposite situation. We have much to learn about how schools and community agencies can work together to restore victims of crisis to agency and, for that matter, how schools and community agencies can work together to support literate citizenry during even normal times. Laurie MacGillivray and her collaborators are to be thanked for focusing our attention on moments when needs are most sharply defined and action must be taken. We all stand to profit from their work and from the future research and practice this book will certainly inspire.

Works Cited

Brandt, Deborah. *Literacy in American Lives*. Cambridge: Cambridge University Press, 2001. Print.

Gee, J. P. "New people in new worlds: networks, the new capitalism and schools." *Multiliteracies: Literacy learning and design of social futures*. Eds. Bill Cope and Mary Kalantzis for the New London Group. London: Routledge, 2000. 43-68. Print.

Community Literacy and the Rhetoric of Public Engagement

Linda Flower

Carbondale: Southern Illinois UP, 2008. 281 pp.
ISBN: 9780809328529. $35.00.

Reviewed by Christine Martorana
The Florida State University

In 2009, the Rhetoric Society of America (RSA) awarded Linda Flower the RSA Book Award for producing that year's best work in rhetorical study. Flower's book *Community Literacy and the Rhetoric of Public Engagement* spotlights her experiences with Pittsburgh's Community Literacy Center (CLC), an innovative project in community literacy initiated in 1990. The 2008 book details a rhetorical model of engaging the privileged and marginalized voices of community leaders, academics and urban teens into meaningful dialogue that values all perspectives and embraces differences as valuable resources. According to Flower, the discourse of academic cultural critique has taught "us how to *speak up* [and] *speak against*" (2 original emphasis). However, what we lack and what this text provides is a model that teaches us "to *speak with* others [and] to *speak for* our commitments [...] for a revisable image of transformation" (2 original emphasis).

The value of Flower's work rests in challenging prevailing social standards in regards to authority and literacy: who speaks, who is given the right to speak, and who is heard. Primarily, she aims to use her work in community literacy to build a platform upon which those labeled as "voiceless and powerless" can stand (6). Although dominant social structures bestow authority upon a select few, Flower seeks to promote a dialogue model that embraces diverse perspectives and experiences.

The book is organized into three main sections. Part 1 (Chapters 1-2) creates a framework for Flower's investigation into community literacy. Part 2 (Chapters 3-5) presents multiple theoretical perspectives within community literacy. Flower labels Part 2 a section "framed by academic debates", guided by her effort to "show academics, mentors, and activists working to construct situated working theories of engagement, collaboration, and empowerment" (73). Part 3 (Chapters 6-10) concludes the book with specific tools readers can implement into their own community literacy practices.

Chapter 1 introduces the CLC through narrative prose and invites readers to take a tour of Pittsburgh's Northside. Flower's use of vivid anecdotes and participant dialogue sets an informal, conversational tone, a rhetorically-purposeful move as this book challenges readers to consider alternatives beyond traditional academic discourse. In Chapter 2, Flower calls upon her definition of community literacy as "an intercultural dialogue *with others* on issues that *they* identify as sites of struggle" (19 original emphasis). She posits the rhetorical agency of "everyday people" (44) central to community literacy. Through rhetorical agency, individuals engage in intercultural rhetoric, a dialogue across cultures that seeks to redefine problems in light of personal and public factors and discuss "what if" statements on possible outcomes (53-54). These discussions may lead to the recognition of cultural differences and power imbalances; however, Flower encourages us to embrace these differences "as a resource" (55).

Part 2, which explores different ideas about community literacy, begins with Chapter 3, where Flower analyzes the current bent within composition towards critique. According to Flower, critique only serves to heighten our awareness of "'others' in our society" (78). She asks, "How do we prepare ourselves to go beyond the safety of critique into the vulnerable stance of reflective, revisable commitment – to speak *for* values or actions even as we acknowledge them to be our current best hypothesis?" (79 original emphasis). Flower calls for rhetoric and composition to "recover the practice of 'doing' rhetoric in its wider civic and ethical sense" (81). Then, Chapter 4 takes a slight turn from the previous chapters. Here, Flower focuses on her position as a researcher rather than the research itself. In this chapter, she appropriately labels herself "a person of privilege" (100) and considers the various ways to ethically balance this position alongside her work with community members and the CLC. Ultimately, Flower concludes that her privileged position is mediated by the relationships she builds with those around her: "So the question of What am I doing here? can take on a special urgency and feel very much like a problem of identity. Yet [...] identity in this partnership is not something you bring with you; it is not about who or what *you* are. Identity is defined by *the relationships you create*" (122 original emphasis). Chapter 5 shifts focus to various sources of empowerment. Flower outlines three common scripts for empowerment, guided by the questions, "Who is being empowered? To what end? By what means?" (123) After presenting the scripts, she identifies components absent within each and offers a revised empowerment script called "Empowerment through Dialogue across Difference" (132). This script is rooted in "speaking with" others (132) by creating "a circle of collaborative meaning makers" (136). Flower then offers a "working theory of empowerment" (137) developed within the CLC, where indicators of success include "acts of personal decision making, reflective understanding, and rhetorical action" (149). She illustrates this working theory through a CLC case study.

Part 3 provides an enactment of Flower's vision of community literacy. Chapter 6 discusses intercultural inquiry, a dialogue at the heart of community literacy. In intercultural inquiry, different viewpoints are embraced, participants are collaborative equals, and community partners are viewed as agents rather than recipients (157).

Conflict is inevitable – and welcome – in intercultural inquiry; Flower writes that conflicting voices are necessary in order to arrive at "mutually transformative" negotiated meanings (159). Within Chapter 6, Flower offers three CLC case studies to exhibit times when students used intercultural inquiry to effectively construct "meaning through the eyes of difference" (160). Chapter 7 moves the discussion of intercultural inquiry one step further. Flower writes that the desire for dialogue inherent in intercultural inquiry must be accompanied by "a dedicated search for difference" (172). This search for difference translates into a search for situated knowledge – the knowledge and understanding each person possesses based upon history and previous experiences (178). Flower reminds us that the situated knowledge within each person can remain unseen (175). Then, Chapters 8 and 9 center upon the function of rhetorical agency. She challenges readers to "move from the familiar roles of teacher, supporter, or nurturer into the role of a *rhetorical researcher* and a *public rhetorician* – whose work is giving a public presence to the expertise and rhetorical agency of *others*" (223 original emphasis). These chapters neatly tie together the main tenets of the previous chapters, specifically Flower's emphasis on collaboration, community, and dialogue. Finally, Chapter 10 provides a practical, hands-on approach to intercultural inquiry, including suggestions on how to frame a question and bring multiple voices to a discussion, a list of significant areas for further research, a checklist for intercultural inquiry, and possible methods for conducting such an inquiry.

The strengths of this book are readily apparent. First, Flower not only calls us to "recover the practice of 'doing' rhetoric in its wider civic and ethical sense" (81), but she also embodies these words in her actions with the CLC. While some academic scholarship remains forever and only on the page, Flower's theories and suggestions for community literacy extend into daily lives and lived experiences. For example, in 2006, Lesley Rex published an article on the interactions between race and literacy in the classroom. Rex offers a detailed analysis of classroom interactions in regards to race, similar to Flower's observations of the interactions within the CLC and the surrounding community. Rex uses her observations to propose a framework for negotiating "conflict when race is a complicating factor" in the classroom (305). While the literacy framework Rex outlines may prove useful for future scholarship, she does not discuss first-hand experiences employing this framework in the classroom. However, when Flower proposes a framework for community literacy, she calls her readers to "draw out silenced voices and to document the unacknowledged expertise" (224), and she does so alongside her own efforts to do just this. Her words and actions are reciprocal: her words explain her actions; her actions support her words. This fluid and graceful movement between words and actions is one of the most notable strengths of Flower's text and supports Flower in reaching one of her main goals: to ground abstract theories into real practice in order "to construct situated working theories of engagement, collaboration, and empowerment" (73).

Flower's call to engage in community literacy joins a chorus of other voices. The majority of these calls, similar to Rex's research, are situated within classroom walls. Writing teachers are encouraged to engage issues of social justice in order to increase students' community awareness (Camangian; Chapman, Hobbel, & Alvarado), utilize drama pedagogies to encourage student awareness of dialogue

(Gallagher and Ntelioglou), and refer to biographical novels to address matters of resistance and promote cultural responsibility (Hansen). While Flower undoubtedly supports the aforementioned goals, her text moves beyond the classroom confines. Instead of asking students to *write* about social justice issues and the role of dialogue, for example, Flower provides a platform for CLC participants to *engage* in dialogue with community members about social justice issues. Flower's community literacy work responds to Ellen Cushman's recognition of the need to create "long term, well resourced, stable collaborations in inquiry that connect the university with the community" (41). In working with the CLC, she fosters a connection between the classroom and the community, or, as she describes it, "the town and the gown" (101).

Another strength is Flower's distinct style of writing that regularly shifts between narrative, informal writing and traditional, academic discourse. The personal stories about everyday people add familiarity to the text while the academic discussions lend reliability to the theories presented. As readers, we are moved to action because the success of the rhetorical model she presents is evident in the anecdotes, dialogue, and research she shares. Third, a valuable characteristic of the book is Flower's ability to navigate her role as an academic scholar within her CLC work. It is complicated to balance an elevated status as a researcher and scholar with a desire to give a voice to the marginalized outside academia. This is a battle many researchers face, and much can be gleaned from Flower's own struggles in this area. Flower offers us an honest glimpse into her thought progression as she grapples with her positionality. She describes how the privileged must use their voices to speak what the marginalized want to say because culture hears and recognizes the voices of the privileged (216). This book is Flower's attempt to lend the volume of her respected voice to those who are otherwise silenced. However, that respected voice also poses a potential problem.

Given the thoughtful organization of Flower's text, it is worth considering why Flower saved the discussion of her positionality for Chapter 4 instead of discussing this earlier. Possibly, starting with recognition of her elevated status might have detracted from the central components of community literacy she wishes to emphasize. However, from the start of the text, the reading audience is aware of Flower's place of privilege in comparison to the CLC participants, and it might have been effective to acknowledge her positioning earlier than Chapter 4.

Flower may have been more mindful of privilege in Chapter 7, which emphasizes situated knowledge. Here, she assumes an omniscient perspective, one that tends to ignore rather than honor others' situated knowledge. For example, she makes generalizations about thoughts and feelings of others based on age group: "For my generation, [the words] evoked images of Birmingham and Selma, Alabama..." (180), "the young were more likely to envision the police..." (180), there was "angry despair in the middle-aged, and angry shock in the young..." (181). Without explaining how she comes to these conclusions, she teeters on the edge of ignoring each person's unique perspectives, thus distracting from her otherwise fruitful discussion of situated knowledge.

Flower's unintentional omniscience reminds us of the inherent risks within community literacy. Witnessing a researcher as competent and experienced as Flower momentarily slip into this trap reveals how conscious we must be about respecting each person's individual perspectives. Furthermore, as readers, it is imperative we remember that Flower is the writer documenting the CLC experiences. The text, although inclusive of community members' voices, is Flower's perspective and her situated knowledge impacts the creation of the text.

Regardless of the minor weaknesses, Flower's work is invaluable to CLC participants, literacy studies, and rhetoric and composition. Her experiences with the CLC offer an effective platform for discussing community literacy in action. In offering her own experiences as an example of a scholar stepping into the community beyond academia, she provides a useful template for engaging in and promoting community literacy. Her book offers guidelines for organizing a community literacy project, steps for bringing disparate groups of people to the same conversation, and potential results from such a project. Her position as both a participant within and the author of this book makes the text useful for various audiences. Community literacy scholars will benefit from Flower's example of negotiating her role as an academic community leader, even the moments when her negotiation falls short. Furthermore, those seeking institutional support for a project similar to the CLC will find Flower's research a useful resource. Her in-depth exploration of rhetorical agency will intrigue and benefit scholars in rhetoric, and composition instructors can draw from this as well in light of their interactions with diverse and/or struggling students. Finally, community leaders can gain insight into an academic researcher's perspective and consider how a community can benefit from academia's resources – and vice versa. Flower's recollection of gaining new literacy herself as a result of her time with the CLC showcases the reciprocal nature of community literacy projects. Although there is typically a divide between "the town and the gown" (Flower 101), Flower reminds us that this need not be. Gaining a deeper understanding of both academic and non-academic perspectives is a crucial step in community organizing.

While the primary audience is an academic one, Flower's use of anecdotes and first-hand narrative appeals to non-academic audiences as well. She skillfully weaves together community and academic voices to provide an exciting, thoughtful look at the value of community literacy and the potential struggles and successes awaiting those who practice a rhetoric of public engagement.

Works Cited

Camangian, Patrick. "Making People Our Policy: Grounding Literacy in Lives." *Journal of Adolescent and Adult Literacy* 54.6 (2011): 458-460. Print.

Chapman, Thandeka, Nikola Hobbel, and Nora Alvarado. "A Social Justice Approach as a Base for Teaching Writing." *Journal of Adolescent and Adult Literacy* 54.7 (2011): 539-541. Print.

Cushman, Ellen. "Sustainable Service Learning Programs." *College Composition and Communication* 54.1 (2002): 40-65. Print.

Flower, Linda. *Community Literacy and the Rhetoric of Public Engagement.* Carbondale: Southern Illinois UP, 2008. Print.

Gallagher, Kathleen and Burcu Yaman Ntelioglou. "Which New Literacies? Dialogue and Performance in Youth Writing." *Journal of Adolescent and Adult Literacy* 54.5 (2011): 322-330. Print.

Hansen, Faith Beyer. "Building the Bridge Between Home and School: One Rural School's Steps to Interrogate and Celebrate Multiple Literacies." *Community Literacy Journal* (2010): 33-46. Print.

Rex, Lesley. "Acting 'Cool' and 'Appropriate': Toward a Framework for Considering Literacy Classroom Interactions when Race Is a Factor." *Journal of Literacy Research* 38.3 (2006): 275-325. Print.

Writing Home: A Literacy Autobiography
Eli Goldblatt
Carbondale, IL: Southern Illinois University P., 2012. 280 pp.
ISBN: 978-0809330850. $32.00

Reviewed by Rebecca Lorimer
University of Massachusetts-Amherst

The literacy autobiography is often assigned to help writers become more aware of how their literacy pasts affect their written present. In *Writing Home: A Literacy Autobiography*, Eli Goldblatt similarly reconstructs his literacy history to contextualize his current literate commitments. In the process, he stretches what he calls "the clinical-smelling term 'literacy'" until it is pliable and durable enough to account for a lifetime of literate experiences beyond books and schools (5). In its exploration of personal language history, *Writing Home* resembles Keith Gilyard's *Voices of the Self*, Min-Zhan Lu's *Shanghai Quartet*, and Victor Villanueva's *Bootstraps*. But Goldblatt's book uses less academic theory than these and lets the social tumult of literacy acquisition speak for itself. The humor and raw candor with which he tells his stories pulls literacy theory out into the daylight of lived experience, showing the full pleasure and pain of finding one's home through writing.

Writing Home is built around the tension between writing alone and writing with others. The desire to bridge community, school, and personal literacies is familiar ground for Goldblatt, but here the taut stretch among these literate realms is given the context of one full life. While the book's chronological chapters follow the phases of Goldblatt's life, the narrative within the chapters often jumps forward and circles back, resembling oral more than written storytelling. As it moves through specific literacy events and practices, the narrative spirals around explorations of gender, race, religion, and class, as one might expect from a writer who takes the social grounding of literacy seriously.

The first two chapters detail Goldblatt's childhood and schooling, beginning on the army base in Germany where his father was employed and ending in a suburban U.S. high school where he finds his poetic aspirations. These two chapters span the longest period of time in the book and contain as many life-altering realizations as any childhood might. Here, Goldblatt's insights are mostly literate: he comes to appreciate school as something he "always knew how to do" no matter where his army family was relocated (29); he comes to understand literary analysis as construction of meaning "deeply embedded in context but careful in respect to text" (37). The scenes in which religious literacies come to the fore—Goldblatt and his uncle analyze the *kaddish* prayer together after his father's death; he learns to lay *tefillin*, the leather strap wound around the hand to form Hebrew letters in prayer—are beautiful and resoundingly significant, showing Goldblatt's growing awareness of literacy as routine and pain, "brute work" and "mystical event" (42). Here he comes to know how the daily activity of literacy "requires considerable devotion but rewards effort with an ineluctable sense of belonging" among others who practice literacy with a shared sense of history (43).

The third and fourth chapter narrate the evolving split in Goldblatt's identity as a solitary "brooding intellectual" and public, social writer. Here we see Goldblatt as college student: following historical threads through literature, aligning himself with William Carlos Williams, transferring colleges, specializing in classics, working at a printing press. We watch him creating a myth of himself as the hard-working poet/manual laborer, which in doses of authorial self-consciousness he both treasures and gently self-mocks. The chapters expand the tension between the "ordinariness" of public working life and the liveliness of an inner literary life, with Goldblatt's ascetic tendencies running up against his real world literacy encounters. The period culminates in a resigned understanding that he "didn't need to be a monk for poetry" and might instead look outward to cultivate what he calls a poem-life (94).

Throughout the next three chapters, Goldblatt's narrative wanders along with his post-college experiences. He criss-crosses the U.S. for work and romantic relationships, doubling back to revisit childhood understandings of Judaism and his father's medical profession. He enters and leaves medical school, struggles to find work in recession-era Philadelphia, commits to teaching and a marriage, all the while developing a meta-awareness of his everyday encounters with language. He begins to take his literary self more seriously, dating his journal entries and keeping "as full a picture of internal and external developments as [he] could" (133). He winks at the reader by admitting the record was kept partly for future reconstruction, but the passage especially shows his maintenance of an internal and external literate split. As the autobiography crosses its midway point, Goldblatt still defines space and people by their separate literate activities— "We would have to…call to each other across the valley created by our separating literacies" (149)—holding other language users at arms length. Even with all his moving, the chapters show him using words to make walls, distilling a personal literate identity separate from his accumulated life and work literacies.

Goldblatt is pushed beyond his own impasse in the last three chapters when a divorce, feminist movement, and Central American revolution crack him open (241). He travels beyond the boundaries of his classroom, the U.S., and of English, finding solitude in writing while simultaneously joining community-driven movements. He repeats that travel taught him to "pay attention" as he was forced to listen across the gulf of languages and upend his ethnocentricity. When his *extranjero* status and fledging Spanish cause an unpleasant sense of isolation, he stops isolating himself to write. He realizes writers don't "need art to distance [them]" since "estrangement in language can happen to anyone at any time" (246). Thus, these final chapters find

Goldblatt realigning his notion of audience: "If I filled my consciousness with as many types of people as I could, then when I wrote I would be writing with them" (194). The more "types" he encountered, the less he wanted to wanted to write alone. By way of much wandering, Goldblatt's travel points him back home to Philadelphia. Once there and teaching again he describes seeing the full landscape of literacy rather than its partitions, and begins to write not just for or about himself, but for the full range of literacy users from his past and in his present.

After moving through so much literate life with him, readers might hope for Goldblatt to make more of his vast experiences. At times the analysis of events is heavy-handed, but at other times it lacks connection—how might the literacy campaign he witnessed in Nicaragua relate to his migrant co-workers in California for example? Very occasionally one hopes for more of the powerful political echoes of literacy to be traced across the phases or locations of his stories. However, the last chapter does this beautifully, including panoramic sweeps of the characters and scenes that populate the book's narrative.

For literacy teachers and researchers, *Writing Home* offers much, reminding us to ask ourselves and our students where our literacy practices come from and why the histories of those practices matter. The book shows the fruitfulness of assigning a literacy autobiography in the first place—accounting for one's literacy experiences reveals how much literacy learning occurs in unexpected settings, across a variety of communities, with strangers as much as with family. Individual chapters of the book could certainly be used as autobiography models in writing classrooms or community writing groups, with the chapters describing Jewish literate routine and central American travel being perhaps the most delicately written.

Literacy researchers will enjoy watching Goldblatt's literacy practices and technologies move with one writer across a specific period of time. We see letter and journal-writing, weavings, lesson plans, recipes, prayers, speeches, and countless notebooks and sketches. We see the struggle and rewards of collaborative literacy projects like political movements, poetry readings, and printing presses, and watch how social situations put pressure on the direction of one person's literate life. For all of these reasons, the autobiography is a pleasure to read. But it is also an important reminder about the hard work of literacy and the ongoing struggle of all writers to find their homes in language.

New Releases . . .

Ready to Wear: A Rhetoric of Wearable Computers and Reality-Shifting Media
Isabel Pedersen. 197 pages. $27 (paperback); $60 (cloth); $20 (digital)

Mics, Cameras, Symbolic Action: Audio-Visual Rhetoric for Writing Teachers
Bump Halbritter. 275 pages. $32 (paperback); $65 (cloth); $20 (digital)

The WPA Outcomes Statement—A Decade Later
Edited by Nicholas N. Behm, Gregory R. Glau, Deborah H. Holdstein, Duane Roen, and Edward M. White. 344 pages. $32 (paperback); $65 (cloth); $20 (digital).

Writing Program Administration at Small Liberal Arts Colleges
Jill M. Gladstein and Dara Rossman Regaignon. 290 pages. $32 (paperback); $60 (cloth); $20 (digital)

Rewriting Success in Rhetoric and Composition Careers
Edited by Amy Goodburn, Donna LeCourt, and Carrie Leverenz. $30 (paperback); $60 (cloth); $20 (digital)

The Uses of Grammar 2e
Judith Rodby and W. Ross Winterowd. 352 pages. $40 (paperback); $20 (digital)

Read more about forthcoming releases for the iPad and tablet computers, events celebrating our tenth year as a scholarly publisher, and more at

www.parlorpress.com

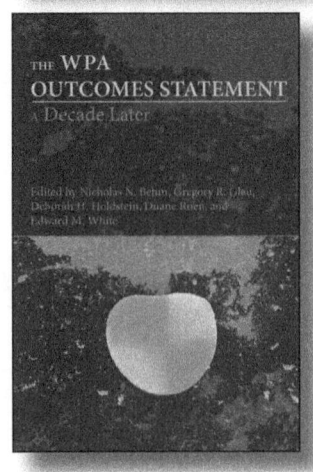

DePaul University
Chicago, IL

Department of
Writing, Rhetoric, & Discourse

Master of Arts Degrees in
New Media Studies
Writing, Rhetoric, & Discourse
with concentrations in
* Professional & Technical Writing
* Teaching Writing & Language

Graduate Certificate in TESOL
Combined BA/MA in Writing, Rhetoric, & Discourse

Graduate Faculty
Matthew Abraham
Julie Bokser
Darsie Bowden
Antonio Ceraso
René De los Santos
Lisa Dush
Sarah Read
Christine Tardy
Peter Vandenberg

wrd.depaul.edu

www.ingramcontent.com/pod-product-compliance
Lightning Source LLC
Chambersburg PA
CBHW031631160426
43196CB00006B/364